NEW WORLDS, OLD WARS

The Anglo-American Indian Wars 1607–1678

David Childs

'This is the Century of the Soldier', Fulvio Testi, Poet, 1641

Helion & Company Limited
Unit 8 Amherst Business Centre
Budbrooke Road
Warwick
CV34 5WE
England
Tel. 01926 499 619
Email: info@helion.co.uk
Website: www.helion.co.uk
Twitter: @helionbooks
Visit our blog http://blog.helion.co.uk/

Published by Helion & Company 2022
Designed and typeset by Mary Woolley, Battlefield Design (www.battlefield-design.co.uk)
Cover designed by Paul Hewitt, Battlefield Design (www.battlefield-design.co.uk)

Text © David Childs 2022
Photographs and Images as individually credited
Front colour artwork by Giorgio Albertini © Helion & Company 2022
Maps by George Anderson © Helion & Company 2022

Every reasonable effort has been made to trace copyright holders and to obtain their permission for the use of copyright material. The author and publisher apologize for any errors or omissions in this work and would be grateful if notified of any corrections that should be incorporated in future reprints or editions of this book.

ISBN 978-1-915113-99-3

British Library Cataloguing-in-Publication Data.
A catalogue record for this book is available from the British Library.

All rights reserved. No part of this publication may be reproduced, stored in a retrieval system, or transmitted, in any form, or by any means, electronic, mechanical, photocopying, recording or otherwise, without the express written consent of Helion & Company Limited.

For details of other military history titles published by Helion & Company Limited contact the above address or visit our website: http://www.helion.co.uk.

We always welcome receiving book proposals from prospective authors.

Contents

Glossary		iv
Preface		v
1	From Harmony to Hostility	8
2	Firearms and Fortifications	26
3	The Powhatan Wars of Virginia	
	Smith's War 1607–1609	43
4	Dale's War 1609–1613	
	Powhatan's High Water	56
5	The Sky Falls Twice	71
6	New England	
	The Pequot War	
	Massacre at Mystic	88
7	King Philip's War: Part 1	
	Ambushing Amateurs 1675	107
8	King Philip's War: Part 2	
	The Slaying of the Sachems 1676	129
9	Maine	
	The First Abenaki War: 1675–1678	152
10	Conclusion and Consequences – How the East was Won	175

Appendices:

I	The Virginia Charter of 1606 (extracts)	184
II	Extracts from letter of John Rolfe to Sir Thomas Dale (extract) 1613, published in Hamor's *True Discourse,*	186
III	Letter to Massachusetts Governor John Leverett	188
IV	Petition of Thomas Dutton to the General court in Boston, 1678	190
V	Statement by Robert Roules concerning the slaying of captives at Marblehead by the Fisherwomen	191
VI	Thadeus Clark to His Mother, 14 June 1676	194
VII	Joshua Scottow's relation to the Massachusetts Council, August 1677	195
Bibliography		198

Glossary

Mamanatowick	Paramount chief of the Powhatan Confederacy
Pniese	Elite warriors especially of the Pokanoket Wampanoag tribe
Sachem	A North American tribal chief
Sagamore	A subordinate chief among the tribes in New England
Sunksqu	A native woman who serves as a *sachem* or chief
Wampum	White and purple beads strung together, often as decorated belts, crafted from quahog or clam shells found only on Long Island or Narragansett Bay. Used for ceremonial purposes, for a period they became a form of currency within New England.
Werowoance	A tribal chief of the Powhatan Confederacy

Preface

For God did make the world to be inhabited with mankind, and here in Florida, Virginia, New England, and Canada, is more land than all the people in Christendom can manure [cultivate], and yet more to spare than all the natives of those countries can use and culturate [cultivate] … for a copper knife and a few toys, as beads and hatchets, they will sell you a whole Countrey; and for a small matter, their houses and the ground they dewell upon.

The Complete Works of Captain John Smith (1580–1631)

Seventeenth-Century Colonial America existed in an historic orphanage. England, the parent, having thankfully waved away its troublesome Pilgrim and Puritan offspring, breathed a sigh of relief and promptly forgot about them until they became rebellious over a century later. Their descendants, happy to claim an ancestry from the new arrivals, had little interest in their story until they clamoured for independence. Yet the outcome of the seventeenth-century wars between these immigrants and the indigenous population made them, without question, the most significant battles in the history of the whole world not just in the century of the soldier.

Even an observant traveller passing through England, Ireland and western Europe will see little evidence of the wars, both civil and national, that raged across the continent during the seventeenth-century. Indeed, all the anger and the suffering made scarcely a noticeable change to the land or its people, whatever their temporary irreconcilable views on politics or religion had been. However, on travelling to the eastern seaboard of the United States, whichever the port of entry, the changes wrought by the contemporaneous conflicts are immediately apparent in the language, landscape, land use, literature, law, religion and the colour of the people's skins.

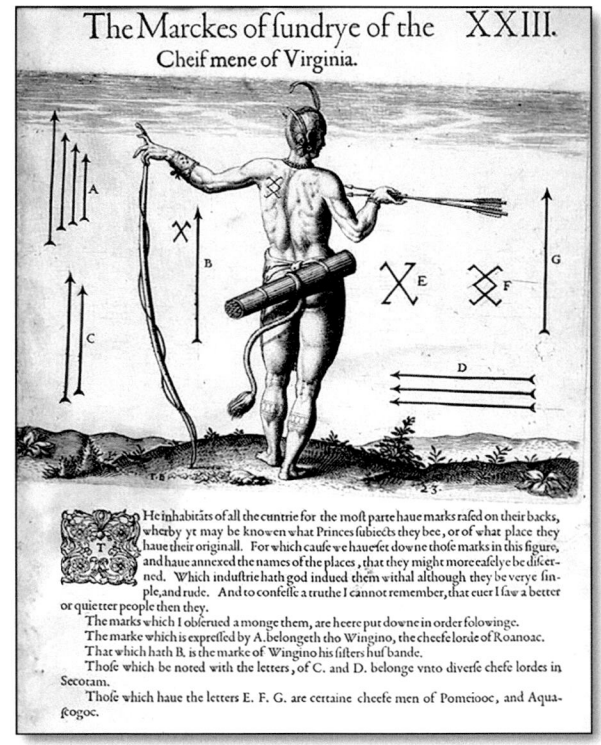

Theodor de Bry's engraving in 1590 of a native American armed with bow and arrow shows an inhabitant of an exotic and as yet, not a threatening world. (Public domain)

The seventeenth-century witnessed four types of war in the New World: the traditional, Amerindian versus Amerindian; European versus European; European versus Amerindian and European and allied tribe against a similar rival group. Although involving far fewer people than in Europe, these were conflicts where two, apparently irreconcilable, civilisations contended for a control that could only be achieved by an annihilation of their adversaries. So savage was the struggle, so dreaded the outcome, it is not surprising these wars were the deadliest conflicts, per capita, of any fought in North America, including the Civil War. The result had far more influence on the world of today than any battle, war or campaign being waged in Europe that century and yet, what these wars were, who was involved and how they were fought, is both largely ignored or forgotten.

There is a good reason for this; the English settlers of the seventeenth-century dwelt in an historic orphanage. Their English parents, glad to be rid of problematic Pilgrims and Puritans, said their farewells and were glad to ignore them until they became pesky revolutionaries. Their descendants, although proud to acknowledge their ancestry, do not consider them as Americans until they demanded independence. Sadly, there is little to boast about in the way the killing Christians behaved towards the native peoples they encountered.

Apart from the obvious outcome, the conduct of these campaigns established in the settlers a long-lasting acceptable method of treating indigenous people; the concept of an armed militia; the right of all to bear arms; the formation of the 'Rangers'; and a fundamental belief that the God of the Old Testament justified their methods of warfare. Quite a legacy. The seventeenth-century in America may well have been the century of the settler but it was also the century of the soldier without whom their settlements would not have been a success.

Rather than considering that on their arrival in North America, they had come in contact with another, very different but equally valid, civilisation, the English viewed the 'naturals' as savages or even devil's spawn. Yet had it not been for the help provided by these people, the colonists, both in Virginia and New England, would have died of starvation being unable, despite their sophistication, to feed themselves. The indigenous population were not only able to do this but were able to manage their environment in a sustainable way; the wisdom and practice of which took the white western world many further centuries to appreciate and adopt.

The disregard for these people was sanctified in the name by which they came to be known. When Columbus reached the far shore of the Atlantic, he was further away from India than he had been the day he sailed from Spain. Nevertheless, he considered he had arrived at the sub-continent and thereafter, the native Americans were referred to as Indians; a race with whom they had fewer links than they did with the Aryans.

This work acknowledges that fault by referring to the local population either by a tribal name or as Amerindians. The derogatory way in which the settlers spoke about the tribes was paramount in the way they treated them.

PREFACE

In their justification, they proffered to rationalise this behaviour and that towards other people of colour.[1]

The English considered the land on whose shores they disembarked (even before they had planted a flag) to be theirs for several reasons: firstly, it had been granted to them in give-away generosity by a monarch, none of whose subjects had any previous association with the country; secondly, the land was empty of permanent settlement; and thirdly, this was the new promised land and they were the new children of Israel.

Each of these 'rights' was centred upon land, its ownership and exploitation and thus became the primary cause of conflict between the indigenous and the incomers. To win these wars, the colonists had to adopt new tactics and new weapons as well as learn new skills. They were so deeply fundamentalist that they saw their campaign not as a new war but as a recreation of the ancient struggle that God's chosen people had fought long ago to claim the original promised land.

The conventional timeline for early colonial North America lists a series of short wars interspersed by periods of peace. In Virginia these were: the First, Second and Third Powhatan Wars, 1610–1614, 1622–1626, 1644–1646. New England experienced the Pequot War, 1636–1638 and King Philip's War, 1676–1678.

This disguises the fact the seventeenth-century was part of a four-hundred-year long period of continual inter-racial strife throughout the Americas. For the English, it began the destruction of both of Sir Walter Ralegh's Roanoke groups in 1586 and 1587, continued when arrows thudded into the jerkins of the Jamestown settlers on their first evening ashore in late April 1607 and would eventually end at Wounded Knee in 1890.

A native village (John White, 1585). Contrary to what the English would later claim, this shows a settled, agrarian community, not a world of transitory hunters and gatherers. (Public domain)

In Anglo-America, the conflict rippled through the colonies so that although there might be a period of peace in Virginia (such as that following Pocahontas's marriage), elsewhere in New York, New England or Canada, the struggle between incomers and indigenes was seldom quiescent. Although these were wars between two races, it is worth noting that the European colonists fought equally fiercely between themselves. Ultimately these were wars about land, its ownership and exploitation. The inevitable results were clear from the moment munificent European monarchs granted acquisitive adventurers' rights to a land they held no sway over, occupied by a people over whom they held no authority.

---

1 J. Lepore, *The Name of War* (Knoft, 1998).

1

From Harmony to Hostility

We were entertained with all love, and kindness, and with as much bounty, after their manner, as they could possibly devise … We found the people most gentle, loving and faithful, voids of all guile, and treason, and such as lived after the manner of the golden age.– Philip Amadas, 1584.[1]

We, greatly commending, and graciously accepting of, their Desires for the Furtherance of so noble a Work, which may, by the Providence of Almighty God, hereafter tend to the Glory of his Divine Majesty, in propagating of Christian Religion to such People, as yet live in Darkness and miserable Ignorance of the true Knowledge and Worship of God, and may in time bring the Infidels and Savages, living in those parts, to human Civility, and to a settled and quiet Government …– The First Charter of Virginia: 10 April 1606.[2]

'Treacherous villains, the dregs and lees of this earth, and the dross of mankind' - William Hubbard, 1677.[3]

There can be no doubt that King James was feeling generous during April 1606. In his charter granted to the two companies and two colonies of the land comprising Virginia and New England, he awarded them:

> … all the Lands, Woods, Soil, Grounds, Havens, Ports, Rivers, Mines, Minerals, Marshes, Waters, Fishings, Commodities, and Hereditaments, whatsoever, from the said first Seat of their Plantation and Habitation by the Space of fifty Miles of English Statute Measure, all along the said Coast of Virginia and America … and may also build and fortify within any the same, for their better Safeguard and Defence.[4]

Thus, he guaranteed a clash between two civilisations.

---

1. R. Hakluyt, *The first voyage made to the coast of America*, in *The Principal Navigations, Voyages, Trafficks and Discoveries of the English Nation*, 1598.
2. Appendix I. For the full wording of all the relevant charters see: <www.Avalon.law.yale.edu>.
3. W. Hubbard, *A Narrative of the Troubles with the Indians in New England* (Boston: 1677).
4. This became a long enduring template. The 1889 Charter of the Royal Niger Company ceded all the Niger Basin and any lands beyond they wished to occupy to the company in an identical way.

James was also endeavouring to be as magnanimous as his illustrious predecessor Elizabeth I. She had granted the first American settlement charters to Sir Humphrey Gilbert in 1578 and Sir Walter Ralegh in 1584. Her less loquacious grandfather Henry VII had promised much the same to John Cabot in 1498 although he had also been invited to 'subdue, occupy and possess all such towns, cities, castles and isles of them found'.[5]

Cabot took no advantage of the free gift of America; he ventured just 'inland beyond the shooting distance of a crossbow', took fright, and sailed away never to return. Sir Humphrey Gilbert drowned. Ralegh never set foot in North America. In 1584, he had the foresight to send a reconnaissance party to the New World to report back before a larger group was despatched to the same coast to establish a pirate base from which attacks could be launched upon Spanish treasure ships.

The two-ship expedition, jointly commanded by Captains Philip Amadas and Arthur Barlowe, departed on 27 April 1584, returning to the West of England in mid September to deliver a very favourable report of the land and its people. Of the land on which they came ashore (possibly Bodie Island, now a narrow peninsular at the northern end of the Carolinas Outer Banks) they wrote: '[It] had many goodly woods, and full of deer, conies, hares, and fowl, even in the middle of summer, in incredible abundance'. Thanks to the local king's generosity, they feasted well, for the king sent them:

> ... every day a brace of fat bucks, conies, hares, fish, the best of the world, he sent us diverse kinds of fruits, melons, walnuts, cucumbers, gourds, peas, and diverse roots, and fruits very excellent good, and of their country corn, which is white, fair and well tasted.[6]

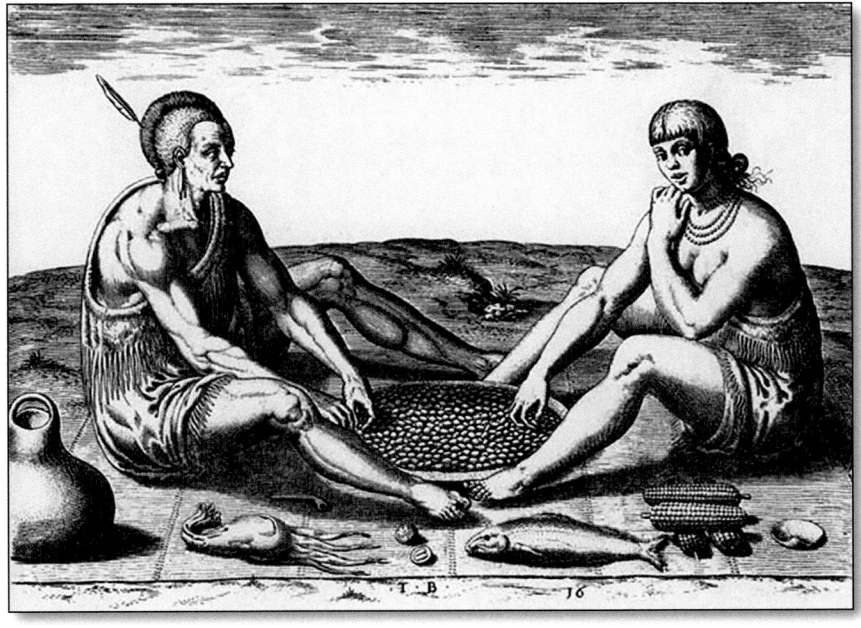

Their sitting at meals (John White, 1585). The first English colonists at Roanoke wrote about the civil domesticity of a people with whom they felt safe to dwell among. (Public domain)

---

5   D. B. and A. M. Quinn, *The English New England Voyages, 1602–1608* (Hakluyt Society, 1983).
6   T. Harriot, *A Briefe and True Report of the New Found Land of Virginia*, New York, 1972.

According to the travellers, the corn was harvested three times a year.

The people in this demi-paradise had welcomed them enthusiastically and even if there was going to be a dispute between the two groups, the captains considered any hostility would end in favour of the visitors:

> When we discharged any piece, were it but a harquebush [early musket], they would tremble thereat for very fear, and for the strangeness of the same: for the weapons that they themselves use, are bows and arrows: the arrows are but of small canes, headed with a sharp shell, or tooth of a fish sufficiently enough to kill a naked man. Their swords are of wood hardened: likewise, they use wooden breastplates for their defence. They have besides a kind of a club, in the end whereof they fasten the sharp horns of a stag, or other beast.[1]

What the two captains failed to realise was they had not arrived at a continuous cornucopia and the Amerindian diet varied between feast and famine. Generous when food was plentiful, they naturally had no desire to share with strangers. They had to eke out a precarious living in the wintertime, especially once they realised the settlers (who arrived the following year) had no provisions or skills of their own to hunt, fish, sow or harvest and sought only to scrounge or seize their succour.

The result was failure; Ralegh's first colony was evacuated by Francis Drake in 1586 shortly before a tardy re-supply arrived under the command of Richard Grenville. Finding the settlement at Roanoke abandoned, Grenville ordered 15 hapless soldiers to man the site until reinforcements arrived. They did not survive. Neither did the small group that came ashore in 1587 under the inadequate command of the artist John White. He returned home to seek assistance but on his delayed return, found no sign of the settlers including his daughter and granddaughter – the first English child to be born in the New World.

During this time, admiration of the Amerindian continued. The more humane, better educated, enlightened English did not disparage the differing social mores. Even the women, despite their scant clothing, were considered ladylike:

> Their women have shoes and stockings to wear likewise when they please, such as the men have, but the mantle they use to cover their nakedness with is much longer than that which the men use, for, as the men have one deer skin, the women have two sewed together at the full length, and it is so large that it trails after them like a great lady's train; and in time I think they may have their pages to bear them up; and where the men use but one bear skin for a mantle, the women have two sewed together, and if any of their women would at any time shift one, they take that which they intend to make use of, and cast it over them round, before they shift away the other, for modesty, which is to be noted in people uncivilised; therein they seem to have as much modesty as civilised people, and deserve to be applauded for it.

---

1 For all the relevant first-hand accounts see, D.B. Quinn (ed.), *The Roanoke Voyages 1584–1590* (Hakluyt Society, 1954, 1955).

FROM HARMONY TO HOSTILITY

Thomas Harriot, who had accompanied John White on Ralegh's first expedition, wrote:

> I have given the opinions of the native inhabitants in detail to show you that there is good hope that they may be brought to embrace the truth through discreet handling and wise government and consequently will come to honour, obey, fear, and love us. Although towards the end of the year some of our men were too harsh with them and killed a few of their number for offences which might easily have been forgiven, still the natives thought the punishment just and did not change their friendly attitude toward us. I do not believe that they are likely to change their general good opinion of us, and if we are careful at all, they need not be feared. Nevertheless, we must hope for the best and try to do our best, taking care to remove the causes for any discontent among them.[2]

Mother and child (John White 1585). The child is playing with a toy given to her by an English settler. (Public domain)

Already, one can see the off handed way in which it was felt appropriate, or at the least permissible, to kill the occasional native for a mere peccadillo.

Twenty years later in 1607, on his reconnaissance voyage to the coast of what was to become known as New England, Brereton was also impressed by the locals. After several meetings with some fierce and naked men, he noted another group were:

> … exceeding courteous, gentle of disposition, and well-conditioned, excelling all others that we have seen; so for shape of body and lovely favour, I think they excel all the people of America; of stature much higher than we; of complexion or colour, much like a dark olive … their eye-brows and hair black, which they wear long, tied up behind in knots, whereon they prick feathers of fowls, in fashion of a coronet … They are quick eyed and steadfast in their looks, fearless of others harm, as intending none themselves; some of the meaner sort given to filching …[3]

This term 'filching' was to cause the greatest initial misunderstanding between a society based upon ownership and one which held all in common and little in person. The native people had only a vague concept of private property, limiting this principally to a person's clothing; all else was treated in common

---

2 D. B. and A. M. Quinn, *The English New England Voyages, 1602–1608*.
3 D. B. and A. M. Quinn, *The English New England Voyages, 1602–1608*.

and available for any who would wish to make use of it. Combined with a social order where status was not defined by personal possession of land or property, their attitude to such objects irritated and confused settlers. They had come from a society defined by such outward show, where to remove without consent, was theft. This friction started at the beginning.

In April 1578, Francis Drake met up with a group of Amerindians near to the River Plate, about whom Edward Cliffe wrote:

> They be much given to mirth and jollity, and are very sly, and ready to steal anything that comes within their reach. For one of them snatched our General's cap from his head (as he stooped) being of scarlet with a golden band. Yet he would suffer no man to hurt any of them.[4]

When one of his party threatened to shoot the offender, Drake stretched forth his hand to forbid it, saying he was 'not to kill a man for a cap'. Would there have been more Drakes; in the centuries to come, many natives were to be killed for a cap – or a cup. Far too often, the explorers and settlers responded to filching with a ferocious overreaction which spread fear and friction rather than friendship.

On 29 June 1585, the hothead Sir Richard Grenville landed near Roanoke and carried out a voyage of exploration and acquaintance in the local area. On 12 July, a villager of Aquascococke stole a 'silver' cup. By the 16th when it was not returned, Grenville sent a boat over to the settlement to set fire to the village and its field of corn.[5] It is difficult to say what the equivalent, legal response would have been in England to the theft of a similar object.

In October 1609, while Henry Hudson was voyaging up the eponymous river it was recorded on one afternoon:

> … one canoe kept hanging under our stern with one man in it … who got up by our rudder to the cabin window and stole out my pillow, and two shirts, and two bandeliers. Our master's mate shot at him, and struck him in the breast and killed him … We manned our boat and got our things again. Then one of them that swam got hold of our boat, thinking to overthrow it but our cook took a sword and cut off one of his hands and he was drowned.[6]

There were those who cast a wry smile at this native proclivity. The writer of *A Brief Description of the People* reported:

> The people steal anything that comes near them, yea are so practiced in this art that looking in our face they would move with their foot between their toes convey a chisel, knife, piercer, or any indifferent light thing: which having once conveyed they hold it an injury to take the same from them.[7]

---

4   R. Hakluyt, *The Principal Navigations, Voyages, Trafficks and Discoveries of the English Nation*.
5   Ibid.
6   G. M. Ashler, Henry Hudson the Navigator: the Original Documents in which his Career is recorded, 1860.
7   *CSP Colonial*, Vol. I, 1574–1660, May 1607.

Filching apart, most of the early contacts were positive. In 1603, Martin Pring sojourning at Cape Cod during his reconnaissance, wrote:

> The people of the country came to our men sometimes ten, twenty, forty or threescore, and at one time one hundred and twenty at once … We had a youth in our company that could play upon a gitterne [a type of guitar], in whose homely music they took great delight, and would give him many things … and danced twenty in a ring.[8]

Brereton was prepared to overlook their inquisitive acquisitiveness for the greater good, considering it most important to establish:

> … principally, by what means the people of those parts may be drawn by all courtesies into love with our nation; that we become not hateful unto them, as the Spaniard is in Italy and in the West Indies, and elsewhere by their manner of usage: for a gentle course without cruelty and tyranny best answereth the profession of a Christian … maketh our seating most void of blood, most profitable in trade of merchandise, most firm and stable, and least subject to remove by practice of enemies … and to be known to be more able to scourge the people there, civil or savage, than willing to offer any violence …[9]

Meanwhile, John Morton in New England admired:

> Their Reverence, and Respect to Age: It is a thing to be admired, and indeed made a precedent, that a nation yet uncivilised should more respect age than some nations civilised, since there are so many precepts both of divine and humane writers extant to instruct more civil nations: in that particular, wherein they excel, the younger are always obedient unto the elder people, and at their commands in every respect without grumbling; in all counsels (as therein they are circumspect to do their actions by advise and counsel, and not rashly or inconsiderately) the younger men's opinion shall be heard, but the old men's opinion and counsel embraced and followed. Besides, as the elder feed and provide for the younger in infancy, so do the younger, after being grown to years of manhood, provide for those that be aged.[10]

Even as late as 1649, a group of English voyagers were rescued, despite being abandoned on an offshore island in such dire straits that they resorted to cannibalism. They were revived by friendly Amerindians who fed, watered and warmed them and then guided them on their way. The party could easily have been assaulted for their guns were 'most of them unfix'd and out of order and our powder much decayed'. The group's leader, Henry Norwood, wrote of the support:

---

8   M. Pring, *A voyage … for the discovery of the North part of Virginia*, in Purchas, *Pilgrimes, iv*, 1654.
9   *Ibid.*
10 T. Morton, *Manners and Customs of the Amerindians of New England* (Boston: 1637).

The village of Pomeiooc (John White 1585). The palisade was probably less regular and more closely staked. The depiction allows the artist to better show the buildings inside. (Public domain)

> The ears of Indian corn they gave us for present sustenance, needed no other interpreter to let them know how much more acceptable it was to us than the sight of dead and living corpses, which raised great compassion in them, especially the women, who are observed to be of a soft tender nature.[11]

Yet once settlement was underway, it did not take long for the newcomers to realise that they were not going to get on with their neighbours. John Smith was not long at Jamestown before he formed the opinion that they:

> … are inconsistent in everything, but what fear retraineth them to keep. Crafty, timourous, quick of comprehension and very ingenuous. Some are of disposition fearful, some bold, most cautious, all Savage. Generally covetous of copper, beads, and such like trash. They are soon moved to anger and so malicious, that they seldom forget an injury.[12]

Seemingly unable to learn lessons from the failure at Roanoke, the Virginia Company's settler parties of 1607 and 1608 were manned neither for conflict or continuity. They consisted of 234 of whom none were described as 'farmers'. However, there were 92 gentlemen, seven tailors, two goldsmiths, two refiners, a jeweller, a perfumer and a pipe-maker; all unproductive mouths to feed. The practical team consisted of only two blacksmiths, three masons, four carpenters and 44 ordinary labourers. This diverse group then chose to establish their base, called Jamestown, on a low-lying mosquito-infested headland whose water source was brackish and impure.

---

11   H. Norwood, *A Voyage to Virginia* (Gale: Sabin America, 2012).
12   J. Smith, P. Barbour, (ed.), *The Complete Works of Captain John Smith (1580–1631)* (University of North Carolina: 1986).

It is not surprising that illness, disease and starvation soon arrived to despatch the majority of them. They owed their survival to one man, Captain John Smith, who bullied and persuaded them and their Powhatan neighbours sufficiently enough to ensure this barely credible group clung on until help arrived.

It was to be a similar story in New England in 1620, where the Pilgrims, ignoring a map provided by John Smith that clearly showed the advantages of neighbouring Massachusetts Bay, chose to settle at less suitable Plymouth in Cape Cod. Here, their pathetic attempts at survival would have failed had not the Amerindians taught and supported them.

They should not have been so ill-prepared as by 1607, the sponsors of adventurers had built up a reasonable idea of what to expect from this bountiful land and the reports were most favourable. Brereton, wrote of his sights of Maine:

> God & Nature hath bestowed on these places, in comparison whereof, the most fertile part of all England is but barren; we went in our light-horseman from this island to the Maine … where coming ashore, we stood for a while like men ravished at the beauty and delicacy of this sweet soil; for besides divers clear lakes of fresh water (whereof we saw no end) meadows very large and full of green grass; even the most woody places do grow so distinct and apart, one tree from another, upon green grassy ground, somewhat higher than the plains, as if Nature would shew herself above her power, artificial.[13]

Pring also described an empty Amerindian village which gives a clear indication the land had been under recent cultivation and was not *vacuum* as the Puritans later claimed:

> We beheld their gardens and one among the rest of an acre of ground and in the same was sown tobacco, pompions, cucumbers and such like; and some of the people had maize or Indian wheat among them. In the fields we found wild peas, strawberries, goose-berries, raspberries, hurts [blueberries] and other wild fruits.

So where did it all go wrong? The answer is surprisingly simple; it went wrong when the English turned from being sojourners to settlers bringing with them the promise of and demand for land. Even the most biased and xenophobic of the English would be forced to admit that their boorish behaviour must accept much of the blame. For a people so willing to exact stern punishment for light-fingered peccadilloes, the English were very relaxed about their own theft of Amerindian belongings – especially food and later, more importantly, land.

On the third day of their exploratory walk along the coast of Cape Cod, following their arrival on 11 November 1620, Miles Standish and his team found four bushels of maize carefully stored in a buried larder. They took away as much as they could carry back to the *Mayflower*. A few days later

---

13   D. B. Quinn and A. M. Quinn, (ed.), *The English New England Voyages*.

they went back and stole some more and desecrated a few graves and looted a wigwam.

Further south, the Jamestown settlers also saw no contradiction in taking food away from Amerindians (by force if necessary) when their own incompetence and of their sponsors, left them starving. Initially, they had traded trinkets for corn but became understandably wary when the Amerindians asked for axes and even weapons. Barter was to remain a major aspect of intercourse between the groups all along the coast, but mainly in New England where the Amerindians did have access to valuable beaver fur. Down in the south, there was little that one side possessed that the other was desirous to obtain – apart from food. For this, the English were prepared to commit robbery with violence.

This was the recommendation of the most forceful of all the Jamestown settlers, John Smith, whose knowledge of the Amerindian's wiles and ways far exceeded that of any of his companions. Throwing aside the Royal Command that they should endeavour to live in love and charity with their neighbours, Smith advocated a consistent show of force, reprisals for wrongs received, and raids for rations. Necessary as these might have been in the short term, they were the type of policy that would build up resentment within the weaker community until they felt they were able to respond in kind.

Following his capture by Powhatan in 1607 and his subsequent release, thanks to the famous and dramatic intervention of Pocahontas, Smith sailed up the Chickahominy to seek out and seize corn. Unaware that the Amerindians were experiencing one of the worst droughts for centuries, which would account for their reluctance to trade, he forced them to hand over a hundred bushels adding a further hundred to his haul when George Percy arrived in a shallop to collect even more.

Such behaviour not only caused an understandable resentment but also did much to alter the respect in which the settlers, due to their many seemingly godlike attributes including firearms, had previously been viewed. Harriot had earlier witnessed at Roanoke:

> … all the natives throughout the country began to have a wonderful opinion of us, and they were not sure whether to consider us gods or men. Their wonderment increased when they saw that not one of our number became ill during their sickness, nor did any of us die. They also noted that we had no women with us, nor did we care for any of theirs. Some of them were of the opinion that we were not born of woman and were therefore not mortal but were men of a past generation who had risen again to immortality.[14]

When the Jamestown settlers died like flies, any ideas of their godlike immortality died with them and with it any respect the Amerindians might have had for them as either immortals or mortals. Neither, when the starving English were saved by succouring Amerindians, did they have the grace to acknowledge a debt, thanking God for their deliverance instead:

---

14   H. Harriot, *A Brief and True Report of the New-found Land of Virginia*, 1588.

And in those days, in our straits, though I cannot say God sent a raven to feed us, as he did the prophet Elijah, yet this I can say, to the praise of God's glory, that he sent not only poor ravenous Amerindians, which came with their baskets of corn on their backs to trade with us (which was a good supply unto many,) but also sent ships from Holland and from Ireland with provisions, and Indian corn from Virginia, to supply the wants.[15]

Once the English had survived their first famines, in part from the seizure of food, they felt strong enough to barter and then take that which they most desired – land. In this quest, paradoxically, they used the Amerindians' lack of personal ownership to argue in favour of the incomers' land grab. For this, two complementary factors worked in their favour – European disease and European law.

In the years before the settlers arrived, many fishermen and traders had landed temporarily on the coast and made fleeting contact with the local population. However, in that short period, they had managed to infect them with diseases to which they had no resistance – measles, smallpox and plague being the deadliest. So devastating were these diseases that the native populations in some parts were reduced by some 90 percent. Vast acres of once well populated lands were abandoned, villages left deserted while the population turned inland and away from the unhealthy coast. It was thus easy for the settlers to believe that they had arrived in an uninhabited wilderness. This was certainly the King's view, his charter for New England stated that:

> We have been further given certainly to knowe, that within these late Yeares there hath by God's Visitation reigned a wonderfull Plague, together with many horrible Slaugthers, and Murthers, committed amoungst the Sauages and brutish People there, heertofore inhabiting, in a Manner to the utter Destruction, Deuastacion, and Depopulacion of that whole Territorye, so that there is not left for many Leagues together in a Manner, any that doe claime or challenge any Kind of Interests therein, nor any other Superiour Lord or Souveraigne to make Claime.[16]

The settlers were additionally guided by an ancient law which stated that land lying waste could be treated as a *vacuum domicilium*, free for the taking by anyone willing to enclose, till, plant, fertilise and generally domesticate it. As Massachusetts governor, John Winthrop, stated:

> That which is common to all is proper to none. This savage people ruleth over many lands without title or property; for they enclose no ground, neither have they cattle to maintain it, but remove their dwellings as they have occasion, or as they can prevail against their neighbours. And why may not Christians have

---

15 R. Clap, *Memoirs*, in Young A. (ed.), *Chronicles of the First Planters of the Colony of Massachusetts Bay* (Baltimore: 1845).
16 Charter for New England, 1620. <Avalon.law.yale.edu/17th-century/mass>
    The same opinion was expressed in the Charter of Newfoundland of 1610 which stated: 'we being well assured that the same land … remaineth so destitute and so desolate of inhabitance that scarce any one savage person hath in many years been seen in the most parts thereof … and being so vacant … we may possess ourselves and make grant thereunto without doing wrong'.

> liberties to go and dwell amongst them in their wastelands and woods, leaving them such places as they have manured for their corn, as lawfully as Abraham did among the Sodomites? For God hath given to the sons of man a two-fold right to the earth; there is a natural right and a civil right. The first right was natural where man held the earth in common, every man settling and feeding where he pleased; then, as men and cattle increases, they appropriate some parcels of ground by enclosing and peculiar manurance, and this in time got them a civil right.[17]

Both Pilgrims and Puritans also held true that the biblical injunction to 'be fruitful and multiply, and replenish the earth and subdue it', did not apply to nomadic hunters and gatherers.

Winthrop, wishing to see a land flowing with milk and honey and promised to him and his followers, was convinced, 'Now thou the hope of Israel, and the sure help of all that come to thee … Carry us into thy Garden, that we may eat and be filled with those pleasures, which the world knows not'.

The only obstruction was the 'pesky' natives whom the English were too obtuse or reluctant to realise, worked the land in a way that was legitimate and viable without the introduction of European methods of agriculture favoured by Winthrop and his followers. For millennia, the Amerindians had lived in harmony with their surroundings by carrying on a form of farming that kept them and the land in a symbiotic relationship. Around their villages they grew the 'three sisters', tall maize, around which beans would entwine, while ground hugging squashes kept the soil moist. Once harvested, shucked and dried, corn could be stored in underground silos where it could keep indefinitely unless stolen by the English.

Closer to their dwellings the natives planted tobacco; the fatal attraction to this plant destroyed the hope of an amicable relationship when it led to a major land dispute with the Powhatan. Of its charms, Harriot, who dying in 1621 may have been the first European victim of lung cancer, wrote:

> There is an herb called *uppowoc*, which sows itself. In the West Indies it has several names, according to the different places where it grows and is used, but the Spaniards generally call it *tobacco*. Its leaves are dried, made into powder, and then smoked by being sucked through clay pipes into the stomach and head. The fumes purge superfluous phlegm and gross humor from the body by opening all the pores and passages. Thus, its use not only preserves the body, but if there are any obstructions it breaks them up. By this means the natives keep in excellent health, without many of the grievous diseases which often afflict us in England.[18]

These crops were seasonally supplemented by fish, fowl and flesh in such a way that the land had maintained its fertility and bounteousness for millennia. Within a couple of centuries, the woods would be cleared and the mountain slopes turned into mudslides. Today, descendants of those English

---

17   J. Winthrop, *Journal, 1630–1649*, R. S. Dunn, J. Savage and L. Yeandle, (ed.), (Harvard University Press, 1996).
18   D. B. Quinn, and A. M. Quinn, (ed.), *The English New England Voyages, 1602–1608*.

settlers, campaign for sympathetic, sustainable, fertiliser free, land use – those very qualities that their ancestors deplored and destroyed. Ironically, it was the denial of access for settled agricultural planting that would contribute significantly to the defeat of the tribes in each of the several wars to come.

The failure to comprehend the natives' ownership and sustainable management of the land is easy to understand from the viewpoint of a country man raised in a land of enclosed fields and pastures surrounding villages and farms. Amending the words of Kate Grenville, when writing of another land where two worlds collided, Australia:

> There were no signs that [the aboriginals] felt the place belonged to them. They had no fences that said this is mine. No houses, this is our home. There were no fields or flocks that said, we have put the labour of our hands into this place.[19]

Nevertheless, the English wanted land and would use any justification or means to get title from a people who could not comprehend that such a natural resource could be owned by one person. The mass appropriation of native land was achieved by many methods most of which were given a legal gloss to what was, for the most part, theft. This may best be summarised in a long paragraph by Francis Jennings:

> Within the limits of jurisdiction, as well as across boundary lines, colonials everywhere used numerous identifiable devices to seize Indian property with some show of legality. One method was to allow livestock to roam into an Indian's crops until he despaired and removed. Even when the Indian uncharacteristically fenced his cropland, he found that there was something nocturnally mysterious that did not love an Indian's wall. The Indian who dared to kill an Englishman's marauding animals was promptly hauled into a hostile court. A second method was for an Englishman to get an Indian drunk and have him sign a deed that he could not read. A third method was to recognise a claim by a corrupt Indian who was not the legitimate landlord and then 'to buy' the land from him. A fourth method … was a simple threat of violence. A timorous Indian – there were many – would turn over his property for no other reason than the 'Love and goodwill' he bore the man behind the gun; he was then permitted to remain as a tenant on a corner of the land he formerly owned. A fifth … was the imposition of fines for a wide variety of offences, the Indian's lands becoming forfeit if the fines were not paid.[20]

Underlying all those options was the force of the Charters and the Law. The first charters had made mention of the indigenous population if only in the need to convert their benighted souls. But the 1629 Charter of Massachusetts granted the governors the right:

> … for their special defence and safety, to encounter, expulse, repel, and resist by force of arms, as well by sea as by land and by all fitting ways and means whatsoever,

---

19 K. Grenville, *The Secret River* (Canongate Books, 2006).
20 F. Jennings, *The Invasion of America* (Institute of Early American history, 1975).

all such person and persons, as shall at any time hereafter, attempt or enterprise the destruction, invasion, detriment or annoyance to the said Plantation of inhabitants, and to take and surprise by all ways and means whatsoever and every such person or persons, with their ships, armour, munitions and other goods, as shall in hostile manner invade or attempt the defeating of the said plantation or the hurt of the said Company in Inhabitants.[21]

A reconstructed Amerindian wigwam, Wendat, Québec. (Author's collection)

This could readily be interpreted as allowing them to attack the natives should they feel threatened by them and if they could not bring them to heel through the application of law.

English law was as alien to the Amerindians as sheep and cattle, but was enforced by the newcomers, not even-handedly but for the benefit of the white man. This flagrant inability to treat co-habiting peoples as equal under the same law or better, leaving each to practice justice as their own codes dictated, did much to cause the friction that sparked the flame.

The English recognised crimes which Amerindians could never imagine. They were spelt out in a remarkable set of laws promulgated by the recently arrived marshal and governor of Jamestown, Sir Thomas Dale, in June 1611. Seeking to install backbone into the survivors of the 'starving time', his 69 page document proscribed capital punishment for: blasphemy, treasonous utterings, murder, robbery, sodomy, swearing false oaths or bearing false witness, illegal trading with or stealing from Amerindians, cheating the Virginia Company or trading on the side with sailors. Like some modern states in today's United States, it also had a 'three strikes and out' policy for hanging. This would occur following three lesser offences, such as non-attendance in church, fornication, adultery, gambling or theft, for which the punishment might have been: having a bodkin driven through one's tongue, a whipping, standing in the stocks or other physical punishment the sadistic Dale might enjoy and employ.

This is not to say that the Amerindians were not subject to their own severe laws which were both customary and arbitrary with the chiefs having power of life and death over their subordinates. The Powhatan considered theft from the tribe, murder and infanticide, punishable by death, whilst disobedience of the tribal leaders could result in a severe beating or even a death by clubbing. The youth, Henry Spelman, who John Smith 'gave' to the Powhatan as both an apprentice and a spy, witnessed five executions in his time with them, four of them linked to an infanticide.

---

21 <Avaolon.law.yale.edu/17th-century/mass>

English law also imposed a Puritanical code that was gobbledegook to the Amerindians. They found that they could be executed for blaspheming a God in whom they did not believe and prevented from working on Sundays, a day of which they had no concept. When they were called in front of the magistrates, often to face a most biased judge and jury, they could claim, with some justification that:

> If twenty of their honest Indians testified that an Englishman had done them wrong, it was as nothing, and if but one of their worst Indians testified against any Indian or their king when it pleased the English that was sufficient … [22]

Along with land and law came liquor, of which many Amerindians could never get enough. Sadly, they had little tolerance. This was a weakness the English were only too willing to exploit claiming legitimacy for deals with a drunken native who would be horrified of his actions once sober.

The inability to handle drink was noticed very early on. In 1578 onboard the *Golden Hind*, Fletcher noted the sudden impact that the smallest sniff of alcohol had on the unaccustomed natives when one of them snatched a glass of wine and tried to drink it:

> It came not to his lips when it took him by the nose, and so suddenly entered into his head, that he was so drunk, or at the least overcome with spirit of the wine, that he fell flat upon his buttock, not able to stand any longer, so that his company began to startle as if we had slain the man … [23]

In a way, they had and would continue to do so, by using the native's genetic inability to handle the drug as a simpler way of arranging land deals than force of arms. In many ways, alcohol was a lethal weapon, made more heinous because it imposed killing through seeming kindness.

There was a notorious practice of forcing Amerindians to hard labour as a penalty for drunkenness, only to get them drunk again on the day before their discharge so that a further period of labour could be imposed. Of this 'barbarous usage' which he witnessed in 1676, Captain Wynborne wrote, 'made not only those poor sufferers, but the other Indians, to vow revenge'.[24] Equally as notorious were the cases (there appear to be more than one) where under the guise of friendship, Amerindians were fed alcohol laced with poison.

That drink was very much a one-sided weapon, can best be judged by the fact that during her period of captivity well away from the English, the preacher's wife Mary Rowlandson, saw only one drunk Amerindian. This was only after he had been provided with it by the man negotiating her release.

Drink was to remain a powerful English weapon throughout the confrontation with the Amerindians. At Concheco in Maine, warriors were

---

22 J. A. Easton, *A Relation of the Indian War*, 1675, in C. Lincoln, *Narratives of the Indian War 1675–1699*, C. H. Lincoln (ed.), (New York: 1913).
23 R. Hakluyt, *The Principal Navigations, Voyages, Trafficks and Discoveries of the English Nation*.
24 T. Hutchinson, *Hutchinson Papers* (Harvard University Press, 1936).

NEW WORLDS, OLD WARS

tricked into an unconditional surrender in 1676 by being plied with alcohol. As one of them wrote, 'Major Waldin do lie. We not minded to kill nobody. Major Waldin did wrong to give us cloth & powder, but he gave us drink & when we were drunk killed us'.[25]

In short, subordination was to be the role of the savage, considered useful only as a servant, a hewer of wood and a drawer of water. They were often sold into slavery in the West Indies or elsewhere, having in all innocence, either surrendered or voluntarily entered English domains despite not having committed any offence.

There were also punishments including imprisonment, fines, whipping, the stocks, banishment, burning, hanging, mutilation, execution, hanging, drawing and quartering, ducking, and branding, all with the possible preliminary of torture. The latter was, of course, practised by the Amerindians especially to unfortunate captives in inter-tribal wars but even here there were dissimilarities. Those tortured by the state in England were expected to yield some vital piece of information and were afflicted until they did so or died. For the Amerindians, the tortured man was expected to display great fortitude and the nobler qualities of man. When such treatment crossed cultures, it was the accounts of cruelty, sometimes inflicted by women that unnerved the new arrivals.

In 1607, William White had 'jumped ship' and moved upstream from Jamestown to live with the Powhatans at Quiyoughcohannock. From here, in the winter he sailed with them to a winter camp on the adjacent Chickahominy. In early December, George Casson was dragged into this camp. He had been seized from a boat in which John Smith had been conducting a foraging expedition.

The interior of a reconstructed native wigwam: a sophisticated building that took many months to construct. (Author's collection)

---

25 S. King, *Subjects under the Same King* (University of Pennsylvania Press, 2005).

There is a question as to whether Casson had raped an Amerindian woman and thus could have brought the punishment he was about to endure, upon himself. Naked, and stretched upright between two stakes, he was flensed with mussel shells before each limb was hacked off, while using 'shells and reads the skin was eased off from his head and face, after which they ripped up his belly and tore out his bowels', until his head and trunk were left squirming on the ground where it was scalped and the inners drawn out.[26] Not knowing the stoicism required, he quite understandably, screamed loudly for mercy.

Horrifying as White's account is, there are two reasons to doubt its accuracy. Firstly, the shear unlikelihood of a limbless torso still being alive and writhing and secondly, another tale told by White. Earlier he claimed to have witnessed a three day long tribal ceremony involving fire and dancing by heavily made-up participants, 'some of whom were black as devils, with horns'. On day three, 14 teenage boys were made to run a gauntlet and at this point, White states that he was forced to leave. However, the next day, he saw their corpses piled up awaiting immolation in a funeral and sacrificial pyre.

Given that White records no earlier tribal warfare, these youngsters could only have come from that village. There is no way such a sacrifice could have been made of such a scarce commodity as young braves. In fact, the young men were going through an initiation ceremony which involved their imbibing with hallucinatory drugs. The suspicion must be present that White, a renegade whose behaviour was so frowned upon that in 1612 it was made a capital offence, was playing the prodigal using his lurid stories to avoid punishment. Be that as it may, the colonial record includes only two accounts of such torture being employed.

The collision of two cultures was not smoothed by the English concern that they should not, by any germ of association, become like the 'other'. Indeed, the settlers had a powerful biblically based belief that any form of intimacy would be sinful. Did not the Book of Ezra teach that it was an abomination for the children of Israel to mingle their seed with that of other groups? While Deuteronomy stated: 'Neither shalt thou make marriage with them: thy daughter thou shalt not give unto his son, nor his daughter shalt thou take unto thy son.' Texts from which John Rolfe was very aware when he applied to marry Pocahontas.

Renegades were considered to have committed a capital offence while few if any, showed a willingness to learn either the native language or customs. Those who did, or who showed a sympathy to the 'savages', were held in contempt, roundly criticised and even persecuted.

Thus, in a matter of years the 'noble savage' of Harriot and Brereton had become a creature on whom no epithet was too vile to apply. 'Perfect children of the Devil', Hubbard called them while their *powwows* were said to conjure up that creature (of whom they had no concept) during their incantations.

---

26   S. Purchas, R. Hakluyt, *Hakluytus posthumus, or Purchas his pilgrimes: contayning a history of the world in sea voyages and lande travells by Englishmen and others.* Volume 4 (Cambridge University Press: Cambridge, 2014).

In his introduction to her book about her captivity, Increase Mather wrote that Mary Rowlandson had been, 'captivated, enslaved to such atheistically proud, wild, cruel, barbarous, brutish, diabolical creatures'. Yet she, who would have agreed with every word, stated that, 'not one of them ever offered me the least abuse or unchastity, in word or action',[27] which might have been different had she been taken prisoner in a European war.

In 1643 when the Royalists plundered Birmingham, the troops:

> … beastly assaulted many women's chastity and impudently made their brags of it afterwards, how many they had ravished; glorifying in their shame … were outrageous, lascivious and lecherous.[28]

Almost uniquely, this was one wartime barbarity that does not seem to have crossed the Atlantic, indeed, the anonymous adviser to Walter Ralegh suggested to him that his settlers should apply the following humane laws when associating with the natives:

> First that no soldier do violate a woman.
> That no Indian be forced to labour unwillingly
> That none may strike or misuse an Indian.
> That none shall enter any Indian house without leave.[29]

Of these laws, only the first seems to have held favour and this was surprisingly in colonies consisting largely of unaccompanied men many miles from the lasses they had left behind. However, for her unimpaired purity, Mary Rowlandson did not thank her captors but rather her God.

Nevertheless, there was both the opportunity and desire for peaceful coexistence, especially in New England's Plymouth Colony. Here on 21 March 1621, it was agreed that a League of Peace between the Plymouth Pilgrims and Massasoit, the *sachem* of the local Pokanoket Wampanoag tribe, should be agreed. It stated:

> That neither Massasoit nor any of his people should injure or do hurt to any of the colonists.
> That if any of his did hurt to any of the colonists, Massasoit should send the offender, and the colonists would punish him/her.
> That if anything were stolen from the colonists, Massasoit would see to it that it was returned. The English would do the same.
> If Massasoit came under "unjust" attack, the English would give aid; and vice versa.
> Massasoit would send to other Native nations "to certify them of this, that they might not wrong [the English], but might be likewise comprised in the conditions of peace".

---

27 M. Rowlandson, *Narrative of the Captivity of Mrs. Mary Rowlandson* (Cambridge: 1682).
28 C. Hibbert, *Cavaliers and Roundheads* (London: Harper Collins, 1993).
29 Quinn.

That the Native people who came to visit would leave their bows and arrows behind.[30]

Ironically, it was the even-handedness of agreements such as this that chafed the colonists when it came to taking control. They had started their settlements with a grudging acknowledgement of some sort of equality by crowning Powhatan and referring to both sides as 'citizens under the same king'. When it came to usurping the native's rights, they had to justify their actions by abuse, not only of the legal position, but by using disparaging terms to describe the locals, to indicate their unworthiness to be treated as equals to the civilised interlopers.

It was harder to reach agreement with Canonicus, *sachem* of the more powerful and warlike Narragansett. He sent a bundle of arrows, wrapped in a snakeskin to Governor William Bradford, the threatening meaning of which lacked any subtlety. However, when it was returned along with a package of gunpowder and bullets, Canonicus also opted for peace. He remained friendly throughout his life, even granting Roger Williams, outlawed from Massachusetts Bay, a large tract of land in 1636 which became the kernel of the Colony of Rhode Island. One year later, it was Canonicus who took the English side in the war against the Pequot. This peace with the settlers lasted until King Philip's War when Canonicus's nephew and successor Pessicus, found that the English coveted his land more than his friendship.

Fifteen years after that first attempt at peaceful coexistence was signed, the New Englanders were at war with the neighbouring Pequot. Fifteen years after the settlers arrived in Jamestown in 1607, the Powhatan would rise in a major attempt to drive the English back to the coast. The identical timescale might be coincidental, or it may show how long it took the smouldering kindling of resentment, fed by the application of unjust land claims, law and liquor to burst into flames.

Yet for all the differences that created distrust, demeaning behaviour and double-crossing, the cause of conflict can be reduced to one word – land. When conflict (as opposed to gang warfare) broke out, both sides became very aware that they had different ideas as to how fight and their weapons of choice. They also realised that if they were to win, they would have to adapt to or neutralise the tactics of their opponents. The land would be witness to a conflict not just between two tribes but between string-power and firepower.

---

30 J. H. Pulsipher, *Subjects unto the Same King: Indians, English, and the Contest for Authority in Colonial New England* (University of Pennsylvania Press, 2005).

2

Firearms and Fortifications

'If frontier wars there chance to arise, and if thereupon we shall fortify, yet will occasion the training up of our youth in the discipline of war, and make a number fit for the service of the wars and for the defence of our people there and at home'.

Hakluyt, *Voyages*, 1589.[1]

The England that the pioneer settlers in America left behind them was an agricultural, settled and for the most part, peaceful country. There was little waste-land or wilderness, the royal forests being one of the few areas where wildlife roamed freely. The overwhelming majority of the population made their living from the land but in a hierarchical structure stretching down from the crown through various levels of peers, gentry, yeomanry, freeholders, copyholders to peasantry. Enclosed fields dominated the landscape due to the demand for wood for fuel, construction and to build ships, both royal and merchant. The wood was also needed to make charcoal for the cannon foundries and the sound of axe and saw was common throughout the country.[2]

What woods remained were generally closed to the public. The medieval Law of the Forest was both enforced and reinforced during the reign of Charles I covering such expanses as the New Forest and Forest of Dean. In 1637, the boundary of the Forest of Rockingham was extended from six to 60 miles with massive fines being awarded against trespass. Thus, for many of those seeking to make a new life in America, their silvan and swampy surrounds were alien to their way of life.

Alien also was the idea of hunting which was considered the preserve of the great landowners who hunted on horseback with hounds. Shooting was considered unmanly while traps were used only by and for, poachers, including the Lincolnshire ones that embarked on the *Mayflower*. In most of the realm, hunting for game was a preserve of the aristocracy and those excluded could be severely punished if caught so doing. Thus, most

---

1 R. Hakluyt, *Voyages*, 1589.
2 A medium size warship might require over 600 trees to be felled for her construction.

FIREARMS AND FORTIFICATIONS

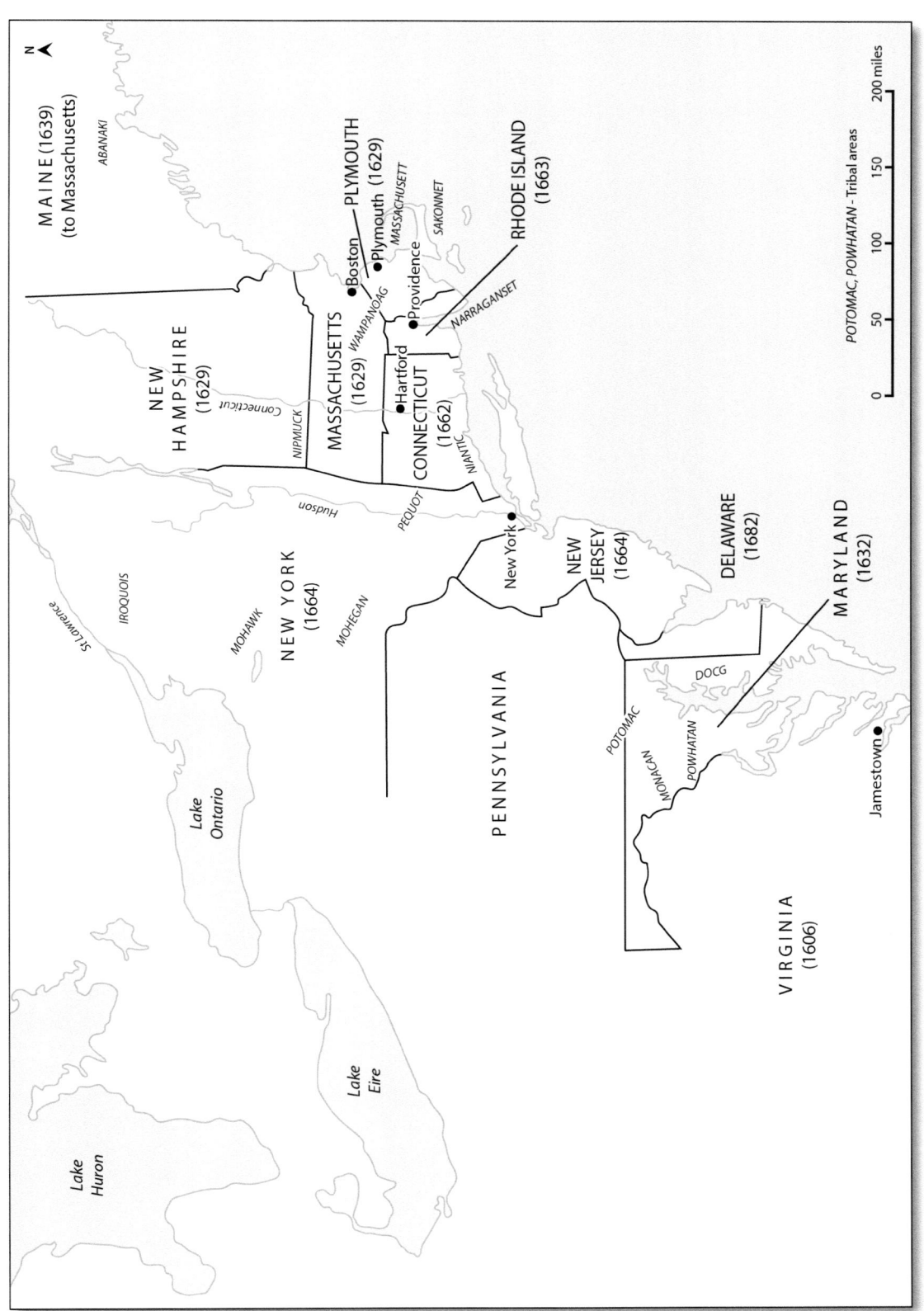

Early Colonial North America

Englishmen viewed both hunting and fishing as recreational past times and when they saw the Amerindian men engaged in such pursuits, considered them to be idle. This meant that the immigrants for the most part, were neither experienced or competent in the handling of weaponry nor the pursuit of game, both essential skills for survival. Nor mainly, were they people with military experience.

Amerindian bowmen (Theodor de Bry, 1590) It is noteworthy that the warriors in the background are engaged in hunting animals rather than in tribal warfare. (Public domain)

England had no standing army and would not have one until the short-lived New Model Army was formed during the Civil War. To make up for this deficiency, all men between the ages of 16 and 60 were expected to be available to form a militia and have weapons to hand. Being a structured and hierarchical society, the country also created trained bands which the more refined citizens were expected to join, although the most famous member of this organisation was to become the hapless train-band captain, John Gilpin.[3] The 'meanest sort' within the militia were those whom the sovereign's representative (each county's Lord Lieutenant), would summon for service abroad; the trained bands, a sort of early Territorial Army, were expected to serve on home soil only.

Much the same system was to be adopted in America where the idea of an armed militia incorporating all adult males (except clergy and magistrates) established an enduring root. This required the employment of men, such as John Smith, Miles Standish, John Underhill and John Endecott who had some military experience, to organise and train the very-inexperienced settlers. The latter arranged for 100 uniforms to be shipped to Boston to kit out his company. Along with the uniforms came eight cannon, 100 muskets (flintlock and matchlock), 100 swords, 83 types of pike and 60 corselets

---

3   See: William Cowper's poem, *The diverting history of John Gilpin* (Boston: Frederick Warne and Co 1796)

or breastplates. Similar arrangements took place elsewhere although the pikestaffs were soon discarded.[4]

Local companies were created with their terms of service confining them to their home environs. If a general campaign was required, troops were raised from volunteers or impressment with local committees deciding who should be sent, usually the unmarried, the poor, the miscreants, the anti-social or newcomers. The regiments were headed by a major/sergeant major with the local council also appointing the other officers although some places elected their leaders. Each seventy-strong company of foot had a captain, a lieutenant, ensigns, sergeants, corporals and a drummer. The cavalry also employed a trumpeter. Companies deploying away from home were accompanied by a surgeon, a chaplain and quartermaster. Soldiers were paid, on average, about six shillings with Plymouth paying privates 2s. per day, drummers 2s. 6d., sergeants 3s., ensigns 4s., lieutenants 5s., captains 6s.

The existence of trained bands did not necessarily mean that a country-wide competent militia existed either in England or in America. Few bands could claim to have any degree of proficiency. Little experience travelled with those heading to the New World.

Apart from the occasional badly organised and soon squashed rebellions, armed men had not marched through the English countryside for decades; the need for which having been much-reduced through the unification of the two crowns in 1603. Although Charles I did mismanage to go to war against the Scots in 1639.

There was also a well-established rule of law which dealt with grievances and was generally considered capable of policing the law-abiding citizenry for whom blood-feuds or vigilante action was a foreign concept. These circumstances meant that most Englishmen's arms rusted unburnished, for they were seldom used. Long gone were the early Tudor times when all able-bodied men were required to be proficient in archery. Now, these seventeenth-century travellers were heading for a land where archery was practised for survival. There was very little else familiar apart from the fact that their new world was occupied by an overwhelmingly agricultural people.

The agriculture that met the settlers was very different from their experience; the English villager saw wheat, oats and barley growing in his field; he saw horses, cattle and sheep grazing as well as the sails of windmills whirling; he heard the clacker of waterwheels and the banging of the blacksmiths hammer. His house, whether wattle and daub, mud, wood or stone was permanent and past it a road led to a market he could travel to without being molested.

None of those common crops or animals would he encounter in the land where he intended to settle. Instead, he had to learn to grow maize, squashes and tobacco. To retain his way of life he would need to clear land, drain swamps, build houses and mills, all of which meant reducing or destroying the eco-system which up until now, had supported the Amerindians. Rather than appreciate how this alien civilisation was managing to live in harmony

---

[4] R. K. Wright, *Massachusetts Militia Roots* (Army Historical Services,1986) <www.history.army.mil>

NEW WORLDS, OLD WARS

with its surroundings, the English viewed this peripatetic people's way of life with scorn and an excuse to take-over their lands.

To defend their settlements, the English arrived armed in much the same way as their trained bands were at home with matchlock, pike and sword. The elegant, accurate, quick firing and almost fool proof, lightweight longbow had been replaced as the infantry weapon of choice by the cumbersome, unreliable, heavy and inaccurate matchlock musket.

The changeover had taken place very recently in June 1578, when Drake, his gunner and some gentlemen carrying bows and muskets, rowed ashore at Port Julian, in Patagonia. There they held a friendly bow and arrow contest with some locals but the event was interrupted by another group of Amerindians arriving with hostile intent. They reached the beach at the very moment when the gentleman Winterhay's bow string snapped. Immediately the Patagonians loosed a shower of arrows at the English to deadly effect. When the gunner Oliver, tried to prime his fowling-piece to fire at the enemy, the damp powder failed to ignite and Oliver fell dead transfixed by an arrow while the equally defenceless Winterhay was fatally wounded.

As the triumphant tribesmen closed on the hapless group, Drake managed to get the matchlock to fire and killed the enemy leader. The shock, surprise and awe of this strange and lethal, noisy instrument was sufficient to make the tribesmen flee. Thus, did string-power and musket power come into conflict in one short confrontation. The strengths and weaknesses of both weapons being clearly illustrated, made the conflict in the Americas one between firepower and string-power. That is, until the Amerindians learnt the value of the former and became adept in its use.

Matchlock & Flintlock. Firing a matchlock. These awkward weapons were not suited for those travelling in small boats or marching through marshes and woodlands. (Author's collection)

A flintlock. The English were slow to adopt the more reliable flintlock but the native tribes soon saw the advantages of adopting it and became very skilful marksmen. (Author's collection)

FIREARMS AND FORTIFICATIONS

The matchlock musketeers along with a weapon and armour, needed: 'a musket rest, powder flask and a bandoleer with 12 charges, a prymer, a pryming wire, a bullet bag and a belt two inches in breadth'[5]. They would also have carried short swords or axes (not an easy outfit to trudge through the wilderness with) but then the matchlock was a weapon devised to be used en masse in the open. Tactically, the musketeers were not required to aim their weapon at a particular target, rather they were kept close together in a line discharging a volley of shot at the charging cavalry or approaching infantry. It was rightly considered that round shot emerging from a smooth-bore weapon, lacked accuracy beyond a few dozen yards. A mass discharge was more likely to be effective and would also compensate for any of the frequent misfires.

Matchlocks were both slow to load and unreliable in the discharge. To finally reach a firing position, the musketeer needed to pour powder down the barrel, ram it home and then insert a ball which was prevented from rolling out by the further ramming down of a small wad. Having primed his weapon, he then needed to light a length of flax impregnated with saltpetre. Through the action of the trigger, this was then brought into contact with the powder once the barrel of the weapon had been placed on the musket rest. A shower of rain was a highly effective way of neutralising this firearm.

De Gheyn's engraving of a soldier with a matchlock illustrates how difficult it would have been to move through woods with dripping boughs, wade through streams or trudge through snow whilst all the time endeavouring to burn your match at both ends. It did not take long for the natives to realise that the English, noisy and fearsome weapon called the matchlock, was useless without a light.

During Robert Davies's 1607 exploratory voyage to North Virginia, New England, William Strachey recorded an incident when:

> '… the savages … devised how they might put out the fire in the shallop, by which means they saw they should be free from the danger of our men's pieces, and to perform the same, one of the savages came into the shallop and taking the fire brand which one of our company held in his hand, thereby to light the matches, as if he would light a pipe of tobacco, as soon as he had gotten it into his hand, he presently threw it into the water and leapt out of the shallop.[6]

But Captain Gilbert called their bluff by having his men raise their muskets which made them flee.[7]

A similar incident happened to John Smith and his company as their boats lay grounded before Powhatan's town of Werowocomoco. Having been warned by Pocahontas that their lives were at risk, they made sure that their match cords were smouldering only for the group of strong-armed tribesmen who approached them bearing food, to complain that the smoke got in their eyes and should be extinguished. Smith did not comply.

---

5   C. Hibbert, *Cavaliers and Roundheads*.
6   D. B. Quinn, and A. M. Quinn, *The English New England Voyages, 1602–1608*.
7   Ibid.

A more reliable musket existed in the form of the flintlock for which the spark was provided by striking iron against flint. These were more expensive to produce and their distribution was often limited to those guarding the ammunition train where the presence of burning matchlocks could not be tolerated. Thus, they were ideal replacements for the Amerindians' bows and arrows.

There was no tradition among the English of employing marksmen. The private ownership of weapons for hunting as a necessity for providing food, had all but disappeared. Not so with the Amerindians for whom stalking prey was a regular occupation requiring stealth and accuracy. It did not take them long to realise that the flintlock offered many advantages over their traditional bow and arrows but only if aimed with the same care.

Whilst marksmanship was not a skill with which the English saw a need to be acquainted, amongst the hunting Amerindians it was a constant companion from an early age. Among the Powhatan, young boys were denied their breakfast in the morning until they passed an archery test set by their mothers – often involving hitting a target thrown up in the air. This training meant, as the Virginian John Pory observed: 'it was an ordinary thing to hit a bird flying'. As they grew up, they learnt hunting and tracking skills from their fathers and when it came time for them to marry, they needed to convince their future bride and her family that they had the ability to provide meat for the fire.

By contrast, recent archaeological examination of over 10,000 fragments of bones in the middens of seventeenth-century colonial homes, has found that 90 percent of them were those of domestic animals and most of the rest were from ducks, the downing of which did not require marksmanship.

In 1643, Roger Williams observed a matchlock training day in which all the participants missed-the-mark save only for a watching Amerindian who after asking permission to have a go, scored a hit. It was not until King Philip's War that Plymouth trained its soldiers 'at shooting at marks'. Meanwhile in Connecticut June 1676 it was ordered that: 'not only trained soldiers but also youths under 16 years of age to be instructed in handling guns, charging and discharging at marks'.

The Amerindians were also the first to realise that it was better to load their weapons with up to a dozen small shot rather than a single bullet. This gave a scattering that could better guarantee striking the target. In time, the English would also realise this; they would discharge their flintlocks with fatal consequences into closely grouped 'savages'.

The Roanoke settlers had been advised that they should:

> … never trust the country people with the carriage of their weapons for if they run from you with their shot which they only fear they will easily kill them all with their arrows. And whensoever any of yours shoots before them be sure that they be chosen out of your best Marksmen for if they see your learners miss what they aim at they will think the weapon not so terrible and thereby be bold.[8]

---

8 The Virginia Company of America, *Instructions Given by the way of Advice*, 1607.

FIREARMS AND FORTIFICATIONS

Ignoring such advice, the English did not fear an Amerindian threat, indeed they were dismissive of their native weaponry, the bow and tomahawk. The author of *A Brief Description* wrote: 'their fight is always in the wood with bow and arrows, and a short wooden sword, the celerity they use in skirmish is admirable, the king directs the battle and is always in front',[9] making him thus, an easy target for a musket shot.

This view confirmed that held by Thomas Harriot the raconteur, on Ralegh's sponsored 1585 expedition, who was probably for many years, the most intelligent Englishman to visit these parts. His description of this bounteous land was pure positive propaganda and maybe not a truthful, as the title of his report might suggest. However, he did give an accurate description of the inhabitants:

> So that you may know, how that they in respect of troubling our inhabiting and planting, are not to be feared; but that they shall have cause both to fear and love us, that shall inhabit with them. They are a people clothed with loose mantles made of Deere skins, & aprons of the same round about their middles; all else naked; of such a difference of statures only as we in England; having no edge-tools or weapons of iron or steel to offend us withall, neither know they how to make any: those weapons yet they have, are only bows made of Witch hazel, & arrows of reeds; flat edged truncheons also of wood about a yard long, neither have they anything to defend themselves but targets [shields] made of barks; and some armours made of sticks wickered together with thread.[10]

Neither did Harriot think that they could muster and lead a great army to repel the settlers:

A tomahawk. Lacking any metal, the wooden tomahawk was the native equivalent of the sword or dagger. (Author's collection)

> The greatest Wiróans that yet we had dealing with had but eighteen towns in his government, and able to make not above seven or eight hundred fighting men at the most: The language of every government is different from any other, and the farther they are distant the greater is the difference. Their manner of wars amongst themselves is either by sudden surprising one another most commonly about the dawning of the day, or moon light; or else by ambushes, or some subtle devices: Set battles are very rare, except it fall out where there are many trees, where either part may have some hope of defence, after the delivery of every arrow, in leaping behind some or other. If there fall out any wars between vs & them, what their fight is likely to be, we having advantages against them so many manner of ways, as by our discipline, our strange weapons and devices; especially by ordinance great and small, it may be easily imagined; by the experience we have had in some places, the turning up of their heels against us in running away was their best defence.[11]

---

9   *CSP Colonial*, 1574–1660, Vol. 1, May 1607.
10   H. Harriot, *A Brief and True Report of the New-found Land of Virginia 1588*.
11   H. Harriot, *A Brief and True Report of the New-found Land of Virginia 1588*.

Harriot's main error was his fervent belief that the Amerindians would embrace readily the doctrine of salvation through his Lord Jesus Christ. They were not and the doctrine by which Virginia (most especially New England) justified their dealings with the 'savages', would be Mosaic and not Messianic.

Harriot's account was accompanied by the wonderful drawings of John White, who was to become Roanoke's sad, incompetent and final governor. Back in England, he had created the idea of a strange paradise just waiting to welcome civilising settlers. Brereton wrote during the 1602 Gosnold expedition to North Virginia: 'the savages neither in this attempt shall hurt us, they being simple, naked and unarmed, destitute of edge-tools or weapons; whereby they are unable either to defend themselves or to offend us'.[12]

This disparaging view of the natives' armament did not always act in the settlers' favour. If the potential opposition was so flimsy, why should the colonists be provided with up-to-date weaponry? In 1608 'numerous habiliments of war' were authorised to be sent to Virginia. These included 400 'jerkins or shirts of mail', 2,000 helmets, 50 matchlock muskets, 2,000 pistols, daggers et cetera and 20 barrels of gunpowder.[13] This would appear to be a rustling up of whatever spare bits were lying around the crown's armoury. The welcome they did eventually receive, was far more nuanced and more a reflection of their own incompetence, arrogance and poor planning, than they foolishly anticipated.

As for the Amerindians' bows, Martin Pring on his 1603 voyage to North Virginia (yet to be rechristened New England) went ashore at Cape Cod and wrote a very detailed, observant account of what he saw, including this description of the weapons of the local Massachusetts or Nauset Amerindians he encountered:

> Their weapons are bows of five or six-foot long of witch-hazel, painted black and yellow, the strings of three twists of sinews [probably deer], bigger than our bowstrings. Their arrows are of a yard and a handful long [40 in.] not made of reeds but of a fine light wood very smooth and round with three long and deep black feathers of some eagle, vulture or kite, fastened with some binding matter … Their quivers are full a yard long, made of long dried rushes wrought about two handfuls broad above, and one handful beneath …[14]

James Rosier, in the account of, Captain George Weymouth's 1605 voyage to (North) Virginia described seeing the native weaponry:

> When we went on shore to trade, I saw their bows and arrows, which I took up and drew and arrow in one of them, which I found to be of strength able to carry an arrow five or six score strongly: … There bow is made of witch hazel, and some of beech in fashion much like our bows, but they want nooks, only a string of leather put through a hole at one end.[15]

---

12 D. B. Quinn, and A. M. Quinn, *The English New England Voyages, 1602–1608*.
13 British Library, Cotton MS Otho fol. 121.
14 D. B. Quinn and A. M. Quinn, (ed.), *The English New England Voyages, 1602–1608*.
15 *Ibid.*

FIREARMS AND FORTIFICATIONS

As important as the quality of the native bows was, how the English believed their potential enemy deployed them in warfare was equally significant. Here, the view expressed at the outset by Hariot seems to have changed little until it was found to be terrifyingly wrong. Henry Spelman, who lived among the Powhatan wrote:

> As for Armoure or dissipline in ware the[y] have not any. The weopons they use for offence are Bowes and Arrowes with a weopon like a hammer and then Tomahaucks for defence which are shields made of the barke of a tree and hanged on ther leaft shoulder to cover that side as they stand forth to shoote. They never fight in open fields but always ether amonge reede or behind trees takinge ther oportunitie to shoot at ther enimies and till they can nocke another arrow they make the trees ther defence.[16]

While in New England, Roger Williams, a sympathetic, observant supporter of the tribes considered, unlike the Europeans, who seemed quite content to advance in lines and get shot down, that the Amerindians:

> When they fight in a plain, they fight with leaping and dancing, that seldom an arrow hits, and when a man is wounded, unless he that shot follows, upon the wounded, they soon retire and save the wounded: and yet having no swords, nor guns, all that are slain are commonly slain with great valour and courage: for the conqueror ventures into the thickest, and brings away the head of the enemy.

The Amerindians were also anxious to know how their bows compared with the muskets of the English. When John Smith visited Powhatan's brother Kekataugh, in the village of Menapucunt, a butte was prepared measuring about 100 metres long, at the end of which was placed a target. This was about the accurate range of a native arrow shot and Smith was invited to hit it. Realising that to miss would entail more than just loss of face, Smith declined, stating that his weapon was temporarily broken.

When incidents did occur the results often demonstrated the superiority of English weapons and organisation. During Hudson's voyage up the river that bears his name, Jute noted:

> Then came one of the savages that swam away from us at our going up the river, [he had been taken prisoner and escaped through a porthole] with many others, thinking to betray us. But we perceived their intent, and suffered none of them to enter the ship. Whereupon two canoes full of men, with their bows and arrows shot at us after our stern, in recompense whereof we discharged six muskets, and killed two or three of them. Then above a hundred of them came to a point of land to shoot at us. Then I shot a falcon at them, and killed two of them, whereupon the rest fled to the woods. Yet they manned off another canoe with nine or ten men, so I shot at it also a falcon … and killed one of them.[17]

---

16   H. Spelman, *Relation of Virginia*, 1613.
17   J. Cunningham, (ed.), Jute's *Journal* (New Jersey Historical Society, 1959).

Such confrontations meant it did not take the Amerindian population long to realise they needed to upgrade their weapons – their choice fell on the flintlock. Although this had a similar loading sequence to the matchlock requiring powder and shot to be rammed down the barrel, the firing mechanism was much simpler, swifter and more reliable. It required a trigger to strike flint against an iron frizzen thus creating a spark which fell into a priming pan and igniting the powder to fire the shot. It was also a weapon that could be carried with ease and without embarrassing consequence; through river and swamp, through wet woods and snow, free from any need for a glowing ember to enable it to be discharged.

In time of trade, the Amerindians could use flintlocks with great accuracy to collect the pelts and skins so much desired by the English traders whereas in time of conflict, they could equally lie in ambush for two-legged prey. The peacetime use enabled Amerindians to obtain more of these weapons. More suspicious settlers might have sensibly traded but there were always rogue traders or Dutch merchants, happy to provide both weapons and the all-important gunpowder. This would always be in short supply if the colonies did not have their own powder mills.

The punishment for illegal trading could be severe; in 1632 the Massachusetts Court ordered that: 'Richard Hopkins shall be severely whipped and branded with a hot iron on one of his cheeks for selling pieces and powder and shot to the Amerindians'. However, excuses or exceptions were granted often enough to keep the trade in existence. When the authorities felt it necessary to clamp down and even disarm the Amerindians, their actions caused more resentment than good – for either side.

It took the colonists a little while to change from matchlock to flintlock. At the time of the Pequot War in 1637, John Underhill spoke of a volley being discharged by both 'flint and match'. By 1645, Plymouth's militia appear to have begun the transfer to flintlocks, with a small reserve being kept by each town. It was not until 1677 at the end of King Philip's War, that the colony banned the use of matchlocks by its militia.

The story of the acquisition and spread of weapons gives a clear indication these were never communities that would be living at ease one with another. Defence was always a paramount consideration. Indeed, the first structure that the English settlers ever built in America was a fort, as was the second and the third. However, as the enemy they feared was Spanish, the site of both Roanoke and Jamestown were selected to be invisible from overcurious Spanish vessels. They had reason to be cautious.

Ever since 1494 when Pope Alexander in the Treaty of Tordesillas had divided the world into two spheres of influence –Spanish and Portuguese, either side of a mid Atlantic longitudinal line – the English had known they would need to be circumspect if venturing into lands where they would be regarded as trespassers. Spain had a brusque way of dealing with interlopers.

The French had been less wary. In 1562, they built a pirate base, Fort Caroline, in Port Royal Sound, South Carolina, far too close to Spanish Florida. In September 1565, Don Pedro Menéndez de Avilés descended on the settlers and slaughtered them to a man. Thus, massacre was introduced as a European contribution to American civilisation.

FIREARMS AND FORTIFICATIONS

At Roanoke, the settlers had been advised by Ralegh to build:

> ... a pentangle in this manner. With five large bulwarks, the casements of the bulwarks large and open with a way out of the bulwarks and the other into the street. The collionsides or ocrechons [cullions or shoulders/excretions] large and long, the curtains somewhat slant, that the earth may lie the faster and the ramparts of the curtains very broad. Every bulwark shall have by it a cavalier to beat the field ...
>
> The ditch I would have large with walls, beyond the ditch a twenty foot from the ditch I would have a wall of four-foot high with a rail on the top so as to top of this should be within a three-foot height by cause it shall prevent any sudden scallado [assault].
>
> The fort should be where a landing of reinforcements would always be possible and among its servants should be; a physician, a good geographer and excellent painter, an apothecary, surgeons and "a general to command absolutely within the fort and without on all matters marshal" and a Justice, whose decisions were binding, a High Treasurer and an Admiral.[18]

Excavations at the site suggest that no such fort was erected and by 1589, two groups of ill-equipped and defended inhabitants had twice disappeared without trace.

Despite knowing this, in 1607, the first governor of the Jamestown settlement, Edward Wingfield, decided against palisading the encampment for fear of upsetting the natives. Luckily, when the locals showed their appreciation by attacking the settlers, despite all of them receiving injuries, they were able to hold them at bay until some sailors fired a culverin whose great noise and the felling of a tree with the shot 'caused them to retire'.[19]

Thus inspired, on the bank of the James River, a triangular palisade was constructed from entrenched split logs with a waterfront of 140 yards and two equal inland walls, each 100 yards long. At the angles, semi-circular bulwarks were built, upon which were mounted heavy ordnance with lighter cannon dispersed along the walls. The attackers were now reduced to firing arrows from long-range over tall posts or, with greater success, picking off hapless individuals who wandered outside the defences.

When it was completed, there was a sense of satisfaction until Captain Newport had departed with his three ships. At that point, the colonists realised that they had actually built themselves a prison in which they would suffer hunger, thirst and contract disease. By March 1610, they had had enough and abandoned the by now dilapidated structure, only to be turned back by the timely arrival of a new governor with a military training and a stiffer backbone.

By then, the source of the true real and present danger was obvious and most of the little farmsteads and hamlets that were springing up along the banks of the James River included some palisading or blockhouse arrangement. The new capital Henricus, proposed by Sir Thomas Dale, was

---

18 D. B. Quinn, and A. M. Quinn, (ed.), *The English New England Voyages, 1602–1608*
19 J. Smith, P. Barbour, (ed.), *The Complete Works of Captain John Smith 1580–1631*

constructed with 'timber, pales, posts and rails' to impale the town and 'to secure' it from 'the malice and treachery of the Amerindians'.

When news of this malice (made palpable in Virginia in 1622) reached New Plymouth, it added to local indications of suspicious Amerindian activity. In short order but with much effort, the town was impaled, for as Edward Winslow saw it the natives were:

> … glorying in our weakness, and giving out how easy it would be ere long to cut us off. Now also Massassowat [Massasoit] seemed to frown on us, and neither came or sent to us as formerly. These things occasioned further thoughts of fortification. And whereas we have a hill called the Mount, enclosed within our pale, under which our town is seated, we resolved to erect a fort thereon; from whence a few might easily secure the town from any assault the Amerindians can make, whilst the rest might be employed as occasion served. This work was begun with great eagerness, and with the approbation of all men, hoping that this being once finished, and a continual guard there kept, it would utterly discourage the savages from having any hopes or thoughts of rising against us.[20]

Or, as William Bradford recorded:

> This summer they built a fort with good timber, both strong and comely, which was of good defence, made with a flat roof and battlements, on which their ordnance were mounted, and where they kept constant watch, especially in time of danger. It served them also for a meeting house and was fitted accordingly for that use. It was a great work for them in this weakness and time of wants, but the danger of the time required it; and both the continual rumour of the fears from the Amerindians here, especially the Narragansetts, and also the hearing of that great massacre in Virginia, made all hands willing to dispatch the same.[21]

In 1627, Plymouth was visited by Isaack de Rasieres, chief trading agent for the Dutch West India Company as well as Secretary to the Director-General of New Netherland. He made detailed notes and described the township thus:

> New Plymouth lies on the slope of a hill stretching east towards the sea-coast, with a broad street about a cannon shot of 800 feet long, leading down the hill; with a [street] crossing in the middle, northwards to the rivulet and southwards to the land. The houses are constructed of clapboards, with gardens also enclosed behind and at the sides with clapboards, so that their houses and courtyards are arranged in very good order, with a stockade against sudden attack; and at the ends of the streets there are three wooden gates. In the centre, on the cross street, stands the Governor's house [Bradford], before which is a square stockade upon which four patereros are mounted, so as to enfilade the streets. Upon the hill they have a large square house with a flat roof, built of thick sawn planks stayed with oak beams, upon the top of which they have six cannon, which shoot iron balls of four and five pounds, and command the surrounding country. The lower part they

---

20   E. Winslow, *Good Newes from New England*, 1624 (Applewood books, 1996).
21   W. Bradford, *Of Plymouth Plantation* (Boston: The Massachusetts Historical Society, 1912).

FIREARMS AND FORTIFICATIONS

use for their church, where they preach on Sundays and the usual holidays.[22]

Within this stockade life was beginning to resemble that of a frontier fort not an agricultural settlement. Isaac de Rasieres noted that for Sunday service:

> They assembled by beat of drum, each with his musket or firelock, in front of the captain's door: they … place themselves in order, three abreast, and are led by a sergeant without beat of drum. Behind comes the Governor … on his left hand, the captain with his side-arms … and so they march in good order, and each sets his arms down near him. Thus, they are constantly on their guard night and day.[23]

Reconstruction of Burial-Hill Fort, New Plymouth, built in 1622, the year of the massacre in Virginia. (Author's collection)

When the English and the Dutch moved rival ventures into the Connecticut Valley, the former rushed a holding group of 20 men to the river mouth to erect a temporary fort. Here, the threat of their two guns was sufficient to prevent a Dutch sloop landing troops to make alternative arrangements. Later, its presence even deterred Governor Andros of New York from landing to claim the area for his patron the Duke of York.

In 1635, a fort designed by Lieutenant Gardener (a military engineer recruited for this project by Lord Saye and Sele) and Lord Brook, was constructed. The appropriately named Fort Saybrook comprised: 'Two cannons on a ten-foot high mound within a palisade commanded the channel through which shipping had to move slowly because of shallow nature and shifting sands'. The grounds enclosed a water supply from a pond and space to grow provisions including an orchard. Within the palisade Gardiner erected a great hall, a barracks and a storehouse.

Whilst Gardiner thought big, his sponsors back in secure England thought small. He had been promised his fort would be manned by 300 sturdy Puritans of which 200 would attend the fortification, 50 till the ground and 50 builders. When it came to war, he had only 24 people inside the fort including men, women and children with only two months supplies. Nevertheless, Fort Saybrook managed to withstand a siege.

Further upstream, the Dutch were ensconcing themselves at a trading post they named House of Good Hope. This was described as being:

> … upon a plain on the margin of the river. The stockade protecting the trading house included two high platforms upon which were mounted small cannons aimed at the river. Within the compound the Dutch traders kept cattle, poultry,

---

22 E. Altham, J. Pory, I. De Rasieres, *Three Visitors to Early Plymouth* (Applewood Books, 1997).
23 *Ibid.*

hogs, oxen and draft horses. Outside was a farm with a kitchen garden planted with beans, pumpkins, a field of maize and an orchard with a variety of fruit trees.[24]

These forts and stockades were never as important for the defence of the settlements as the garrisons built to protect the members of isolated towns. In May 1667, the General Court of New England, ordered militia committees: 'to erect or cause to be erected within their towns, either enclosing the meeting houses, or in some other convenient place, a fortification … in which the women, children and aged persons may be secured in case of any sudden danger'.[25]

It would be no exaggeration to state these fortified garrisons were instrumental in keeping inland settlers alive while the rest of their towns were razed and the unsheltered unfortunates slaughtered.

Thus, by the time simmering local resentment was brought to boiling point by incomer greed, the settlers from South to North had constructed their defensible positions, not realising that the tribes had no intention of storming the larger palisades. Indeed, the palisades that were to witness major actions, were those built by the natives themselves.

Internecine strife, as well as the threat from local wildlife, meant that many of the tribes lived within fenced villages. These varied from the single simple structures drawn by John Smith, to complicated double rows of tall timbers with sophisticated defensives at the entrances. Within these, the various tribal groups lived in wigwams; long huts cunningly built to keep out the cold and wet and in which several fires were kept forever burning.

In 1615, Champlain laid siege to just such a fort held by the Onodagas at the eastern end of Lake Ontario. This was a moated structure with a high walkway built between the double walls from which the defenders could rain arrows down on their attackers. Champlain resorted to building a siege-tower but even then, he had to retreat leaving the Onodagas triumphant.

In New England, the Pequot and Narragansett built less sophisticated protected villages. The former's villages, such as that at Mystic, were described by Philip Vincent in 1638, in his narrative of the Pequot War:

> They choose a piece of ground dry and of best advantage, forty or fifty foote square. (But this was at least 2 acres of ground.) here they pitch close together, as they can young trees and halfe trees, as thicke as a man's thigh, or the calfe of his legge. Ten or twelve foote high they are above the ground, and within rammed three foote deepe, with undermining, the earth being cast up for their better shelter against the enemies dischargements. Betwixt these pallisadoes are divers loope-holes, through which they let flie their winged messengers. The doore for the most part is entered side-waies, which they stop with boughes or bushes as need requireth. The space within is full of Wigwams wherein the wives and children live with them. These huts or little houses are framed like our green arbours, something more round, very strong and handsome, covered with close wrought mats, made

---

24   A. A. Cave, *The Pequot War* (University of Massachusetts, 1996).
25   K. F. Zelner, *A Rabble in Arms: Massachusetts Towns and Militiamen during King Philip's War* (New York University Press, 2009).

by their women, of flags, rushes, and hempen threads, so defensive that neither rain, though never so bad and long, nor yet the wind, through never so strong, can enter. The top through a square hold giveth passage to the smoke which in rainy weather is covered.[26]

Unlike the English, the native forts did not have cannons mounted on the walls. Indeed, cannons were not to feature in the century long wars to command and control coastal North America, being far too cumbersome to cart through wood and swamp. It is no coincidence that the two major assaults on Amerindian villages took place within swamps. In time of trouble, the indigenous population would often move their squaws, elderly and children into the natural security of these watery terrains so that, in the words of Increase Mather, 'every swamp is a castle to them'. Nathaniel Saltonstall described such landscapes as: 'a Moorish place, overgrown with woods and bushes, but soft like a quagmire or Irish Bog which horses cannot at all, or English foot use'. Indeed, the Amerindians had a special way of moving through such marshy terrain bending their legs, putting their shins in contact with the ground thus spreading the load.

As a result, two civilisations were established, ill-at-ease with each other and for the most part, content to live their separate lives. Indeed, the English distrusted and punished those who decided that native life was more acceptable than the officious, religiously controlled white settlements.

The most notorious of these apartheid actions took place in Plymouth where Miles Standish, the arrogant, quick-tempered military leader, led a group of his men to nearby Wessagusset where a crowd of English hippies appeared to have settled down comfortably to live alongside the Massachusetts. Rather than admonish the settlers, Standish (on what appears to have been dubious evidence of murderous intent by the Amerindians) tricked the native leader into a hut for a meal and then stabbed him to death along with his fellows. They then spread out to kill any others tribesmen that failed to flee – although they did spare their captive women.

Not surprisingly, seeing the slaughter, the hippies embarked in their ship *Swan*, and sailed away to the island of Monhegan. Standish returned home with the head of his chief victim, the *pniese* Wituwamat, which he then stuck on a pole – the first of many to be so displayed.

In both Virginia and New England, there was one other weapon equally available to both sides and if ruthlessly employed, could have won the war for either of them – famine. The settlers in Virginia and New England, had been subject to this horror shortly after their arrival.

In Virginia, the aptly named 'starving time' winter of 1609–1610, would have ended in defeat had not help arrived; just as the disillusioned, skinny, skeletons who had already witnessed an act of cannibalism, were about to depart. Yet, in both colonies the English averted famine principally because their enemy fed them (although in Plymouth their salvation was attributed to a good God, not a charitable Amerindian). Having failed to make full

---

26 P. Vincent, *A True Relation of the Late Battle Fought in New England, between the English and the Pequot Savages*, in Orr, *History of the Pequot War*: 1897.

use of this weapon of mass destruction, the Amerindians found it would be turned against them and with dire consequences.

The wars that broke out in the seventeenth-century were short in duration but frequent. The settlers were seldom free from fear, be it of the Amerindians, the Dutch or the French. To begin with, they responded by erecting wooden palisades and ended, in the middle of King William's War in 1692, with Governor Phipps at Boston ordering a fort to be built at Pemaquid, 'which was the finest thing that had been seen in these parts of America'.

At a significant cost of £20,000, Fort William Henry was built of stone with its outer walls being seven hundred and 37 foot 'in compass' and the inner walls, 108 feet square. On these walls were mounted 18 cannon, manned by a garrison of at least 60 men. It was considered to be unassailable, giving rise to the epithet that, 'It may be given up but it cannot be conquered'. In the end it was neither for it was surrendered on 6th August 1696, to a small company of French and Indian besiegers who proceeded to demolish it.[27]

For over a century, the English had fortified their settlements in North America and by the end of the seventeenth-century were no more secure than they had been since the end of the sixteenth. Perhaps, the wise, sad words of the elderly Powhatan to John Smith would indicate that there might have been another way of resolving conflict:

> Think you I am so simple, not to know it is better to eat good meat, lie well, and sleep quietly with my women and children, laugh and be merry with you, have copper hatchets, or what I want, being your friend: then be forced to fly from all, to lie cold in the woods, feed upon acorns, roots, and such trash; and be so hunted by you, that I can neither rest, eat, nor sleep; but my tired men must watch; and, if a twig but break, everyone crieth there cometh Captain Smith: then must I fly I know not whither: and thus with miserable fear, end my miserable life.[28]

By the end of the century the lives of many people from both civilisations would end in miserable fear.

---

27 Cotton Mather, *An History of Remarkable Occurrences in the Long War, which New England hath had with the Indian salvages, from the year 1688, to the year 1698*, in C. Lincoln, (ed.), *Narratives ... Thus.*

28 E. W. Haile, *Jamestown Narratives: Eyewitness Accounts of the Virginia Colony, the First Decade, 1607–1617* (Champlain, Virginia, Round House, 1998).

3

The Powhatan Wars of Virginia Smith's War 1607–1609

Having crossed the Atlantic in 1607, the pinnace *Discovery* remained at Jamestown carrying out many exploring and foraging expeditions for the settlers. John Smith, almost single-handed through his energy, leadership and negotiations with Powhatan, saved Jamestown from starvation and destruction.

> Gentlemen, what shame would it be for you to force me to returne with a months provision, scarce able to say where we have been, nor yet heard of that wee were sent to seeke. You cannot say but I have shared with you of the worst that is past; and for what is to come, of lodging, diet, or whatsoever, I am contented you allot the worst part to myself. As for your fears that I will lose myself in these unknowne large waters, or be swallowed up in some stormie gust: abandon those childish fears, for worse then is past cannot happen, and there is as much danger to returne, as to proceed forward.
>
> Captain John Smith, 1608 [1]

In 1577, the polymath John Dee published *The General and Rare Memorials pertayning to the Perfect Arte of Navigation*, in which he advocated an increase in the naval strength of England. He also coined the term 'British Empire'. Admirers of the influential Dee were quick to seize on his ideas and as these included Walter Ralegh, they were able to refer to his wisdom in their plans for settlements in the New World. Thus, was born the expansion that led to a global empire. Unfortunately, in 1607, the second attempt at establishing an initial foothold in Virginia, trod on land that owed allegiance to an empire already in existence – that of Powhatan.

By 1597, Powhatan's journey from the high chief of six tribes to the *mamanatowick* (or emperor) of many, was complete. By that time, he had conquered the Kecoughtans whose lands lay at the seaward end of the

---

[1] J. Smith, P. Barbour, (ed.), *The Complete Works of Captain John Smith 1580–1631*, (University of North Carolina: 1986).

peninsular created by the James and York Rivers. Ten years later, over 30 tribes to the westward of the Chesapeake, acknowledged his supremacy and his right to appoint sub-chiefs or *werowances*. They could be either male or female and acted as overlords to extract a tribute. This could amount to about 80 percent of their annual harvest of furs, corn, copper and game. Centrally stored, this bounty was then re-distributed to where it was most needed and most useful for the emperor to display his largesse.

However, extraneous elements over which Powhatan had no control, made his timing problematical. The harbingers were the arrival of hitherto unknown diseases; before whose onslaught the Amerindians – having no immunity – became fatal victims. Often introduced by a short acquaintance with transitory European adventurers, plague, measles, smallpox and the like, prepared the way for those that came after. These adventurers had come to look at the (by now) thinly populated land and declare it 'virgin' and available for possession.

Decimated though his people might have been, by the time Christopher Newport brought his 104 adventurers into the James River in April 1607, Powhatan still had some 14,000 subjects, including 3,200 warriors available to repulse these interlopers. The emperor's problem was that although he could command, he could not necessarily control any braves who were not organised into a disciplined army, nor even regiments based on tribal affiliations. Nevertheless, the ragbag of settlers disembarking on the low-lying, marshy, mosquito ridden peninsula that was to be their base, had Powhatan to deal with if they were to survive.

Although the First Charter of Virginia issued by James I, referred to the enterprise as a 'colony', its purpose was not (primarily) to establish a self-sufficient settlement which would thrive and expand in time. Indeed, the settlers were there to make a profit for gentlemen in England who had created the Virginia Company and whose main aims were to find gold and a route to Cathay. These two objectives were ones of which the geography and geology of the Chesapeake region was singularly ill-equipped to deliver.

Equally ill-equipped and ill-prepared were the ill-assorted passengers onboard *Susan Constant*, *Godspeed* and *Discovery*; many of whom were 'gentlemen', unprepared and unsuited to dig and delve. However, two men braced themselves for the very different challenges that lay before them. Firstly, the company's man Captain Christopher Newport, strove to find both the fabled route to Cathay and the gold that he believed lay beneath the soil. By contrast, the independent Captain John Smith, took upon himself the challenge to keep them alive knowing that the two essential skills of farming and soldiering were poorly represented.

Indeed, it would not be long before the settlers were very aware that they lacked 'some skilful man to husband, set, plant and dress vines, sugar-canes, olives, grapes, hemp, flax, liquorice and prunes'. At the best, this meant that the 'common kettle' contained only a mush of wheat and barley, liberally infested with worm from time spent festering in a ship's hold.

In these circumstances, Smith saw opportunity. His opinion was that the uncultivated land around them was ripe for cultivation being 'more land than all the people in Christendom can manure, and yet more than all the natives

THE POWHATAN WARS OF VIRGINIA SMITH'S WAR 1607–1609

John Smith's map of Virginia (John Smith, 1612). This remained the most accurate representation of the Chesapeake region for six decades. (Public domain)

of these Countries can use'.[2] Yet developing such land would have taken a huge bite out of Powhatan's empire. He was not consulted, being thought of as one of the 'Infidels and Savages' who lived in 'darkness and miserable ignorance …' This seems ironic given the miserable darkness into which the ignorant English were soon to be plunged. For the immediate crisis, Smith was neither in charge nor in favour.

Although the word omnishambles was not one coined by William Shakespeare, he would have been hard put to find one more appropriate to describe the English attempt at colonising Virginia. The word aptly describes their actions between 14 May 1607 (when the adventurers disembarked at what was to become Jamestown) and 22 May 1610 when the starving remnants abandoned the settlement and came within hours of repeating the earlier failure at Roanoke. When almost at the mouth of the Chesapeake, they were turned back by the timely arrival of the martinet Lord Delaware whose brief sojourn in the colony salvaged Jamestown.

Those who came ashore on the Chesapeake coast in the spring of 1607 were greeted by a hostile volley of arrows discharged by 'savages creeping

---

2 J. Smith, P. Barbour (ed.), *The Complete Works of Captain John Smith (1580–1631)*.

upon all fours … with their bows in their mouths'. This could not have been considered an omen for peaceful co-habitation. Nevertheless, peace is what they wished for and in a misguided endeavour, to demonstrate their trust of the locals, President Wingfield eschewed the construction of palisades to protect the unimpressive collection of tents christened Jamestown.

No sooner ashore then the captain/commander of the expedition, the ex-privateer Newton, reduced their strength by sallying forth to explore upstream in search of both gold and the head of the river. He was led to believe it flowed from a lake – the other side of which would prove navigable to the other side of this inconveniently placed continent and a short sea voyage to Cathay.

The natives whom Newport had made contact with, were happy to act as guides and provisioners. They escorted the English onto the great cataract on the James River that ended their boat journey, close to the major town of Powhatan which confusingly, was not the seat of the *mamanatowick* himself. They did not meet Powhatan in person but were entertained by several of his chiefs, including the great queen, Appamatuck and Powhatan's brother, Opechancanough.

Returning towards Jamestown, Newport must have felt that he had established good relations with the local chiefs; even the perennial problem of theft by an Amerindian had been settled amicably. What he did not know, was how their arrival had been reported and viewed by Powhatan; he had been warned by his advisers that a foreign incursion into the Chesapeake region would result in 'subjection and conquest' by the settlers.

Back in Jamestown, these settlers were lulled into a sense of security by gifts of food delivered to them by the Paspahegh *weroance* Wowinchapunke. They soon discovered his visit was by way of a recce when they found themselves assailed by some 200 at Chiskiack, Quiyoughcohannock, Weyanock, Appamatuck and Paspahegh Indians on whose territory the settlement was perched.

With few weapons and little shelter available, most suffered some sort of injury and one boy was killed. They might all have been slain had not a quick-witted sailor fired off one of his ship's culverins bringing down a branch above the advancing horde. The noise, the flash and the destruction spooked the attackers and they fled leaving three dead. The defenders rapidly constructed a triangular fortification on whose battlements were placed both cannon and culverin – the noise from whose discharge would, for the moment, provide a shock and awe superior to the accuracy of the shot itself.

Despite this, sporadic attacks continued. On 29 May, the attackers, creeping through the long grass, fired over 40 arrows into the new fort. Two days later, they fatally wounded a gentleman who had passed beyond the palisade to relieve himself.

Sometime that summer, Powhatan ordered his subordinate tribe to cease their attacks. Another period of calm descended over Jamestown whose settlers proved themselves capable of organising their own destruction without the aid of the Amerindians. Indeed, with a winter famine claiming many of their number, those that survived only did so because the Paspahegh were prepared to give the supplicant John Smith, some corn and other produce from their stores.

By mid December, with wildfowl available on the river, the survivors were feasting on bread, peas, pumpkins, plums as well as venison. Realising that their fate was more in the hands of Powhatan than they had previously been prepared to admit, John Smith sallied forth to meet the emperor in his capital.

In the first century of English settlement in Virginia, New England and Newfoundland, the names of only two people are widely remembered today: John Smith and Pocahontas. Their fate, and that of their people, closely intertwined with their interaction. Without them it is more than likely that the Jamestown inhabitants would have died or dispersed and abandoned this latest attempt at colonising Virginia.

John Smith was an awkward, argumentative, totally self-confident, soldier, sailor, cartographer, visionary who was utterly convinced (and not bashful) that his leadership skills made him and no other, the best choice for the presidency of the Virginians. It was an attitude that won for him few friends, probably because his rivals realised the rightness of his claims – this included the belief that he knew best how to handle the Amerindians. In December, he set off with nine companions and two guides to try and negotiate a more reliable arrangement for the supply of victuals with Powhatan himself.

They had a rough journey. When the shallowness of the Chickahominy River meant the barge could not progress further, Smith went on ahead in a canoe with just two Englishmen and the two Amerindians. Shortly after their departure, one of the rear-party, George Cassen, was seized, bound to a tree and skinned alive with sharp mussel shells before being eviscerated, disjointed and burnt alive. Unaware of this incident, Smith himself left his comrades in the canoe while he waded ahead through the marshes. They too were attacked and either pierced with arrows or bludgeoned to death.

The Capture of John Smith (*The Generall Historie of Virginia*, 1624). Smith was also a skilled artist although prone to exaggerating the events of his career for dramatic effect. It is worth noting that, even at this critical moment, the warriors appear to be dancing with their bows and arrows. (Public domain)

Smith, finding himself surrounded, broke free, only to become embogged, needing a helping hand from his attackers to haul him out of the deep swamp. Death seemed imminent but the quick-witted Smith produced his compass from his pocket and bewitched his captors with the magic of the magnetic needle. As a result, he found himself being feted and fed so much food that he thought he was being fattened up as a feast for these people who, it was still rumoured, might be cannibals. They were not. In fact, their leader Opechancanough, was Powhatan's half-brother and after a few days, he helped Smith achieve the objective of his journey by marching him off to meet the emperor.

Powhatan was found, sitting on 'a bedstead a foot high, upon 10 or 12 mats richly hung with many chains of great pearls about his neck'. He was surrounded by his wives and in Smith's opinion, 'naked savage' as he may be, he had 'a grave and majestical countenance'.[3]

---

3   *Ibid*.

John Smith saved by Pocahontas (*Generall Historie*) the most famous incident in the early history of the English settlement of Virginia and one which may have been exaggerated or misinterpreted by Smith. (Public domain)

One can assume that the muddy, red-whiskered Englishman did not produce the same feeling of awe in Powhatan; for having asked a few questions of his captive, he made it clear that Smith was to be executed with his head being laid on a rocky pillow and his brains bludgeoned out. Just as the clubs were being raised, Powhatan's favourite daughter Pocahontas, flung herself across Smith's body and pleaded with her father for his life.

Given the awe in which the emperor was viewed by his subjects, this defiance was so extraordinary that Powhatan considered it to be some sort of miracle and Smith was not only released but created the *weroance* of Capahowosick – a settlement about an hour away downstream and not part of Paspahegh territory. In return, Powhatan requested the release of any captives and the gift of a grindstone and two 'great guns'. Readily agreeing, to secure his release, Smith was escorted homeward with his guards/guides carrying ample supplies for the journey and as handouts for the hungry settlers.

Smith, modestly writing of his adventures in the third person (like Caesar) concluded his report of this mission by stating:

> Six or seven weeks those barbarians kept him prisoner, many strange triumphs and conjurations they made of him, yet he so demeaned himself amongst them, as he not only diverted them from surprising the fort but procured his own liberty, and got himself and his company such estimation amongst them that those savages admired him more than their own Quiyouckosucks [gods].

Smith kept to his side of the bargain by offering his guides two culverin for them to take back to Powhatan yet knowing full well that they would be too heavy for them to transport. Powhatan kept his word, sending regular supplies down to the fort until the spring.

Pocahontas was to save Smith's life yet again when a plan was hatched to murder him and his companions while they slept during a visit to Powhatan. In saving Smith's life, she unwittingly guaranteed the loss of her own people. Without Smith's drive, initiative and ruthlessness, Jamestown would have been lost.

The town came close to being abandoned shortly after Smith returned home badly burnt by a gunpowder explosion which might not have been accidental. If Powhatan had carried out either the execution or the assassination, he would have been rewarded by the self-destruction of the colony. As it was, he almost achieved this aim with little effort; watching from the woodland while the ill-led intruders committed suicide through disease, dearth and despair.

Smith did his best to keep morale high. Commensurate with his own desire to be seen as the man-in-charge, a position that the visits by Christopher Newport (who Powhatan regarded as the 'King of the Waters') did much to deflate. In turn, Smith took to drilling soldiers in preparation for an assault on Powhatan's capital. This attack however, never materialised.

Having exhausted most other contenders for President, Smith was grudgingly elected to this role just in time to prevent the settlement from total collapse. Before taking up his office, he sailed away again for some six weeks to continue his exploration of the Chesapeake. On this occasion he received a hostile reception from the Rappahannock who rained a great volley of arrows down upon them leaving the unfortunate Anas Todkill (who had been acting as a hostage) 'all bloody'. Rather than flee, Smith endeavoured to protect his shallop from attack by raising a barrier of shields above the gunwale through which his protected crew could point their muskets. From this floating, armoured, personnel carrier, shots were exchanged with the Amerindians with both sides content with the result.

Continuing up the river, the explorers came yet again under attack, this time from the independent Mannahoack. When captured, one explained that they had been hostile because they had heard that the English 'were a people come from under the world to take their world from them'. Smith could not persuade them otherwise and the shallop departed under a hail of arrows.

On the return journey, Smith came close inshore to a Nansemond village when the inhabitants showed friendly intent. This soon changed when seven canoes filled with armed men paddled fiercely towards them, only to back off having received a volley of musket shot and several of the crews abandoning their boats and taking to the water. Smith saw an opportunity. He recovered the canoes and out of range but in sight of the Indians, began chopping the canoes apart. This was too much for the tribesmen who called over that they wished to talk peace and save their boats.

To give an idea of what was at stake for the Nansemond, each canoe was the product of many hours of work. Amadas and Barlow described this well:

> Their manner of making their boats is this: they burn down some great tree, or take such as are wind-fallen, and putting myrrh and rosin upon one side thereof, they set fire into it, and, when it has burned it hollow, they cut out the coal with their shells, and everywhere they would burn it deeper or wider … and by this means they fashion very fine boats and such as will transport twenty men.[4]

Making a boat was an operation that could take several months of hard work. Smith played from his strength. In return for saving their canoes, he demanded of the Nansemond that at harvest time, they present the settlers with 400 baskets of corn or else 'we would break all of their boats, and burn their houses, corn and all they had'. A threat which, sadly, would be carried out. With this satisfactory arrangement, secured Smith headed back to Jamestown for his all too short, reign as President.

On 10 September, he took his oath of office and immediately set about reforming the colony which included drilling the men and repairing the store houses. Shortly after this work began, Christopher Newport sailed in from England with 70 more mouths to feed, some supplies and instructions to locate a gold mine and to 'crown' Powhatan as a tributary ruler subordinate

---

4 R. Hakluyt, *The first voyage made to the coast of America*.

to King James. Both ideas which Smith, had he possessed a sense of humour, would have found laughable as well as ludicrous. He saw Powhatan at best a fickle friend – at worst, a fiendish foe. A mock coronation was not going to change this opinion in any way as Smith suspected it would make the emperor more imperious. However, his views did not count. He was ordered to brief Powhatan on the forthcoming investiture which the proud and wily *mamanatowick* would insist took place at his capital, rather than at Jamestown.

Smith, humbled by Newport, set off. However, on reaching Werowcomoco, he found Powhatan was away on a hunting expedition. Instead, he and his two companions were entertained, most royally, by Pocahontas. She arranged a sensual dance to be performed before them by a bevy of naked ladies who, 'casting themselves in a ring about the fire, singing and dancing with most excellent ill variety, oft falling into their infernal passions', sidled up to the Englishmen. What then transpired is, in Smith's account, silent.

Newport and his party were not offered such pleasures. Instead, Powhatan grumpily allowed the crown to be forced onto his head and accepted the present of a large bed. Newport then tried to assemble the prefabricated barge he had brought from England, to launch above the James River rapids but found it was too bulky. He pressed on by foot but found no gold thus failing two goals in one trip.

When Newport departed for England, he carried with him a sensible letter from Smith to the Virginia Company. This made it clear that he felt their 'get rich' objectives were unrealisable and they would be better to send him 'thirty carpenters, blacksmiths, masons and diggers up of trees, roots, well provided'. Smith knew these would be far better than the idle gentlemen with whom he was encumbered and with whom he would have to survive another winter.

First, he called in an enforced favour by sailing down to the Nansemond village and demanded his 400 baskets of corn. When it was not forthcoming, he scared the villagers away with a volley of shot and then set fire to one of their homes. Before the roof had caught ablaze, the villagers returned with an offer to share half of their harvest. This Smith accepted and supervised the loading of his barge.

They were less lucky elsewhere as village after village was abandoned as the English gleaners appeared. Only the Appamatuck were able to add a few more baskets to Smith's haul. Smith returned to Jamestown blaming Powhatan for ordering his subjects not to trade with the settlers but there was a far more pertinent reason for the lack of corn – there was no surplus.

The past three years had seen Virginia suffer its worst drought for generations. The Amerindians, who relied on harvesting a surplus to see them through the long winter and early spring, had gathered far less than they needed for their own use. Smith's strong-arm tactics were creating an implacable foe as he stole from the starving.

With little to show from his journey, Smith considered that the solution lay in attacking Powhatan's capital with its storerooms of grain. He was given an ideal opportunity to make a reconnaissance visit without creating suspicion. Powhatan had invited him to make a deal in which he would provide food aplenty if in return, Smith would arrange to build him an English-style house along with giving him some 50 swords, a few guns, a cock and hen. Smith had the skilled artisans available to build the property and these he sent willingly to begin work and to spy out the land. He set out after them minus the weapons but was warned by friendly Amerindians that Powhatan's proffered friendship was a cunning plan to capture and kill the English party.

Being so alerted, Smith acted with caution although this did not exclude verbal fencing with Powhatan whose main argument was that the English, were 'coming hither not for trade, but to invade my people and possess my country'. This fact Smith could not refute and his lack of a bargaining position was emphasised when he found the German tradesmen, impressed by Powhatan's plenty as opposed to Jamestown's dearth, changed sides. Yet Powhatan it seems, was also keen to return to an armed neutrality, saying to Smith, in another earlier quoted speech, that rings clearly through the centuries as a *cri-de-coeur*:

> Captaine Smith, you may understand that I having seene the death of all my people thrice, and not anyone living of these three generations but my selfe; I know the difference of Peace and Warre better than any in my Country. But now I am old and ere long must die, my brethren, namely Opitchapam, Opechancanough, and Kekataugh, my two sisters, and their two daughters, are distinctly each other's successors. I wish their experience no lesse then mine, and your love to them no lesse then mine to you. But this bruit from Nandsamund, that you are come to destroy my Country, so much affrighteth all my people as they dare not visit you. What will it avalle you to take that by force you may quickly have by love, or to destroy them that provide you food? What can you get by warre, when we can hide our provisions and fly to the woods? whereby you must famish by wronging us your friends. And why are you thus jealous of our loves seeing us unarmed, and are willing still to feede you, with that you cannot get but by our labours? leaving my pleasures to such youths as you, which through your rash unadvisednesse may quickly as miserably end, for want of that, you never know where to finde. Let this therefore assure you of our loves, and every yeare our friendly trade shall furnish you with Corne; and now also, if you would come in friendly manner to see us, and not thus with your guns and swords as to invade your foes.

John Smith foils an ambush by seizing the werowance Opechancanough (*Generall Historie*) [top right] The proud chief, Powhatan's brother, never forgave Smith for seizing his sacred topknot. (Colonial Williamsburg Foundation)

The fact that while he was uttering this speech, Powhatan was also planning the slaughter of his guests, does not detract from the sentiment. The first attempt went wrong when the alert but isolated Smith, drew his pistol and firing it at the warriors, gained sufficient space to run back to his party of 20 – all armed. The would-be attackers withdrew, explaining that there had been a misunderstanding and no hurt had been intended.

That night, before the murderers crept towards the barge, a lone figure slipped down to the river-side – Pocahontas. At great risk to her own life, the princess

An even more dramatic, less accurate but legend enhancing, depiction of Pocahontas pleading for the life of John Smith. (Alonzo Chapel, 1861, Public domain)

advised the Englishmen to stay alert. They did and the night-attack failed to materialise. The next morning, alive but unreplenished, the party sailed down to where Powhatan's half-brother Opechancanough, was in residence at Pamunkey.

The *weroance* welcomed Smith warmly and arranged for some supplies to be carried down to the boat with more to follow if Smith wanted to stay for longer. All was going well until Smith's companion John Russell, ran into the hut crying out that they had been betrayed – hundreds of warriors had surrounded the hut. Leaping to his feet, Smith challenged the tall warrior to a duel and then, seizing him by his long lank of hair, dragged him outside. In a scene that would be repeated in many a western and gangster movie, holding his pistol to Opechancanough's breast, Smith threatened to shoot him if anyone spilt 'one drop of blood of any of my men'.

The bluff worked and shortly afterwards, Smith and his men sailed into the stream where the captain considered the option of returning to Werowcomoco to carry out his planned raid. In this he was unsuccessful; the two men he sent ahead to reconnoitre returned to say that Powhatan, his wives, family and retainers, had moved away taking all their supplies with them. Smith now had no option but to return to Jamestown with what little food he had gleaned.

He was in no mood to be reconciled with the indolent men he had left behind to sit around and make little contribution to their own welfare. He cleared the camp and addressed them thus:

> I speak not this to all of you, for divers of you I know deserve both honour and reward, better than is yet to be had here. But the greater part must be more industrious, or starve, how ever you have been heretofore tolerated by the authority of the council … You see now that power resteth wholly in myself; you must obey this now for a law, by that he that will not work shall not eat … for the labours of thirty or forty honest and industrious men shall not be consumed to maintain an hundred and fifty idle loiterers …[5]

---

5 W. Symonds, (ed.), *The Proceedings of the English Colonie in Virginia since their first beginnings from England in the year of our Lord 1606, till this present 1612, with all their accidents that befell them in their Journeys and Discoveries* (London: 1624).

THE POWHATAN WARS OF VIRGINIA SMITH'S WAR 1607–1609

Below is another key historic speech, recalling that delivered by Francis Drake in 1578, shortly before entering the Straits of Magellan on his circumnavigation. In similar circumstances, he told his mutinous, disgruntled and divided crews:

> For by the life of God, it doth even take my wits from me to think on it. Here is such controversy between the sailors and gentlemen, and such stomaching between the gentlemen and sailors, it doth make me mad to hear it. But, my masters, I must have it left. For I must have the gentleman to haul and draw with the mariner, and the mariner with the gentleman. What! Let us show ourselves to be of a company and let us not give occasion to the enemy to rejoice at our decay and overthrow. I would know him that would refuse to set his hand to a rope, but I know there is not any such here.[6]

Both men achieved their objective. They were very similar in their character and the leadership they displayed in time of crisis. Both realised that sometimes, words were often more powerful than whips.

Somehow, the English made it through the winter only to discover in the early spring, that rats had eaten the rations. Taking a lesson from the native population, Smith decided that their best hope lay in sending away groups to live off the land elsewhere. Some 30 he sent downstream to survive on shellfish; another group had to camp out and fish, while a third party were sent away to live with a friendly tribe. It worked but Smith won little praise from many of the 'lubberly gluttons' who would rather have traded away all their goods for food rather than work.

The pinnace *Discovery*, having crossed the Atlantic in 1607, remained at Jamestown carrying out many exploring and foraging expeditions for the settlers. (Author's collection)

In the summer, a ship commanded by Captain Samuel Argall arrived. The ship had trailed a more direct route across the Atlantic that avoided the semi-circular traditional passage via the West Indies. Argall brought with him (along with a large number of unwelcome settlers) news that a new temporary governor – Sir Thomas Gates – would soon arrive and be followed by the governor-for-life, Thomas West, also known as Lord De La Warr or Delaware. A month later, four more ships arrived – part of the massive, third re-supply that had sailed under the command of Admiral Somers. Sir Thomas Gates, an experienced soldier was being ferried onboard the *Sea Venture* commanded by Christopher Newport. Slowly, three more of the eight-ship fleet hauled into the Chesapeake, bringing even more mouths requiring feeding. There was no sign of *Sea Venture* and most must have

---

6 D. Wilson, *The World Encompassed* (London: Hamish Hamilton, 1977).

thought that she had gone down in the great hurricane that had roared across their path.

In fact, *Sea Venture* had gone aground on the Bermudas, a cluster of low-lying islands that lay unmarked and perilously close to Argall's new route. All succeeded in scrambling ashore, a feat and a tale that was to inspire the opening scene in Shakespeare's *The Tempest*. What was even more remarkable, the shipwrecked survivors under the joint determined leadership of Gates and Somers, set to work and built two new ships sufficiently sea-worthy for them to carry on their voyage to Jamestown.

Meanwhile, Smith, having argued his way to retain the presidency in the absence of Delaware, decided that the best plan to provide for all the new colonists, was to continue his idea of dispersal. Two major moves were decided upon; the younger brother of Thomas West (the absent governor) was despatched upstream to establish a settlement near the falls while John Martin and George Percy took 60 colonists with them to settle close to the Nansemond.

It did not go well. Very soon after their arrival Percy led an attack against the Nansemond, accusing them of killing two of his team who had been negotiating for the purchase of Dumpling Island, a sacred place where the tribe's temples and sacred items were kept. In the absence of agreement, Percy beat the savages out of the island, burnt their houses, ransacked their temples, took down the corpses of their dead kings from off their tombs, and carried away their pearls, copper, and bracelets, 'wherewith they do decorate their king's funerals'.

He did not justify his action, as might the Puritans, by quoting Deuteronomy: 'and ye shall overthrow their altars, and break their pillars, and burn their groves with fire; and ye shall hew down the graven images of their gods, and destroy the names of them out of that place'.[7] All these atrocities Percy had enacted but unlike the New Englanders, he did not require a biblical justification for his gross behaviour.

Neither was West winning the trust of the river Amerindians who carried out several fatal attacks on his group. He had decided to build his settlement on a low-lying, flood-prone stretch of land rather than sweat up the valley side to a more defensible and healthier site. He even spurned taking over an existing but abandoned native village to which Smith tried and failed to direct him. Smith, on one of the few occasions he did so, had to admit himself defeated and abandoning West to his fate, headed back down stream.

As he lay sleeping in the drifting boat, a spark ignited the powder-bag which lay across his body. There was a flash and Smith, his clothes on fire, leapt into the river to douse the flames and the pain. He was hauled back onboard but he had been badly burnt. His injuries were so bad, he realised that he could no longer continue to exercise the authority he felt was rightly his – especially once the new governor, brother to one of Smith's most implacable foes, arrived. With a sad heart, he decided it was time for him

---

7 *Deuteronomy* 12:3.

THE POWHATAN WARS OF VIRGINIA SMITH'S WAR 1607–1609

to leave Jamestown and he organised a passage for himself on one of the returning supply ships.

Smith had been Jamestown's saviour. No more fitting eulogy reflects his value to that community than the one penned by William Fettiplace:

> What shall I say? But thus we lost him, that in all his proceedings, made justice his first guide, and experience his second; ever hating baseness, sloth, pride and indignity, more than any dangers; that never allowed more for himself, than his soldiers with him; that upon no danger would send them where he could not lead them himself; that would never see us want what either he had, or could by any means get us … whose adventures were our lives, and whose losses our deaths.[8]

John Smith who almost single-handed through his energy, leadership and negotiations with Powhatan saved Jamestown from starvation and destruction (Author's collection)

---

8 W. Symonds, (ed.), *The Proceedings of the English Colonie in Virginia …*

4

Dale's War 1609–1613
Powhatan's High Water

> And now famine beginning to look ghastly and pale in every face that nothing was spared to maintain life and to do those things which seem incredible, as to dig up dead corpse[s] out of graves and to eat them.
>
> George Percy, *A True Relation*, 1612

The eulogy on Smith penned by William Fettiplace, could have served as the colony's epitaph. During the departing Captain's time, proportional response and purposeful action had been the benchmark. Smith had begged, bartered, bargained and when necessary, bullied his way to obtaining food for his fellows. He had succeeded in keeping their tenuous hold on the beachhead at Jamestown, both by negotiation with and threats to Powhatan. Maintaining, it must be said, a mutual respect between the two warriors and the remarkable relationship that the Englishman had with Princess Pocahontas. With his leaving, no man remained who had the capability to keep the peace. Smith's departure thus signalled an outbreak of a war in which Powhatan came close to total victory by driving the English out of Virginia.

Smith's successor as President was the aristocratic, effete, epileptic George Percy. He was the younger brother of the ninth Earl of Northumberland who had despatched his sibling to Virginia – as much as to be rid of him as to further his own career. The youth might have liked elegant footwear but he was unable to fit into the boots of the departing plebeian Smith.

The Powhatan offensive began almost immediately. It was led most willing by the Nansemond who were still smarting from the violent onslaught that Percy himself had made on their sacred places. Near their village, the English encampment established by Smith, was looking sufficiently isolated for one of its leaders, John Martin to abandon it and return to Jamestown. That cowardly move saved his life. A short while afterwards, following more desertions, the new commander Michael Sicklemore, set out to barter for bread. They were found by a search party – dead with the bread crammed

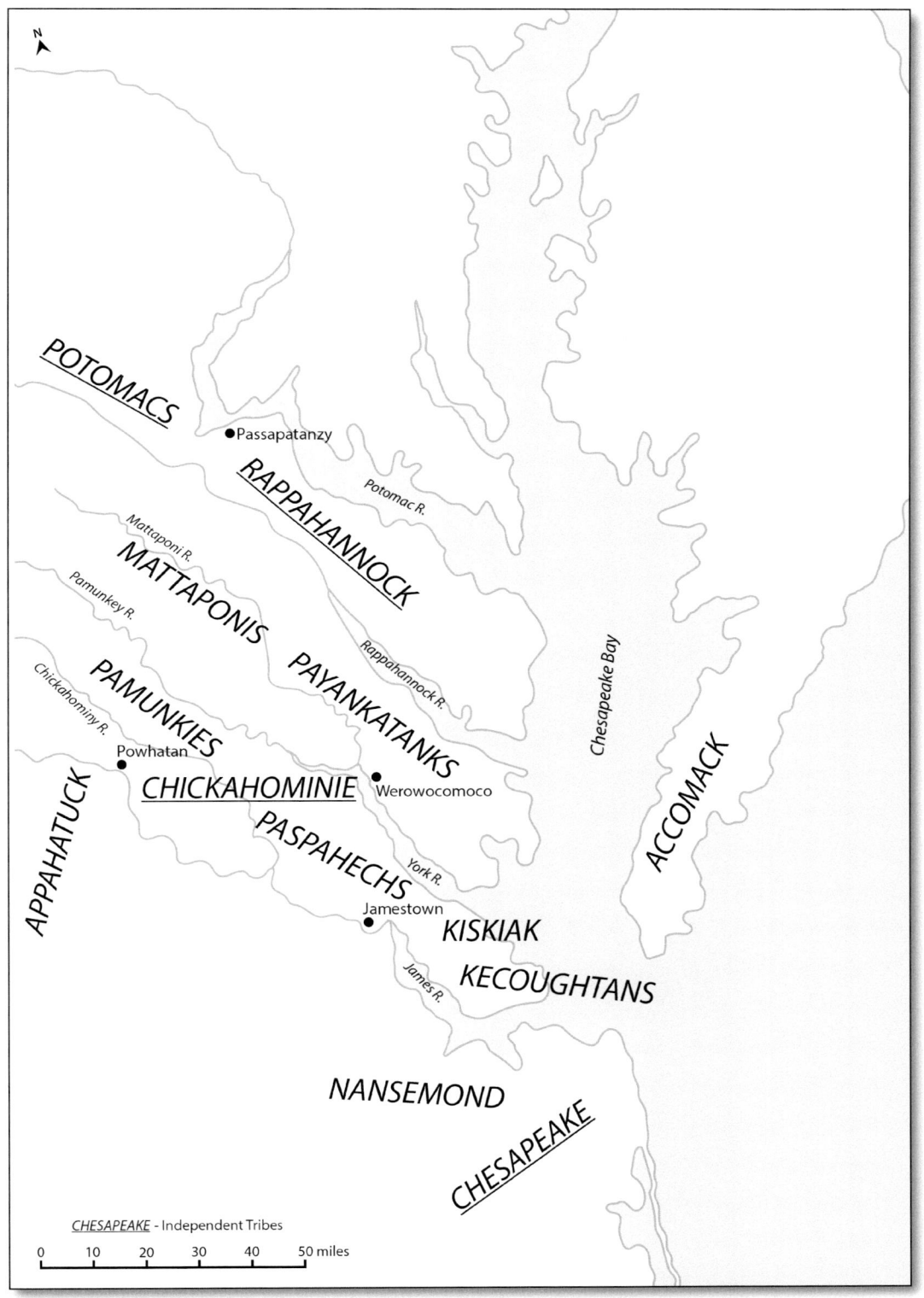

Tribal Virginia – the Empire of Powhatan

NEW WORLDS, OLD WARS

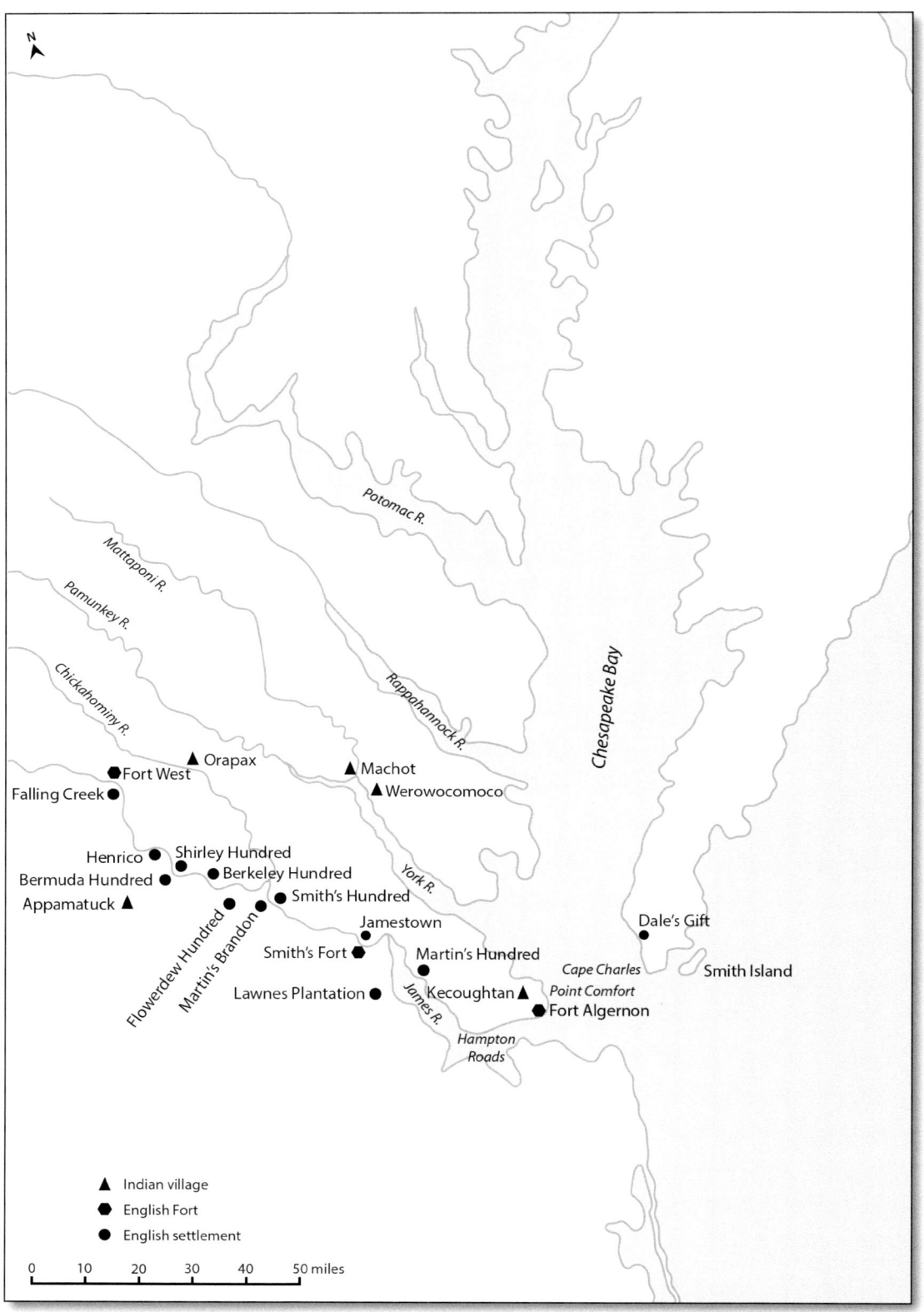

Early Colonial Virginia

into their mouths. Starvation was to be Powhatan's weapon of choice and this was the first scornful indication as to its effectiveness.

Aware of the change of circumstances following Smith's departure, Francis West decided to abandon his beleaguered settlement at the falls. This had been under sporadic attack and retreat to Jamestown thereby increased the number of mouths needing to be fed in the provision-light fort which was now under siege.

Just as a muster of provisions showed how short the rations would be over the next few months, a chance for relief appeared to have been offered by Powhatan. Along with a gift of venison, he came with an invitation for a delegation from the settlers to call on the *mamanatowick* and trade for food. The decision was made to send the experienced John Ratcliffe with 50 men upstream to take advantage of the offer.

Powhatan could not have been more welcoming. He escorted Ratcliffe and a number of his men, to a house for their evening quarters and the next day, took them to his storehouse to begin trading. Some banter about the size of the baskets took place but when business was finished, the English loaded their baskets on their backs and began the half-mile trudge down to the ship. Somewhere on the way, they were ambushed and all individuals except Ratcliffe were slain. For the leader, the Amerindians had a special death; Ratcliffe was tied to a stake and flensed with sharpened mussel shells, his skin being flung onto the fire before he too was placed in the flames. A mixture of arrogance and trust had led to the death of Ratcliffe and his men; Smith would probably have not let his guard drop and [may have] out wiled the wily Powhatan.

The Amerindians now felt bold enough to attack the ship, careless of what heavy guns it might carry. Not one seems to have been fired as its commander, Smith's great admirer William Fettiplace, tried desperately to get underway. He succeeded but at the cost of several lives. When his empty vessel berthed at Jamestown it was carrying just 16 survivors of the 50 who had set out.

The horrific manner of Ratcliffe's death was considered to show just how savage and ungodly the Amerindians were. However, contemporary Christians had little to justify their wearing a cloak of moral superiority. In 1606, the Gunpowder Plot perpetrators were told that they would be drawn backwards to their death by a horse, their heads nearest the ground and that they would be 'put to death halfway between heaven and earth as unworthy of both'. Their genitals would be cut off and burnt before their eyes, and their bowels and hearts removed. They would then be decapitated, and the dismembered parts of their bodies displayed so that they might become 'prey for the fowls of the air'.

With Ratcliffe dead, Percy turned to his other trusty lieutenant, Thomas West, to provide support. He was ordered to the Potomac River to barter corn from the Patawomeck, a tribe with whom the English had not fallen out – not yet. Enforcing his bid by cutting off two of the Amerindians' heads, West was able to sail with a full hold. But he did not travel to Jamestown. He and his crew of 36 decided to turn east in Chesapeake Bay and abandoning their colleagues, headed for England.

Percy, inadequate in every aspect of leadership, now had to lead his people into winter without the wherewithal to avoid famine. The months that followed became known as 'The Starving Time', but it might be more truthful to refer to them as 'The Starving War' – as Powhatan watched his strategy wreak its anticipated effects without him having to risk a warrior.

A Wikipedia entry states:

> … some sources say that the colonists were under siege by the Powhatan Native Americans, but the lack of primary documentation reveals the hastiness in that conclusion.

This view can hardly be justified. Men do not boil their leather belts to chew on as an indigestible pemmican (a mix of tallow and dried meat); they do not eat cats and rats and dogs when there are fish in the river and pigs a short boat journey away – unless they are prevented from sallying forth to catch them. They do not, as one man is recorded as doing, kill their pregnant, throw away the foetus and joint a mother's remains for future consumption. Archaeological evidence has found the remains of a teenage girl whose bones show the marks of her having been butchered. Neither did Percy manage to send men down to the outpost at the aptly named Point Comfort where the isolated group survived the winter on a diet of shellfish and their own pigs. However, he did at some stage, abandon Jamestown for the better life on the coast. Nevertheless, he recorded well the straits in which he and his fellows found themselves:

> Now all of us att James Towne beginneinge to feele that sharpe pricke of hunger wch noe man trewly descrybe butt he wch hath Tasted the bitternesse thereof A worlde of miseries ensewed as the Sequell will expresse unto you in so mutche thatt some to satisfye their hunger have robbed the store for the wch I caused them to be executed. Then haveinge fedd uponn horses and other beastes as long as they Lasted we weare gladd to make shifte wth vermine as doggs Catts Ratts and myce All was fishe thatt came to Nett to satisfye Crewell hunger as to eate Bootes shoes or any other leather some colde Come by And those being Spente and devoured some weare inforced to search the woodes and to feede upon Serpents and snakes and to digge the earthe for wylde and unknowne Rootes where many of our men weare Cutt off of and slayne by the Savages. And now famin begineinge to Looke gastely and pale in every face thatt notheinge was spared to mainteyne Lyfe and to doe those things wch seame incredible As to digge up dead corpses outt of graves and to eate them and some have Licked upp the Bloode wch hathe fallen from their weake fellowes And amongste the reste this was moste Lamentable Thatt one of our Colline murdered his wyfe Ripped the childe outt of her woambe and threw itt into the River and after chopped the Mother in pieces and salted her for his foode The same not beinge discovered before he had eaten Pte thereof for the wch crewell and inhumane factt I aiudged

him to be executed the acknowledgmt of the dede beinge inforced from him by torture haveinge hunge by the Thumbes wth weightes att his feete.[1]

Powhatan did not just watch and wait for the inevitable result. On one raid, his men cut loose many of the boats moored in the river thus further isolating those in the fort. On another occasion, his warriors visited Hog Island and slaughtered the 100 or so healthy pigs snuffling there – a more than adequate source of food, if any durst venture that way.

It is not possible to surmise exactly what the death toll was in that dreadful winter for some, like West, had fled or had sought shelter with the Amerindians. By the time the famine was over, just 60 starving people were alive from an initial population nearing 500 giving a fatality rate of some 80 percent. This far outweighs the losses in King Philip's War which is still cited as the deadliest of all conflicts on the American mainland.

Almost miraculously, salvation was to come from outside. On 10 May 1610, *Deliverance* and *Patience*, the two ships built in Bermuda from the salvaged remains of *Sea Venture*, set sail. The 286-day sojourn of the 180 shipwreck survivors had been brought to a triumphant conclusion by the efforts of Sir Thomas Gates, ably assisted by Admiral Somers. Gates's calm, authoritative but fair style of leadership had been exemplary. It is best summed up by remarks penned by William Strachey early on during the mutinous mutterings of their stay. Strachey wrote:

> Lo, what are our affections and passions, if not rightly squared? How irreligious and irregular they express us! Not perhaps so ill as we would be, but yet as we are. Some dangerous and secret discontents nourished amongst us had like to have been the parents of bloody issues and mischiefs. They began first in the seamen, who in time had fastened unto them (by false baits) many of our landmen likewise, and some of whom (for opinion of their religion) was carried an extraordinary and good respect.
>
> The angles wherewith chiefly they thus hooked in these disquieted pools begat such a murmur and such a discontent and disunion of hearts and hands from this labour and forwarding the means of redeeming us from hence, as each one wrought with his mate how to divorce him from the same.

Then his summary of their having such a good leader:

> It was happy for us, who had now run this fortune and were fallen into the bottom of this misery, that we both had our governor with us, and one so solicitous and careful, whose both example (as I said) and authority could lay shame and command upon our people. Else, I am persuaded, we had most of us finished our days there, so willing were the major part of the common sort (especially when they found such a plenty of victuals) to settle a foundation of ever inhabiting

---

1 <www.virtualjamestown.org>

there; as well appeared by many practices of theirs (and perhaps of some of the better sort).[2]

Despite now being much practised in handling disaster, Gates and Somers surveyed the mess that was Jamestown and after a week of discussions and some fruitless fishing, decided that evacuation was the only option. This was not going to be easy. The colonists had four ships available to them: the Bermudan makeshifts – *Deliverance* and *Patience*; the original shallop – *Discovery* and *Sea Venture*'s tender (which had managed to reach Jamestown having been cast off shortly before the grounding in Bermuda). There was sufficient room to cram everyone onboard but there were insufficient supplies to last a long Atlantic crossing. Instead, the plan was to turn north and sail for Newfoundland where sufficient friendly fishermen might be found to victual them and possibly take on some passengers themselves.

On 7 June, utilising what formal ceremony they could, the survivors marched down to the ships and embarked leaving the shell of the fort to rot or be reprieved by others. In late afternoon, they anchored off Hog Island weighing the next morning to collect the remaining souls from Point Comfort. Following that, there would be no Englishmen left in Virginia. Powhatan had won a decisive victory.

As the evacuation fleet moved slowly towards the open sea, a rowboat was sighted heading in the opposite direction. It drew up alongside *Discovery* and Captain Edward Brewster clambered onboard with momentous news. A few miles in the offing lay a fleet of three ships carrying 300 men and the new governor, Thomas West Third Baron, Lord Delaware. What was more important was that these ships carried a year's worth of supplies. The governor's order was not open to discussion; Gates turned his ships about and, on Sunday 10 June, the colonists returned to their shambolic fort. Powhatan's triumph had lasted from ebb to floodtide.

Delaware was determined to impose his presence on the ramshackle community from the start. He came ashore with a guard of honour and, finding no residence worthy of his status remained onboard ship until his dignity could be preserved.

Virginia now had for the first time, not one but four experienced soldiers leading the settlers. Gates had been knighted by the Earl of Essex for gallantry during the taking of Cadiz in 1596. Delaware had also served with Essex, including during the embarrassing expedition to Ireland. Indeed, he had been rather too close to the mutinous earl (and queen's favourite) and was charged with supporting Essex's insurrection but was later acquitted. Sir Thomas Dale, Delaware's 'high marshal' had served with Elizabeth's other favourite, the Earl of Leicester, in the Netherlands and elsewhere. The fourth senior soldier was the 'general of horse' Sir Ferdinando Wainman, who was also placed in charge of ordnance and had to dig up the cannon earlier buried by Gates before the departure. However, Wainman, did not last long, dying within two months of his arrival.

---

2 W. Strachey, *A True Report of the wreck in the Bermudas*, in *Purchas – his pilgrimage*, 1617. <www.virtualjamestown.org/>

Having formally accepted the presidency from West, Delaware summoned the settlers and clearly stated his position. He blamed them for the mess they were in and stated that should he be dissatisfied, he would be 'compelled to draw the sword in justice to cut off delinquents which I had much rather draw in their defence to protect from enemies'.

However, before any major actions were undertaken, there was an urgent need to find a source of fresh meat. With all the hogs slain, Somers volunteered to sail with Argall in company, back to Bermuda where many swine were roaming free. The mariners departed in *Patience* and *Discovery* but became separated. Somers did make it to Bermuda but died there. His grieving crew sailed back to England with his corpse for proper internment.

Once they had sailed, Delaware turned his attention to the Amerindian threat. He had been briefed that Powhatan's warriors had increased their armament by over 'two hundred swords, besides axes and poleaxes'. This was sufficient weaponry for them to wreak havoc on the still badly defended Jamestown.

His instructions from the Virginia Company were also somewhat equivocal: convert the savages or slay them, would be a reasonable summary. This applied especially to their 'priests' who they felt held their people in thrall to the devil. While they lived amongst them 'you shall never … have any civil peace or concurrence with them'. Gates thought otherwise and felt that peace could be negotiated by 'a more tractable course'. But not for long – on 6 July while sailing past a Kecoughtan village, one of his men was captured and 'sacrificed'.

Gate's response was cunning. Early one morning, he landed close to the village and instructed his taborer to play tunes on his fife and drum. Enchanted, the villagers gathered round the musician only for Gates to spring an ambush and despatch five of them with the sword. The remainder fled while Gates marched into the abandoned village and pillaged just 'a few baskets of old wheat', along with some peas and beans and a few items of women's finery. He then left a party behind to build two forts beside the village. These would be the first port of call for future settlers to refresh themselves after their weary weeks at sea. For the moment, that was his final contribution to the settlement. Two weeks later he was sailing back to England to report on the incredible events in which he had been the leading figure.

Delaware felt that the time had come to negotiate with Powhatan. Unlike Smith, he did not realise the importance of calling on the proud *mamanatowick* in person, sending two emissaries in his place. This did not impress Powhatan. He listened to Delaware's protests about Amerindian outrages and his proposal that he order a cease fire. He also wanted the return of any prisoners and punishment of those who had killed some guards. Powhatan listened before rejecting them all and demanding in turn, that the English either depart from his country or confine themselves to the environs of Jamestown. The attacks continued.

In response, Delaware cut off the right hand from one of two captured Paspahegh and sent him to Powhatan with a threat that should the great chief not see sense, the other captive would surely die. At the same time, a campaign of torching Amerindian villages and fields was introduced along with the taking of more captives including *weroances*.

The Paspahegh were obviously a major irritant to Delaware and in early August, Percy was ordered to take a party of 70 men, plus a renegade Amerindian, downstream in two boats to attack their main town. After some wayward wanderings by the 'spy', Percy deployed his troops so each cluster of Amerindian houses was surrounded. A pistol shot and the attack went in. The early skirmish accounted for 15 dead Amerindians while the rest fled. In pursuit, the English captured – the *weroance*'s wife, her children and an escort. They were brought before Percy who immediately ordered that the man be executed and the village and its fields, rich with the harvest, set ablaze.

His day's work done, Percy re-embarked taking the queen and her children with him. On the voyage home, the troops started chiding Percy for sparing the captives. Never of firm resolve, he invited suggestions as to what should be done with them. As a result, the children were thrown overboard with the men 'shooting out their brains in the water'. This was such thirsty work the boats were rowed ashore so that the men could refresh themselves. However, the Amerindians had been tracking them downstream and no sooner had they landed, arrows began to rain down on them. The English rallied and charged after their attackers driving them away and finding themselves in a sacred grove complete with a temple. This they also set alight before returning satisfied, to the boats.

Percy along with his captive, reported back to Delaware who expressed astonishment that the queen still lived. It was proposed that she should be burnt as a witch but Percy had courage enough to oppose this final act of savagery. Instead, she was put into the care of Captain Davies who took her ashore and slew her with his sword. Any hope the English had of reaching a peaceful settlement, died that night.

Wowinchapunke, the *weroance*, who himself had earlier been captured by the English and escaped, continued his harassment. In February 1611, he was mortally wounded in a fight near Jamestown. After his death, although his followers continued the struggle, the Paspahegh as a tribe ceased to exist; the people dispersed to seek shelter with other groups. In May that year, Sir Thomas Dale found the town abandoned, derelict and overgrown, giving the tribe the sad distinction of probably being the first to be eliminated by the English.

A few weeks after Percy's expedition, Samuel Argall, who had returned to the colony with a hold full of fish, was sent upstream to attack Warraskoyack This was a town that had provided Jamestown with many bushels of corn when the colonists were in great need. The inhabitants had fled but Argall, continuing the English practice, set the houses and fields on fire, thereby depriving the villagers of their winter sustenance. The expedition demonstrated the great advantage that the English had via command of the waterways. Most expeditions they mounted could reach their destination by boat thus avoiding travelling along narrow woodland paths with the constant threat of ambush. In New England, the colonists would have no such advantage and would find themselves constantly ambushed.

Argall's next voyage, a change of direction by both him and Delaware, was to seek Amerindian tribes who might be willing to ally themselves to the English in the fight against Powhatan. Having upset all their neighbours, Argall had to sail north up the Chesapeake and into the Potomac River before he reached a tribe, the Patawomeck with who he could talk alliances.

The chief he met was called Iopassus who indicated that he was no friend of Powhatan. However, he and Argall swiftly struck up a close relationship so that when Argall departed several days later laden with corn, the two men recognised each other as 'brothers'. That contact was to lead to the second most famous story in colonial history after the saving of Captain Smith's life. It was to involve the same heroine – Pocahontas.

In March 1611, the governor-for-life Thomas West, left the colony having been ill for most of his brief time in charge. He appointed the ineffective George Percy as deputy governor. However, Sir Thomas Gates with Sir Thomas Dale as 'marshal and deputy governor' as his subordinate, were probably the more imposing characters. Percy himself lasted another 12 months before returning to England in April 1612.

Dale is one of a select group of military leaders such as Draco, who are better known for their harshness to their subordinates than their mastery over their enemies. The colony already had a set of rules but Dale was to amend 'Lawes Divine, Morall and Martiall' to reflect his own jaundiced view of his fellows – whom he expected to work without shirking from morning to evening drumbeat. Those who failed to measure up would be whipped or, after a repeat offence, enslaved. The harshness of the law being imposed is illustrated in the fate of the ringleader of a small number of discontents who were discovered planning to steal a boat and sail away. As Percy relates:

> My Lord for an example adiudged one of them by marshall lawe to be executed. The execution Pveinge strange And seldome heard of I thoughtte nott to omitt, for the Pty beinge throwen of the Lather whatt wth the Swindge and weighte of his body the Roape did breake and he fell upon the grownde And in Regard of the Accident my Lord Pdoned him althowghe itt nothinge Avayled him haveinge Receved his deathe wth the gerde of the Roape and extremity of the fall so that wthin 2 days after he dyed.[3]

In June 1611, Dale refined the laws concerning personal hygiene. These were much-needed in a settlement where many more were dying from avoidable diseases than from Amerindian arrows. Consequently, washing clothing, dishes and performing 'the necessities of nature' were ordered to take place away from the habitation. It was not the regulations which were draconian, it was the punishment to be inflicted on the offences that gave these laws their reputation.

Criticism was not to be encouraged; those reported for such discontent were to have a spike driven through their tongue. Execution, by several methods, was to be the fate of the blasphemer and any committing murder,

---

3   E. W. Haile, *Jamestown Narratives: Eyewitness Accounts of the Virginia Colony, 1607–1617* (Round House, 1998)

NEW WORLDS, OLD WARS

Captain Argall with the Chickahominy (T. de Bry, America: 1619). Despite the presence of threatening musketry, Argall managed to negotiate a peace treaty with the Chickahominy – a relationship that would assist in the kidnapping of Pocahontas. (Public domain)

sodomy, robbery, perjury, adultery, fornication or trading illegally with the Amerindians, sailors or other merchants. Anyone who slaughtered livestock without permission could also be executed. In the earliest American example of 'three strikes and you're out', death was the penalty for a third offence for which the lesser punishments of whipping or the stocks had been imposed.

One of Dale's objectives was to create a new town to be named Henrico in honour of Prince Henry. This was to be sited some 80 miles upstream from Jamestown in a far healthier environment but in the region of undefeated Amerindian tribes who, as Percy noted:

> weare nott Idle all this Tyme butt hindred their designes as muche as they colde shoteinge Arrowes into the foarte where wth dyvrs of our men weare wownded & others indangered And some haveinge inploymentt wthoutt The foarte did come shorte hoame and weare slayne by the Savages.[4]

A typical confrontation involved the taborer who had featured in Gates's raid on the Kecoughtan. This time, in the continuing fruitless search for valuable minerals, a boat was despatched up to the falls:

> and goeinge by Apoamatake weare called A shoare by the Savages and beinge to fill their Baricoes wth water weare easely thereunto induced and after intysed by the Savages upp to their howses pretendeinge to feaste them butt our men forgetteinge their Subtellties lyke greedy fooles accepted thereof more esteameinge of A Little foode then their own lyves and saffety for when the Indyans had them in their howses And found A fitteinge Tyme when they Leaste dreaded any dawnger did fall upon them Slewe dyvrs and wownded all the rest who wthin

---

[4] G. Percy, *Trewe Relacyon*, reprinted in *Tyler's Quarterly, Historical and Genealogical Magazine III*, 1922.

towe dayes after also dyed onely DOWSE the Taborer who flyeinge to their boate was hardly pursewed butt gayneinge the same he made A vertewe of neccessity useinge the Rudder insteade of A Targett to kepe their Arrowes outt of his body. And so skulleinge of by little and little gott out of their Reache and freed himselfe The Savages be nott Soe Simple as many Imagin who be not Acquaynted wth their Subtellties'.[5]

In such circumstances it is not surprising that some men felt that they would be better off running away to the Amerindians, but:

many of them beinge taken ageine Sr Thomas in a moste severe mannor cawsed to be executed. Some he apointed to be hanged Some burned Some to be broken upon wheles, others to be staked and some to be shott to deathe all theis extreme and crewell tortures he used and inflicted upon them To terrefy the reste for Attempteinge the Lyke and some wch Robbed the store he cawsed them to be bownd faste unto Trees and so sterved them to deathe'.

Another pressing problem remained the shortage of foodstuffs. The re-supply had brought livestock aplenty to replenish the animals that had been killed during the staving time. Unfortunately, the continuing hostility between the two groups meant the Amerindians either shot the animals or those people who ventured from behind the palisades to tend them. For this reason, Argall's friendship with Iopassus was important. In December 1612, this relationship was renewed when the captain sailed up the Potomac to his friend's village taking a prefabricated shallop with him specifically to load with foodstuffs.

He returned to Jamestown in January with 1,000 bushels of corn. A bushel was equivalent to eight gallons or 64 pints. The daily ration in Jamestown had been prescribed as one pint per person. This was hardly sumptuous: one pint of corn was the daily allowance given to captured Athenian soldiers, cooped up in overcrowded and stifling quarries of Syracuse in 412 BC. The advice given to those wishing to travel from England to Virginia was to supply themselves for a year with eight bushels of meal, two bushels of peas and two bushels of oatmeal. Now, no one was now going to starve as long as Argall could continue trading with Iopassus; nor was the colony going to continue to be an unprofitable soaker-up of funds and lives. John Rolfe planted a packet of Caribbean tobacco seeds and produced a crop of the 'tastiest' tobacco to come out of Virginia. Fortunes might now be made – not lost.

On his next voyage, Argall ventured far inland and came across a herd of bison – several of which fell easily to his guns. Things were evidently on-the-up for with food available, Powhatan's deadliest weapon would be blunted. It was to be further dulled by what was to be, the most infamous kidnapping in American history – eclipsing that of the far more recent snatching of the Lindbergh baby and Patty Hearst.

---

5   E. W. Haile, *Jamestown Narratives: Eyewitness Accounts of the Virginia Colony, 1607–1617*

NEW WORLDS, OLD WARS

The kidnap of Pocahontas (T. de Bry, America). The foreground shows the abduction of Pocahontas in 1613 while in the background, the English are shown setting fire to a village in 1614 having been repulsed on a journey to return the princess to her father. (Public domain)

Journeying his way down the river, Argall discovered that Pocahontas was staying at the Potomac village of Passapatanzy. The reason for this being her marriage to the Potomac warrior Kocoum, who may have been Iopassus's brother. This could well have been a political marriage for the Potomac were lukewarm members of Powhatan's confederacy. However, in view of what was about to happen, this speculation is certainly questionable. In the village at the same time was Henry Spelman, the young man who had been sent to live with Powhatan. He was possibly here to woo a Patawomeck woman but his presence gave Argall the use of a friendly interpreter.

No sooner had Argall come ashore than he persuaded Iopassus to connive in the kidnapping of Pocahontas, who would then be used as a bargaining chip to achieve a peace with her doting father. Promising the *weroance* English protection should the plan misfire, Argall got Iopassus and his wife to persuade the girl to join them on a ship visit. Once onboard, they were regally dined and probably well wined, for all three slept onboard. Iopassus probably slept clutching the copper kettle and toys which were his equivalent of 30 pieces of silver of which, as Hamor wrote, 'he would have betrayed his own father'.

In the morning, the guilty couple slipped ashore while the distraught Pocahontas was told that she was 'reserved' and carried back to Jamestown. This town was to serve as her open prison until her father saw sense.

Sense was the return of eight prisoners and any captured weapons. Powhatan procrastinated for at least three months earning his daughter's ire that he loved her less 'than old swords, pieces and axes'. In the end, as was so often the case, the English had to go to Powhatan – not Powhatan to the English.

In March 1614, Dale along with 150 armed men and Pocahontas, sailed upriver and landed at a Powhatan village and repeated his ultimatum; threatening to set the town on fire if the remaining captives and weapons were not promptly returned. They were not and in response to a flight of arrows, Dale's men 'killed some, hurt others, marched inland, burnt their houses, took their corn'.

The next day, having been told that Powhatan was still several days journey away, the English continued their voyage up to the old capital of Werowocomoco hoping to arrange the prisoner exchange there. However, there was one captive the English did not wish to be exchanged.

DALE'S WAR 1609–1613 POWHATAN'S HIGH WATER

During her months as a hostage, Pocahontas had fallen in love with the middle-aged tobacco farmer, John Rolfe and had no intention of returning to her old life or old religion. Till now, few knew of this turn of events. Rolfe, reciprocating the emotions and wishing to do the honourable act of marrying the woman, was acutely aware that such an act might be considered inappropriate because of the biblical precedent from whose teachings he was seeking an exemption.

He had delivered a most grovelling letter to Dale (Appendix II) in which he begged forgiveness for his strange desires but felt that good would come of them. He need not have worried too much, Dale had his eye on Pocahontas's even younger sister but this proposal was rebuffed in no uncertain terms by Powhatan.

The marriage between John Rolfe and Pocahontas was solemnised in April 1614 after which Rolfe took his bride, now christened Rebecca, away for a honeymoon in England, where she had a somewhat frosty reunion with John Smith. However, she did not to return home. Falling ill while the ship carrying the family (including their young son Thomas) was heading back to America and sailing down the Thames, she died on 21 March 1617 and was buried at Gravesend.

The marriage of Pocahontas. The marriage of John Rolfe and Pocahontas led to a short period of amity between the Powhatan and the settlers. This ended in 1618 with the return of Rolfe without his bride who had died at the start of the return voyage. (Library of Congress)

In Virginia, the marriage seems to have had the desired political effect. Ralph Harmor wrote that, 'since the wedding, we have had friendly commerce and trade not only with Powhatan but also with his subjects'.[6]

Sadly, with Pocahontas's death and failure to return to Virginia, the main chance for a peaceful and integrated future between the Amerindians and the English faded. From now on, people of colour in Virginia (including the black 'servants' who would arrive in 1619) would be treated as second-class non-citizens.

The tragedy of the most famous marriage in American history, is that it was so exceptional. Henry Spelman is thought to have married a sister of Pocahontas, a Patawomeck who was given the English name of Martha. In 1638, the settler John Basse married the daughter of the Nansemond *werowance* who was baptised with the name, Elizabeth. Their descendants perpetuated the Nansemond tribe who the English had tried so hard to eradicate. These exceptions apart, the deep cultural divide between the two groups, rather than lessening with time, increased.

In 1924, the Virginian General Assembly enacted the Racial Integrity Act which prohibited inter-racial marriage and classified as white, only those who had no trace of any blood other than Caucasian. It thus enshrined the already existing racial segregation. However, a Pocahontas snobbery caused an amendment to be made. Many of Virginia's leading families had proudly claimed to be descended from the princess and they could hardly be banished from their homes and positions. Thus, was inserted the following exception:

> It shall thereafter be unlawful for any white person in this State to marry any save a white person, or a person with no other admixture of blood than white and American Amerindian. For the purpose of this act, the term "white person" shall apply only to the person who has no trace whatsoever of any blood other than Caucasian; but persons who have one-sixteenth or less of the blood of the Amerindian and have no other non-Caucasic blood shall be deemed to be white persons.[7]

That exception aside, almost all other Virginian Amerindians were classified as 'coloured' and their very history and ancestry was brought into question.

In 1967, following the persecution of another famous mixed marriage (that of the Lovings), the Supreme Court ruled against Virginia's laws. There followed a series of repeals culminating in an apology by the state governor, for previous racially motivated Acts. Pocahontas could rest in peace.

---

6   R. Hamor, *A True Discourse of the Present Estate of Virginia*, 1614, <virtualjamestown.org>
7   *Preservation of Racial Integrity*, 1924. <www. encyclopediavirginia.org>

5

The Sky Falls Twice

> We, who hitherto have had possession of no more ground than their waste and our purchase at a valuable consideration of their own contentment … may now by right of war, and law of nations, invade the country, and those whom sought to destroy us; whereby we shall enjoy their cultivated places.– Waterhouse, 1622.[1]

In 1618, the lives of the two major influences on Virginia's early history, ended in very different circumstances. In October, the axe fell on the neck of the failed founder of the British Empire, Walter Ralegh, through whose enthusiasm the first settlers had been sent to Roanoke. A favourite of one monarch and a fiend for her successor, his was a legacy of ideas rather than results.

Frail and full of years, 1618 also witnessed the death of Powhatan who had challenged the English ever since their arrival at Jamestown but had done so in a way that kept the opportunity for compromise and mutual respect open. Following the marriage of his daughter to John Rolfe, Powhatan told Hamor that the English:

> … should not need to distrust any injury from me or any under my subjection.

Henrico. By 1620, although most settlements had stockades, the tribes were often free to come and go as they pleased, thus lulling the settlers into a false sense of their own security. (Author's collection)

---

1   E. Waterhouse, *Declaration of the State of the Colonyn and Affaires in Virginia; With a Relation of the Barbarous Massacre in the time of peace and League, treacherously executed by Native Infidels upon the English, the 22 March last* (London: 1622).

> There have been too many of his men and mine killed, and by my occasion there shall never be more ... for I am old now, and would gladly end my days in peace. So as if the English offer me injury, my country is large enough; I will remove myself farther from you.[2]

Unfortunately, the country was soon proven to not be large enough and the injury offered by the English was to cut too deep to be healed peacefully.

For a few years, harmony seemed to have returned. In 1619, at the first session of the Virginian General Assembly, it was decided that there should be, 'no injury or oppression wrought by the English against the Amerindians whereby the present peace might be disturbed'.

This was far from acknowledging an equal status between the two groups. By now, many Amerindians had come to the various river settlements and seemed content to work the land with the colonists. The assembly were not relaxed about this development, ruling that:

> As touching the instruction of drawing some of the better disposed Indians to converse with our people and to live and labour amongst them, the Assembly who know full well their dispositions think it fit to enjoin, least to counsel those of the colony, neither utterly to places well peopled, there to do service in killing of deer, fishing, beating of corn and other works, that then five or six may be admitted into every such place, and no more ... Provided that good guard in the night may be kept upon them for generally ... they are a most treacherous people and quickly gone when they have done a villainy.[3]

This disparaging attitude was almost universal, for as George Thorpe (a great believer in harmony) observed, the majority of his countrymen did scarce, 'afforde them a good thought in his hart and most men with their mouthes give them nothing but maledictions and bitter execrations'.

Powhatan was succeeded by his younger brother, the physically weak and unimpressive, Opitchapam. However, the real power resided with another brother, Opechancanough; a proud and strong warrior and the man who had once captured John Smith but was later taken as a hostage by the same man.

Opechancanough had been promoted by his brother to take command of the Youghtanan and the strategic and productive Pamunkey river valley, along which the Powhatan's enemies, the Monacan, were likely to invade. He was thus regarded as a competent warrior and a skilled negotiator. Following the first Powhatan war, he persuaded the Chickahominy to renege on their promises to become allied to the English, pay tribute and to join the rest of the Tidewater Algonquin in opposing the expansion of the alien settlements.

It is likely that Opechancanough deeply resented the way John Smith had manhandled him by seizing his sacred scalp-lock back in 1609, but he proffered peace and this desire was reflected in the fact that he indicated a willingness to convert to Christianity. He also expressed his intention to

---

2   R. Hamor, *A True Discourse of the Present Estate of Virginia*, 1614.
3   <www.historicjamestowne.org>

render the English no harm in the (soon to be) notorious phrase, 'he held the peace concluded so firme, as the Skie should sooner fall then it dissolue'.

Ironically, the fracture when it occurred, ripped along the length of the James River and was in some great measure, caused by the man who had demonstrated his willingness to unite the two communities through marriage – John Rolfe.

It was Rolfe who had managed to replace the inferior local tobacco with the far smoother West Indian variety that would flourish in the Virginian climate. In 1614, Rolfe sent to England, four barrels of tobacco that he had planted, harvested and cured. In 1616, 2,000lbs were despatched; in 1617 it was 18,839lbs and by 1618, he sent 49,528lbs.

There was a tobacco gold-leaf rush underway, bringing all available land into production. Shortly after this came the realisation that tobacco was a greedy crop sucking the goodness out of the land. Production had to spread further and further into previously sustainably managed farmlands of the Amerindians – land which the colonists still regarded as waste.

Huge estates were created. A new charter granted 'Ancient planters' a 100-acre 'headright' and new arrivals would receive 50 acres. Others could invest in almost as much land as their ambition or greed desired. Despite its name, 'Smythe's Hundred', covered over 150 square miles while some estates laid claim to over 80,000 acres. Smaller grants included that to Captain Samuel Argall of 2,400 acres, while the Reverend Richard Buck had 750 acres at Archer's Hope plus other pockets of land.

All of this land was free to be developed as the owners wished but it was mostly tobacco – a monoculture the reliance upon which, was starting to cause concern back in England as London was now using the colony to clear its streets of vagrant children. In 1618, it was noted that 'an hundred young boys and girls that lay starving in the streets', had been shipped to Virginia. They were to be followed by 90 women and over 1,000 'choice men borne and bred up to labour and industry'.

By this time, the enormous profit from tobacco enabled the planters to indulge themselves in a previously absent luxury. In 1621, the ships *Marmaduke*, *Warwick* and *Tiger*, disembarked 56 maids at Jamestown, each purchased as brides for 150lbs of tobacco. Very soon, this addiction to tobacco – a useless but valuable dried weed – would cause many deaths in Virginia long before its cancers grew in the lungs of those who consumed its smoke.

There was one group who would not benefit from this golden harvest – the Amerindians. For a few years, any resentment they felt was not openly expressed. Instead, Opechancanough watched, witnessed and planned, while showing an outward interest in English ideas and expressing a desire to contemplate conversion to Christianity.

By 1621, seeing the great land-clearances, many more settlers arriving and the disembarkation of the brides (which could only mean the birth of more home-grown settlers and the establishment of permanent families), the new *mamanatowick* must have viewed his people's future as uncertain. If so, he was reading the mind of the Virginia Company with accuracy; their stated aim in shipping out the maids was to 'make the men there more settled and less movable who by defect thereof … stay there but to get something and then to return for England'. This 'something' was generally considered to be tobacco, no one without long-term plans for residency would have wasted a season planting anything else. Wives would demand corn and vegetables, as would hungry children. Besides which, as the company clerk wrote:

> We have found that the minds of our people in Virginia are much dejected, and their hearts enflamed with a desire to return for England only through the wants of the comforts of marriage without which God saw Man could not live contentedly, no not even in Paradise.

This sentiment seems to make the segregation of the Amerindian and English sexes even harder to comprehend.

Opechancanough's concerns were supported by the views of the one Amerindian who had accompanied Pocahontas to London and then returned with John Rolfe – Tomocomo.

Tomocomo had been briefed by his chief to observe all he witnessed in London and report back. It is obvious that he was not impressed by what he saw but probably his main warning to the *werowances* must have been descriptions of the vast number of the English population compared with the few thousand Powhatan. Countless hordes could cross the ocean and should such a tidal wave occur, then the natives would be washed away. Opechancanough could not allow this to happen.

On 22 March 1622, a date that would be infamous in colonial Virginia – he unleashed his response. This was to be Virginia's Boudicca moment, the time when the native population rose-up at last to try and throw out the invading force. Like Boudicca with the Romans, the enemy was shaken and disturbed but stout enough to respond and overcome.

The planning was almost perfect but it may have been either tardy or precipitous. In the summer of 1621, word spread that Opechancanough had been trying to obtain a large quantity of lethal poison that could be extracted from water hemlock by the Accomack, a tribe on the eastern shore of the Chesapeake. If he was trying to utilise an early form of biological warfare, he would only have been taking his late brother's plans to a logical conclusion, for Powhatan had experimented with serving the English visitors hallucinatory drugs.

With numerous settlers still dying of disease, Opechancanough might easily have found a way to administer the poison by disguising it as an herbal remedy, but it was not to be. Esmy Shichans, the Laughing King of the Accomack tribe, refused to be bribed by a basket full of blue beads and reported Opechancanough's approach to the settlers. However, as they had no evidence to support their suspicions, the chief was free to think up another scheme. It could not have been too difficult for him.

The years of peace following Pocahontas' marriage and the great desire to grow tobacco, meant the settlers had neglected their defences. Jamestown's own 15ft high triangular fortifications were in a sorry state. At one stage, the four demi-culverin that formed its main armament had collapsed on their rotten carriages and the palisade itself was in urgent need of repair. Many of the outlying settlements were simply not in a state where they could resist an onslaught from a determined foe, although there were exceptions.

In Wolstenholme Town, the main settlement of the 20,000 acres Martin's Hundred, seven miles downstream from Jamestown, stood a fort complete with watch-tower and heavy armament. Inside was accommodation, storehouses and a well, suggesting it would be able to withstand a siege. Nearby, there was another defended compound and a well-palisaded homestead also fitted with small cannon. These might not have offered much protection against a determined raid by the Spanish but would certainly challenge the more-lightly armed and less-disciplined Amerindians.

At this stage, many of the settlers would have been convinced that such defensive measures were unnecessary. Governor Wyatt believed peace had come to stay and looked benignly on those who sought out new rich lands where they could get three seasons of tobacco before clearing more land on unexhausted soil. To help them achieve this, they were very happy to enlist the help of friendly natives who they entertained at table and 'commonly lodged in their bed-chambers'. Wyatt even wrote to the Company saying that:

> … he found the Country settled in a peace (as all men there thought) sure and unviolable, not onely because it was solemnly ratified and sworne … but as being aduantagious to both parts; to the Sauages as the weaker, vnder which they were safely sheltered and defended; to vs, as being the easiest way then thought to pursue and aduance our proiects of buildings, plantings, and effecting their conuersion by peaceable and fayre meanes.[4]

Thus, Opechancanough achieved his first objective; the colony had been lulled into a sense of security – the settlers' guard was down.

There is reason to believe the attack was going to take place to coincide with the 'taking up of Powhatan's bones' for formal burial, but in fact it was the death of another leading tribesman that precipitated the assault. Both Powhatan and Opechancanough had taken spiritual advice from the *shaman* Nemattanow. The settlers referred to him as 'Jack-of-the-Feathers' as he was adorned with feathers and sported a pair of swan's wings attached to his shoulders seeming to indicate that he could fly. To add to his mystique, he claimed that he could not be injured by any gunshot fired by the colonists whose presence he despised.

In early March, Nemattanow ill-advisedly killed a planter with whom he was trading and then returned to his victim's house wearing the dead man's cap. Openly suspicious of his actions, the man's servants proved the fallacy of his claimed invulnerability by opening fire and fatally wounding him. Just before he expired, he asked them to promise not to disclose that 'he was slain with a bullet' and to 'bury him amongst the English'; possibly a hint to Opechancanough to exact a swift revenge. Two weeks later, that revenge was exacted with a highly professional and horrific efficiency.

---

4   <www.virtualjamestown.org>

The coordination of the assault when it was launched on 22 March, must have taken much planning for, as Waterhouse stated in his report:

> These wyld naked Natiues live not in great numbers together, but dispersed, and in small companies; and where most together, not aboue two hundred, and that very rare, in other places fifty or forty, or thereabouts, and many miles distant from one another, in such places among the Woods where they either found, or might easiliest make some cleared plots of ground, which they employ wholly in setting of Corne, whereby to sustaine their liues. These small and scattered Companies (as I haue said) had warning giuen from one another in all their habitations to meete at the day and houre appointed for our destruction, at all our seuerall Townes and places seated vpon the Riuer; some were directed to go to one place, some to another, all to be done at the same day and time, which they did accordingly.[5]

To avoid any suspicion, the Amerindians were ordered to show restraint in the days before the attack, even when they were presented with easy victims. Waterhouse again:

> Even two dayes before the Massacre, some of our men were guided thorow the woods by them in safety: and one *Browne*, who then to learne the language liued among the *Warrascoyacks* (a Province of that King) was in friendly manner sent backe by them to Captaine *Hamor* his Master, and many the like passages, rather increasing our former confidence, then any wise in the world ministring the least suspition of the breach of the peace.

The evening before and early on the selected morning, Amerindians had wandered into settlements on both banks of the winding James River without their bows, arrows, knives and axes; in some cases, bringing venison, fish, turkey and other produce to part with as gifts or to barter for beads. Their hosts and prey were thus further lulled into a sense of security – their own sharp-edged tools being freely available for the assailants to grasp from the moment the assault was launched. Seizing these weapons, the Amerindians attacked all the English they could reach, regardless of age or sex, contrary to their normal rules of engagement that generally spared women and children. Only in Martin's Hundred would the women be spared with 20 of them being taken into captivity – a traditional Amerindian practice.

In settlement after settlement, the Amerindians used the same tactics. Staying indoors until the servants had gone out to the fields they silently and swiftly killed those left in the houses. This made sense as the buildings not only held the weaponry but were also the only protective structures in those open lands. Then they moved out into the fields. Of the 1,240 English settled along the Tidewater, 347 were to die that day in 30 separate locations.

At Falling Creek ironworks (66 miles from Jamestown), along with John Berkley, 21 men, two wives and three children also died. Three miles

---

5   E. Waterhouse, *Declaration of the State of the Colonyn and Affaires in Virginia …*

away at the Sheffield Plantation, nine men, two women and two boys were slain. The death toll at the adjacent Henrico Island was six.

So it went on and few were to be spared. At the Henricus College Lands where George Thorpe had started his project to educate the Amerindians, 17 died. Even Thorpe, the advocate and admirer of the Amerindians, was beheaded at his home in the Berkeley Hundred and died, ironically, because he did not believe the warning from his fleeing servant, that his life was in danger. This was not bone-headed stupidity as Thorpe had not only built for Opechancanough:

Skyfall – the Massacre of 1622 (T. de Bry, *America*). This gory engraving combines a number of incidents during the James River attack of 1622 to create a dramatic, but inaccurate, representation of the massacre. (Author's collection)

> … a fayre house according to the English fashion, in which hee tooke such ioy, especially in his locke and key, which hee so admired, as locking and vnlocking his doore an hundred times aday, hee thought no deuice in all the world was comparable to it.

But also, regarding the Amerindians, did:

> … so truly and earnestly affect their conuersion, and was so tender ouer them, that whosoeuer vnder his authority had giuen them but the least displeasure or discontent, he punished them seuerely. He thought nothing too deare for them, and as being desirous to binde them vnto him by his many courtesies, hee neuer denied them anything that they asked him, insomuch that when these *Sauages* complained vnto him of the fiercenesse of our Mastiues, most implacable and terrible vnto them (knowing them by instinct it seemes, to be but treacherous and false-hearted friends to vs, better then our selues) he to gratifie them in all things, for the winning of them by degrees, caused some of them to be killed in their presence, to the great displeasure of the owners. [6]

Yet:

---

6   G. Thorpe, *Virginia Colonial Records* (Richmond: 1874).

> … all was little regarded after by this Viperous brood … not only wilfully murdered him, but cruelly and felly, out of deuillish malice, did so many barbarous despites and foule scornes after to his dead corpes, as are vnbefitting to be heard by any civil ear.[7]

English commentators considered the mutilation of the corpses to be a particularly heinous crime and an example of what differentiated the savage from the civilised. After all, apart from lopping off a few heads, the English themselves did not show such disrespect to the 'heathen' Irish when they were being massacred. Thorpe was not the only person to be treated in this fashion. Captain Powell, along with his very heavily pregnant wife and family, were butchered at Powle-Brooke and his head was cut off.

The assailing seems to have been effective, for very few appear to have escaped once having been wounded. However, one survivor was Thomas Hamor, who on stepping outside, saw his fellows lying shot and battered before him. He was then pierced by an arrow only to be able to stagger back and barricade himself indoors where a young servant fired off a musket which was sufficient to scare the attackers away. Not far away his brother Ralph Hamor, took shelter in a half-built house and defended himself with a spade and axe. Once armed with some muskets sent up from Jamestown, he and a large body of men were able to break out and join his brother and together retreat with other survivors to Jamestown.

Jamestown does not appear on Waterhouse's list of the 30 sites attacked but without taking the main town, Opechancanough would have been unable to claim a decisive victory. The reason for the failure to take or even to assault Jamestown, has a certain mythical explanation. Waterhouse explained that in a house across the river from Jamestown, an Amerindian had been briefed by his brother that he must kill the houseowner the next morning. Instead, having been kindly treated by the Englishman, the Amerindian warned him of the plan and he in turn, rowed over to Jamestown to alert the governor:

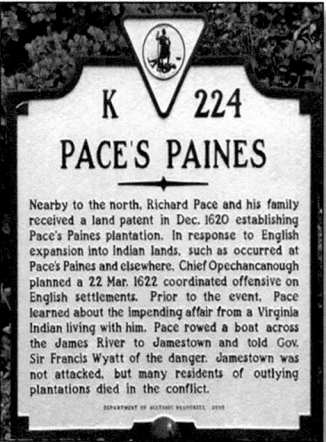

This information sign may well explain the reason why the Powhatan did not attack Jamestown. (Author's collection)

> … by which meanes they were prevented there, and at such other Plantations as was possible for a timely intelligence to be giuen; for where they saw vs standing vpon our Guard, at the sight of a Peece they all ranne away.

This explanation seems too simplistic. It seems improbable that rampaging tribes were foiled from achieving their ultimate aim by a few men waving firearms from feeble palisades. Instead, one would have thought that a major war party, led by Opechancanough himself, would have prioritised an attack on the town and made some effort to inflict damage, such as setting huts and fields alight. Even if they had quailed at the sight of men with muskets on the ramparts, any one of them might have fallen victim to an accurate archer. Having successfully assaulted settlements both up and down stream of the main settlement, one would

---

7   E. Waterhouse, *Declaration of the State of the Colonyn and Affaires in Virginia …*

imagine the victorious warriors would rendezvous to bring their weight of numbers to impact upon the town.

No one knows Opechancanough's strategic plan – there is a lack of primary evidence. It is possible to assume he saw advantages in having the English present as trading partners in Virginia so long as they confined themselves to the lower stretches of the river. If so, he misread the situation. Unlike the tribes of New England and Canada who could become partners with the English in the fur trade, the Powhatan had nothing to satisfy a market in England; Virginia's sole saleable asset was tobacco and this the colonists were growing themselves – each appropriated acre reducing the area available to support the Amerindian's way of life.

Jamestown did endure a state of siege with men loathe to venture out. Fortunately, there was little reason to do so; the fields awaited sowing not harvesting and the livestock would have been driven away by the Amerindians. But no attacks seem to have been pressed home and even in the wider English domain, killings seem to have been desultory. Towards the Chesapeake in Kecoughtan lands, there appear to have been no reports of attacks.

Three weeks after the assault, Governor Wyatt ordered that Kecoughtan and Newport News, along with several other well-defended garrisons, be reinforced. Meanwhile, he evacuated many vulnerable settlements back to Jamestown giving that community a major problem of provisioning the increased population, two-thirds of whom were 'women and children and unserviceable people'.

By the end of his repositioning, Virginia was left with five plantations, in addition to Jamestown, which were considered strong enough to discourage assault. Nevertheless, another starving time had to be endured with over 400 settlers dying from malnutrition and an epidemic that arrived with the supply ship *Abigail*. Those that survived did so in part, ironically, through trade with the Amerindians for corn. Yet survive they did – resilient in the face of disaster.

Wyatt also wrote an urgent letter to London requesting: a year's supply of victuals; sufficient weaponry to fight a war; and spades, shovels, pickaxes and other tools with which to improve the fortifications. All of this would be paid for with good quality tobacco. Sadly, when support did arrive, it included a foul beer the drinking of which, it is claimed, was the death of many. Neither were troops despatched, although John Smith made it plain to the company that if he was:

> … transported with a hundred soldiers and thirty sailors … with victuals, munitions and such necessary provision … we would endeavour downforce the savages to leave the country, or bring them in that feare and subjection that every man should follow their business securely.[8]

---

8   J. Smith, P. Barbour (ed.), *The Complete Works of Captain John Smith 1580–1631*.

London viewed Virginia as one might an eccentric and erratic maiden aunt who, having flounced off abroad still wished her old home to rescue her when, through her own fault, she was in distress. The Virginia Company chided the governor in a letter of 1 August 1622, in which they pronounced:

> We have to our extreme grief understood of the great massacre executed on our people in Virginia, and that in such a matter as is more miserable then the death itself; to fall by the hands of men so contemptible; to be surprised by the treachery in a time of known danger … and almost guilty of the destruction by a blindfold and stupid entertaining of it; which the least wisdom or courage sufficed to prevent even on the point of execution …

In response for the plea for arms, the government searched the dusty depths of the Tower and by order of the Privy Council, unburdened themselves of:

> … certain old cast arms in the Tower, altogether unfit for modern use, are directed to be delivered to the Virginia Company as serviceable against the savages of that country, 400 of the inhabitants having been lately massacred by the treachery of the Amerindians.[9]

A replacement 400 young men were also despatched.

However, there was one point that both the settlement and the company were in concord – revenge. Wyatt directed Sir George Yeardly to 'make war, kill, spoil, and take by force or otherwise, whatsoever boote of corn, or anything ese he can attain unto, from the savages our enemies'. Meanwhile, the company ordered the colonists to wage 'perpetual war without peace or truce' or, as subsequent actions would reveal, rules.

Firstly, the colony needed to recover its strength. Nevertheless, newcomers still arrived. Most must have been appalled by the conditions that greeted them on arrival. The letter home, from the indentured Richard Frethorne, who settled in Martin's Hundred must speak for many:

> Loving and kind father and mother … this is to let you understand that I your child am in a most heavy case by reason of the nature of the country is such that it causeth much sickness … and when we are sick there is nothing to comfort us; for since I came out of the ship I never ate anything but pease and loblolly [gruel] as for dear or venison I never sawn any … there is indeed some fowl, but we must work hard both early and late for a mess of water gruel and a mouthful of bread …
>
> People cry out day and night, Oh, that we were in England without their limbs and would not care to lose any limb to be in England again … if you love me you will redeem me, for which I do intreat and beg.[10]

There was another group who might have been in a worse situation than Master Frethorne. Two months after 'Skyfall', the settlers became aware that about 15 women and half-a-dozen men had been taken captive at Martin's

---

9 S. M. Kingsbury, *The Records of the Virginia Company of London* (Washington: 1906).
10 *Virginia Colonial Records*, vol. 4.

Hundred. The men would be tortured to death while the women, while being treated as slaves, were seen as sentient bargaining chips. For the moment however, Governor Wyatt showed little interest in bartering for their exchange.

As a result, the women captives were left to endure a harsh winter and a major cultural shock. They would live communally in a dark, smoky wigwam made from bent branches shingled with well-cut squares of bark. Amerindian modesty took little notice of nakedness and love-making was not performed in total privacy. As their clothes became tattered, the English women had to cover themselves in robes of skin that exposed hitherto well-covered parts of their anatomy. However, none mentioned any impropriety by their captors.

The deprivations of a hard winter meant Opechancanough needed to trade the women for peace. He expressed himself willing to send home those people 'whom they saved alive since the massacre' provided his people could 'plant quietly in all places'. Before this were to happen, the settlers wanted to press home their advantage. There were those who saw the Amerindian assault as an opportunity.

Waterhouse, having recounted the tragedy, felt the colonists could now throw away any sensitivies they may previously held regarding their dealings with the Amerindians:

> Because our hands which before were tied with gentlenesse and faire vsage, are now set at liberty by the treacherous violence of the Sauages, not vntying the Knot, but cutting it: so that … turning the laborious Mattocke into the victorious Sword (wherein there is more both ease, benefit, and glory) and possessing the fruits of others labours. Now their cleared grounds in all their villages (which are situate in the fruitfullest places of the land) shall be inhabited by vs, whereas heretofore the grubbing of woods was the greatest labour.

While:

> those commodities which the Indians enioyed as much or rather more then we, shall now also be entirely possessed by vs. The Deere and other beasts will be in safety, and infinitly increase, which heretofore not onely in the generall huntings of the King (whereat foure or fiue hundred Deere were vsually slaine) but by each particular Amerindian were destroied at all times of the yeare, without any difference of Male, Damme, or Young. The like may be said of our owne Swine and Goats.

Once they had regrouped, the English, aided as always by their command of the waterways, sallied forth to burn villages and destroy crops. There was even talk of enslaving those captured but the practicalities of so doing dissuaded them. Instead, raiding parties endeavoured to deprive the Powhatan of both food and shelter – it worked. Opechancanough, recognising 'that blood enough had already been shed on both sides, and that many of his people were starved', proposed peace talks. To show his intent, he released Mistress Sara Boyse who returned home bedecked like an Amerindian queen.

Early in 1623, Wyatt wrote to the Virginia Company stating:

> We have slain diverse, burnt their towns, destroyed their weirs and corn … It is now apparent that they are an enemy not suddenly to be destroyed with the sword by reason of their swiftness of foot, and advantages of the wood … but by way of starving and all other means we can possibly devise.[11]

One such means was devised when the two sides agreed to meet on 22 May 1623 to discuss peace in Opechancanough's town on the Pamunkey River. For the English, it was too good an opportunity to miss, their strategy being simply to recover the captives and then 'to follow their example by destroying them' and cutting down their corn. To this end, they followed Opechancanough's earlier plan and brought along with them a butte of liberally poisoned wine prepared by the Jamestown physician, Doctor Pott.

The English contingent of 13 men led by Captain William Tucker, landed before several hundred Powhatan assembled to witness this historic treaty. Once business was concluded, it was time for the betrayal. The drink was produced; the English sipped from a special section and then poured a generous amount into the eager cups of the Amerindians – a hundred or more of whom quaffed and were killed. Fifty more were shot by Tucker and his men who then returned to Jamestown triumphant, brandishing scalps.

There was, however, a small price to be paid for such flagrant breach of etiquette; the ironically alcoholic Pott, was suspended from his post, only to be elected deputy governor in 1629 – a post he filled with ignominy. In between these dates, he organised a further poisoning and held one of the released women, Jane Dickenson, in bondage claiming he had bought her indenture from the Amerindians for two bags of beads. Further misdemeanours included stealing his neighbour's livestock and organising an abortive *coup d'état*.

Pott's memorial stone at Jamestown states:

> In Memory of
> John Pott MA
> Learned Doctor
> Of Medicine
> Physician General
> Member of the Council
> Governor of the Colony
> Resident of Jamestown
> 1621–1635

In some way, the difference between the facts engraved and the truth between-the-lines, summarises the problem of studying early, colonial Virginia. Events are only recorded by the one side who needed to justify their actions and intentions; proselytised through propaganda (including portraying their opponents as savages) makes it difficult to arrive at an unbiased truth.

---

11 S. M. Kingsbury, *The Records of the Virginia Company of London*.

Not surprisingly, hostilities resumed but so did the search for supplies. In the spring of 1623, Henry Spelman, who had arrived in Jamestown in 1609 at the age of 14 and been apprenticed to Powhatan, led a party of 19 men up the Potomac to barter for food. Landing at the settlement of Nacochtanck, Spelman set off inland, presumably trusting that the Amerindians would recognise him as a friend. They did not and he was captured and beheaded by the Pawtuxunt. Those waiting offshore for Spelman's return were also attacked and all but one slaughtered.

Thus died another man who had tried to reconcile the two groups. Like Rolfe, Spelman had married an Amerindian girl, a Patawomeck given the English name of Martha, who tradition has it, was a sister of Pocahontas. History is silent about both her and any offspring.

A year later, the only battle of the campaign was fought when 60 settlers drove away over 800 Amerindians, killing many of their attackers at the cost of just 16 wounded. The colonists were availing but their obvious ineffectiveness against, what England believed was puny opposition, along with their failure to return a reliable profit, meant they were regarded as unfit for purpose. On 24 May 1624, Virginia became a royal colony under direct rule by the monarch.

The change of ownership did not affect the struggle against the Amerindians. This continued with regular incidents of antagonism until in 1632, a sort of peace was achieved. Thereafter, the English sought to segregate the two communities by building a six-mile-long wall between the James and York Rivers. The aim was to keep the natives away from the settlements and to deny the Amerindians access and rights. It was not much of a barrier and was more symbolic than deterrent.

Where possible, the builders erected wooden boards fronted by a six-foot wide ditch. Linked wooden posts formed the structure as it climbed and descended hills. However, as none were charged with its maintenance, the barricade soon rotted away. Yet its very existence must have incensed the proud Opechancanough who, in 1644 made one last attempt to drive the English away.

Although now both elderly and frail, Opechancanough chose his moment well. Civil War had broken out in England in 1642 and the friction between supporters of the King or Parliament was manifest in the American Colonies whose borders were also far from frictionless.

In 1632, King Charles had granted to his friend Lord Calvert (a Catholic), a vast chunk of the lands to both east and west of the Chesapeake. This included islands such as Kent, already occupied and developed by Virginians. In 1635, a mini-sea battle was fought between the resident trader William Claiborne in the sloop Cockatrice, against the Maryland vessels *St. Margaret* and *St. Helen*, in which the latter were victorious. Claiborne however, recovered to become a leader in what was known as the 'Plundering Time' when from 1644 to 1646, he and his partner Captain Richard Ingle invaded Maryland and roamed the colony looting at will.

Perhaps, convinced that the colonial administration was fracturing and that aid from a war-engulfed England was unlikely to be sent, Opechancanough launched his second assault on the settlers with a force consisting of

Nansemond, Chickahominy and Weyanock. Some 450 settlers were killed but the impact was far less than it had been in 1622. In the intervening years, immigration had brought many more people to the Chesapeake region and the core settlements were not threatened by this attack.

Hostilities ended rapidly once Governor Berkeley stormed Opechancanough's stronghold and took him prisoner. Too frail to walk, he was carried into captivity in Jamestown. Two weeks later he was dead, shot in the back by one of his gaolers. His death was also the death of the Powhatan empire; all that was left were a few starving families who had to beg for sustenance.

His successor Necotowance, signed a peace treaty in 1646 in which he stated that, 'the Sun and Moon should first lose their glorious lights and shining, before He, or his People should evermore hereafter wrong the English in any kind, but they would ever hold love and friendship together'. That friendship came at a dreadful cost; by the end of the century many of the tribes had totally disappeared and the few that were left were being confined to reservations. Amerindians in the settled lands were required, on pain of death, to wear a swatch of coloured cloth which was later changed to a copper badge.

The treaty made the King of England the guarantor of Powhatan rights but placed many restrictions upon them. For example, it confined them to lands north of the York River, with any communication with the settlers to be carried out by distinctly dressed messengers. In return for this 'protection' they had to pay a tribute of 20 beaver skins. The Amerindians were henceforth placed in a legal no-man's land. Here, they were treated either as a foreign or a tributary nation, depending on the level of lust for their land expressed by the settlers who could adjust the law to legalise land seizure. In a dainty device, the Amerindians were exempt from paying taxes, a 'kind' gesture that thus denied them the rights afforded to other citizens.

In 1658, the purchase of Amerindian lands was placed in the control of the governor thereby legitimising the transfer of ownership. Steadily, through a series of treaties, Virginia Colony pushed her frontier with the Amerindian Nations further inland. Even the Patawomeck, who had been the colony's allies in the tense times of 1622 and 1644, were pressurised to give up their lands – causing violent disputes to break out in the 1650s. Unable to hold on to any advantage, the *weroance*, who had been captured and then released, agreed in 1655 to sell his remaining land to Virginia in return for a few warm coats. In 1666, following a short campaign by the colony against their northern neighbours, the Patawomeck tribe disappeared.

There were other tribes such as the Doeg, whose lands straddled the border between Virginia and what the earlier colony saw as the upstart, land-grabbing, Maryland. Thus, a three-way friction existed between rival groups which frequently erupted into violence.

Unlike his earlier predecessors such as Wyatt, the fanatical royalist Sir William Berkeley, once having disposed of the Powhatan, had a vision of an economically fruitful Virginia living at peace with its native neighbours. So much did he relish this idea, the settlers felt he was taking the Amerindian side even after they requested help to defend themselves. In 1676, a

Declaration was published against the governor listing a series of complaints that included:

> For having, Protected, favoured, and Emboldned the Indians against his Majesty's most Loyall Subjects; never Contriving, requiring, or appointing any due or proper Meanes of Satisfaction; for theire many Incursions, Murthers, and Robberies, Committed upon Us.
>
> For having when the Armie of the English, was upon the Tract of the Amerindians, which now in all Places, burne spoile, and Murder, and when Wee might with ease, have destroyed them, who were in open hostilitie.
>
> For having expresslie, countermanded, and sent back, our Armie, by Passing his word, for the Peaceable demeanours of the said Amerindians, who Immediatly prosecuted theire Evill Intentions – Committing horrid Murders and Robberies, in all Places … That They are not only become difficult, but a very formidable Enemie Who might with Ease have been destroyed.[12]

The distrust, dislike and mutual antagonism between the groups continued, regardless of Berkeley's desires. One small but significant episode in 1675, was recounted by a settler signing himself 'T.M.' (probably Thomas Matthew):

> My dwelling was in Northumberland, the lowest county on Potomac River, Stafford being the upmost, where having also a plantation, servants, cattle &c, my overseer there had agreed with one Robt. Hen to come thither, and be my herdsman, who then lived ten miles above it; but on a Sabbath day morning in the sumer anno 1675. people in their way to church, saw this Hen lying thwart his threshold, and an Amerindian without the door, both chopt on their heads, arms and other parts, as if done with Amerindian hatchetts, th' Amerindian was dead, but Hen when ask'd who did that? answered Doegs Doegs, and soon died, then a boy came out from under a bed, where he had hid himself, and told them, Amerindians had come at break of day and done those murders.
>
> From this Englishman's bloud did (by degrees) arise Bacons rebellion with the following mischiefs which overspread all Virginia and twice endangerd Maryland, as by the ensuing account is evident.
>
> Of this horrid action Coll. Mason who commanded the militia regiment of foot and Capt. Brent the troop of horse in that county (both dwelling six or eight miles downwards) having speedy notice raised 30, or more men, and pursu'd those Amerindians 20 miles up and 4 miles over that river into Maryland, where landing at dawn of day they found two small paths. Each leader with his party took a separate path and in less than a furlong, both found a cabin, which they (silently) surrounded. Capt. Brent went to the Doeg's cabin (as it proved to be) who speaking the Indian tongue called to have a "matchacomicha, weewhio" i.e. a council called presently such being the usuall manner with Indians) the king came trembling forth, and wou'd have fled, when Capt. Brent, catching hold of his twisted lock (which was all the hair he wore) told him he was come for the murderer of Robt. Hen, the king pleaded ignorance and slipt loos, whom Brent

---

12 N. Bacon, *Declaration of the People of Virginia, 1676*, Wikisource: 2020.

shot dead with his pistoll, th' Indians shot two or three guns out of the cabin, th' English shot into it, th' Indians throng'd out at the door and fled, the English shot as many as they cou'd, so that they killed ten. [13]

The now aroused and endangered Amerindians – Doeg and Susquehannock (Congestoga) – took shelter in Fort Piscataway, downstream from modern Washington D.C. which was robust enough to withstand assault by the militia. It was described as having:

> … high banks of earth, with fflankers having many loop-holes, and a ditch round all, and without this a row of tall trees fastned 3 foot deep in the earth, their bodies from 5 to 8 inches diameter, watled 6 inches apart to shoot through with the tops twisted together, and also artificially wrought, as our men could make no breach to storm it nor (being low land) coud they undermine it by reason of water neither had they cannon to batter itt, so that 'twas not taken, until ffamine drove the Indians out of it.[14]

Before they fled, the Amerindians had sent out a peace party of six of their leaders to negotiate terms. Instead of listening, the besiegers 'beat out the brains', an act considered so despicable by the Amerindians that, on escaping, they:

> … speedily effected in the death of sixty inosscent soules, and then send in their Remonstrance to the Governour, in justification of the fact … that their messingers sent out for peace were not only knock'd on the head but the fact countenanc'd by the governour; for which (finding no other way to be satisfied) they had revenged themselves, by killing ten for one of the English; such being the disperportion between there men murthered, and those by them slane, theres being persons of quallety, the other of inferiour Ranke.

The question the aggrieved Amerindian leader felt the governor needed to answer was:

> What *was it* that moved him to take up arms against him his professed friend in the behalfe of the Marylanders his *professed* enemies contrary to that league made betweene him and himselfe? declares as well his owne as subjects griefe to finde the Verginians, of friends, without any cause given to becom his foes, and to be so eager in their groundless quarrell, as to persew the chase in to anothers dominions?

Unconvinced by the response, the escaped Amerindians went on the rampage so that:

---

13 'T. M.', *The Beginning of Progress and Conclusion of Bacon's Rebellion in the Years 1675 & 1676, 1705,* <www.virtualjamestown>
14 C. M. Andrews, (ed.), *Narratives of the Insurrection, 1675–1690* (New York: 1915). <www.virginiastudies.org>

> ... the most exposed small families withdrew into our houses of better numbers, which we fortified with pallisadoes and redoubts, neighbours in bodies joined their labours from each plantation to others alternately, taking their arms into the ffields, and setting centinels; no man stirr'd out of door unarm'd.

At this point, governor and governed came to the final parting of ways. Berkeley, commentating on the killing of the peace mission, stated: 'If they had killed my father and my mother and all my friends, yet if they had come to treat of peace, they ought to have gone in peace'.

These were not the sentiments of men like John Washington, the great-grandfather of George, who led a party of Virginians to assist Maryland. Nor was this the view of Nathaniel Bacon who stirred up the rebellion that now bears his name. In response to his call to arms, several thousand formed a violent force which killed both Amerindians and drove Governor Berkeley from his capital which they torched in September 1676.

Succour, as so often, came from the sea; first armed merchant ships, then the Royal Navy entered the fray on the governor's behalf. The response was aided by the fact that Bacon died of dysentery in October. Thereafter, the restoration of lawful government was never in doubt. In 1776, the rebellion would serve as a reminder to the colonists that it was possible to revolt against the crown.

What also persisted was the bloody triangle of confrontation between colony and colony and Amerindian. Maryland and Virginia – one free, the other slave owning – remained uneasy neighbours. Eventually, with the Amerindians destroyed, the colonists turned against each other. In 1862, on the killing creek of Antietam in Maryland, they spilt more blood in one day than in the preceding two centuries of conflict.

However, it would be idle to deny that the English were ever other than unwelcome in tidewater Virginia and that their first 100 years were not a perpetual struggle to possess a land to which they were not entitled. Those that had once been free to roam now find themselves curators of 'historic' reconstructed villages where segregated and uncertain of their meagre land rights, they earn money portraying the past which the ancestors of their visitors destroyed.

6

New England
The Pequot War
Massacre at Mystic

> Thus, saith the Lord … Now go and smite Amalek, and utterly destroy all that they have, and spare them not: but slay both man and woman, infant and suckling, ox and sheep, camel and ass.
>
> *1 Samuel* 15:2.3

Nowadays most Britons and Americans might have little idea as to who the Amalekites were and why they deserved to be destroyed. It is difficult to appreciate that it was their fate and everyone else who prevented the children of Israel from occupying the promised land, that provided the justification and the precedent for the action of the settlers against the Amerindians.

Instead of Amalekites and other occupiers of Israel, the English identified Powhatan, Pequot, Narragansett, Wampanoag, Abenaki and many other tribes who lived in the land that God and the King of England, had given to their subjects. Having identified the tribes, the strategy towards them was directed by the Old Testament. For these fundamental Christians, with their unreformed Old Testament attitudes, the Bible (especially the Books of Exodus, Deuteronomy and Joshua) was their guiding light reinforcing the Puritan. It reinforced the Puritan belief that the world and its works was divided into two camps; those possessed by God and those by the Devil. They believed the dark-skinned Devil's spawn owned all the land that the white God's party was manifestly destined to settle upon.

Thus Christianity, as the unconverted Pequot were to discover in 1637, was not synonymous with civilisation nor with loving thy neighbour as thyself. Indeed, it is very seldom that any of the settlers' accounts of the wars they witnessed, full as they are of biblical references, quote from the New Testament Gospels.

The Pequot had two fatal advantages. Firstly, they claimed hegemony over the riverine tribes of the broad Connecticut Valley thus controlling its

NEW ENGLAND THE PEQUOT WAR MASSACRE AT MYSTIC

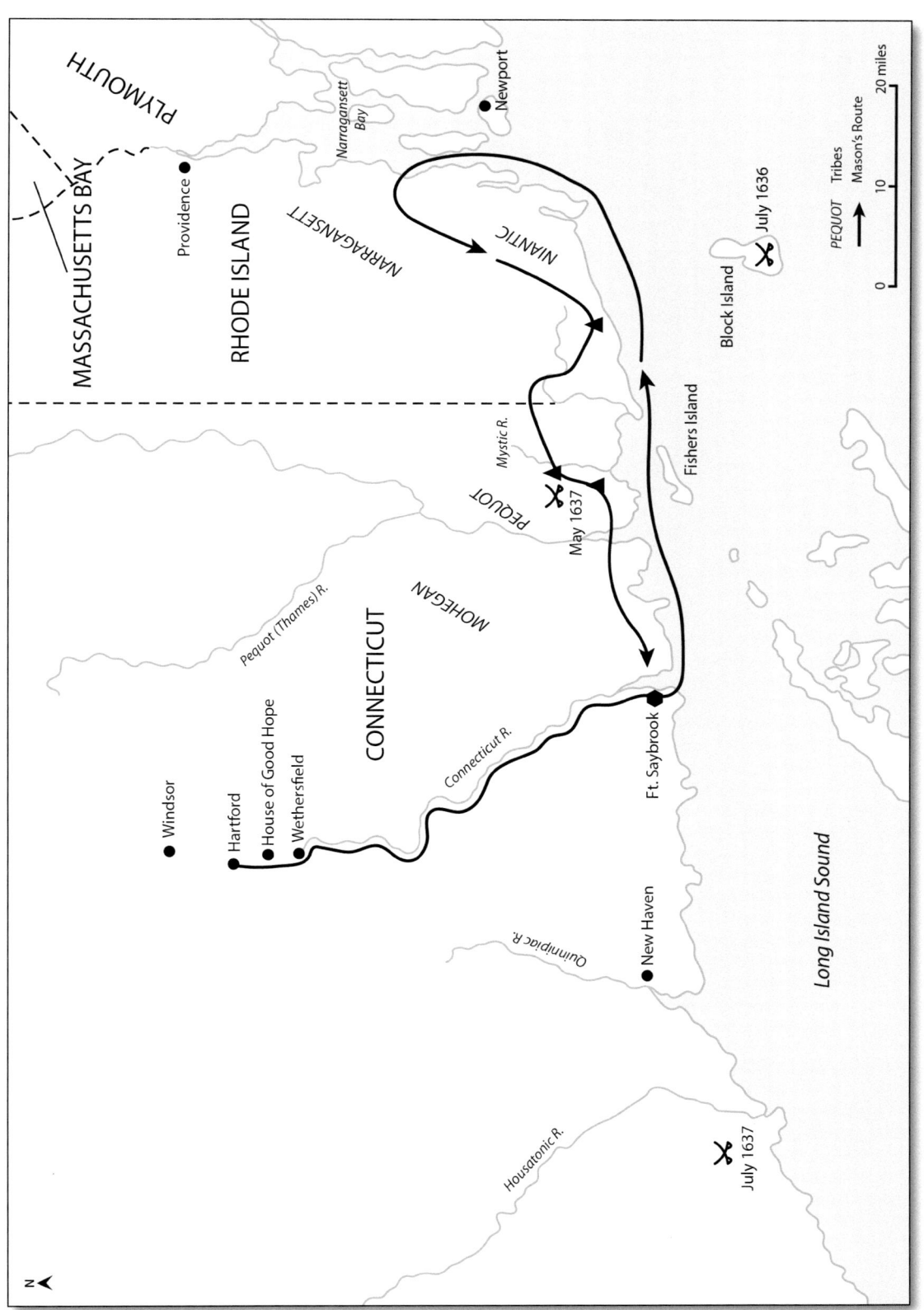

The destruction of the Pequot

NEW WORLDS, OLD WARS

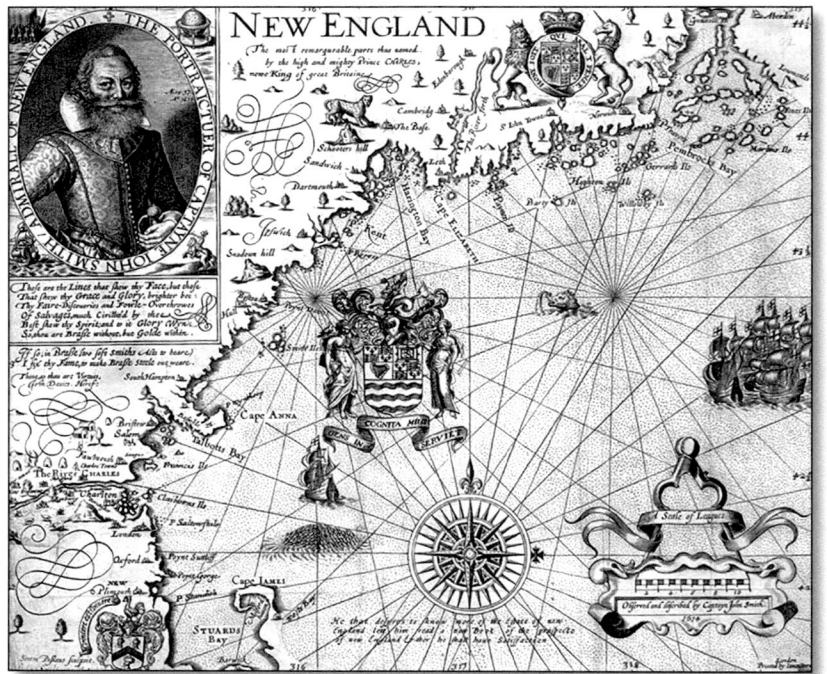

Map of New England, created to encourage the immigration of the many (John Smith, 1614). When the Pilgrims arrived, they retained the name *Plymouth* for their settlement as named on this map. (Public domain)

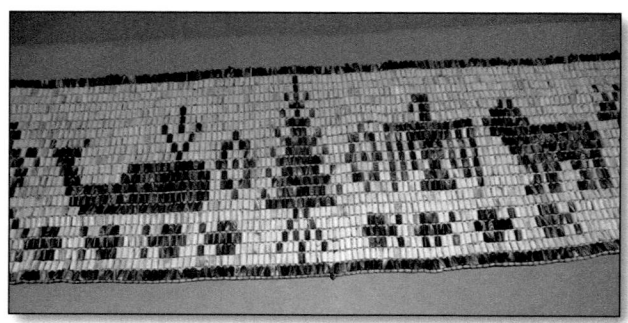

A wampum belt created to commemorate the 400th anniversary of the *Mayflower* landing. Wampum beads, made from a special shell, became the currency of choice in trade between the English and the indigenous; its production became for a while, a Pequot monopoly. (Author's collection)

excellent trading routes and potential green pastures. Secondly, their tributary tribes on eastern Long Island produced *wampum* which had become the standard currency in the all-important fur trade and a significant amount of this passed down the Connecticut Valley. Therefore, the Pequot not only controlled a land which the Dutch, rival New England colonies and even New York, coveted – but also owned the mint that manufactured the currency of choice.

The Pequot were determined to retain dominance over their native neighbours. Besides demanding tribute, they wished to act as the monopolistic middleman with the newly established Dutch and English traders, in the exchange of goods, including fur and *wampum*. Their behaviour, creating anguish rather than allies, saw them friendless when the new arrivals decided to contend as to whom was the mightiest. The Niantic and the mighty Narragansetts would each contribute in their own way, to a war of extermination, as did the Mohegan, a group that split from the Pequot when they saw which way fate was flowing.

The Pequot's own territory lay between the Pequot (now Thames) and Pawcatuck Rivers. This was an area of about 250 square miles in which numerous small, scattered settlements, many near the coast, contained (in their heyday) approximately 16,000 people. Situated some 50 miles West of Plymouth, they were separated by the emerging colonies of Rhode Island, Connecticut and the expanding Massachusetts Bay. These colonies all had their eye on the Connecticut Valley, as did the Dutch and the governor of New York who was looking out for the interests of his royal patron. Each European group was anxious to establish legitimate occupational rights by converting 'rights by discovery' into 'rights by possession' while dismissing the Pequot's own historic 'right by conquest'.

In 1632, the Dutch purchased from Tatobem (the Pequot *sachem*), land on the banks of the Connecticut where present day Hartford now stands. On this tract, they built a trading station which they named the House of Good Hope. When news of this reached Plymouth, a spoiler trading post was proposed a few miles upstream of Hope where it could intercept the furs and other goods moving down the river. Plymouth was motivated by the fact that its posts in Maine had come under French attack – to counter which, they had sought (but not received) the support of Massachusetts.

The Pequot, anxious to maintain both their hegemony and their trading monopoly, murdered some Narraganset who were bringing stocks to Good Hope without their permission. The Dutch responded in kind by seizing Tatobem on board a Dutch trading ship and holding him for a ransom of a bushel of *wampum*. When the payment was promptly paid, the Dutch returned the body of Tatobem whom they had already murdered. However, the Pequot did not turn their wrath upon the isolated settlement which they could easily have overwhelmed. Trade continued and the Pequot, under their new *sachem* Sassacus, seemingly adhered to a philosophy of proportional response.

Before the hostilities did break out, the Pequot were dealt three devastating and possibly, fatal blows. In 1633, disease had spread rapidly through their settlements killing an estimated 80 percent of their number.[1] By the time a strong body of healthy warriors was required, the total population probably numbered less than 3,000. Furthermore, Sassacus's elevation was resented by his brother-in-law, Uncas, who dealt his kin a further blow by withdrawing his supporters, the Mohegan. These were a group bound to the Pequot through intermarriage, and Uncas dedicated himself to the usurping of Pequot authority, even if this meant allying with the hated Narragansetts and ultimately, with the English.

Such tribal disputes were obviously advantageous to the settlers who, from this time forward, were more interested in finding excuses for war with the Pequot rather than reasons for rapport. Two slayings would now set off the already sensitive fuse that caused the ingredients of competition, distrust and rough usage, to explode into war. As so often in such cases, the Pequot were peripheral to the killings, a fact that the colonists would choose to ignore.

Shortly after the Dutch trading house was established, a dodgy West Indian cum-Virginian merchant trader, Captain John Stone, entered the Connecticut River. He engaged two Amerindians to pilot him in a skiff to Good Hope while embarking another group of Amerindians

River trading craft. In such a boat, traders such as Stone, Oldham and Gallop would have carried out coastal and river voyages. (Author's collection)

---

1   W. Bradford, *Of Plymouth Plantation* (Boston: 1912).

whom, it would seem, had hitched a lift onboard his barque. That evening, Stone anchored in the stream but the skiff, with two Englishman onboard, beached so the crew could bed down on the bank. However, when they were asleep, the Amerindians murdered them while the same fate befell Captain Stone and his companions on the ship, who were killed by the passengers.

The barebones of the story as related in contemporary accounts, omit some most relevant details. The first detail being, that at the time, it was believed the killers were not Pequot but Western Niantic, a tributary tribe of the Pequot, but with their own *sachem* who was answerable for their behaviour. Secondly, Stone was not the innocent trader that he made out to be. He was heading South, having been expelled from Boston (presumably with unfinished business), for bedding another man's wife; he had no reason to be nosing into the Connecticut, let alone providing a taxi-service for a dozen Amerindians. It is far more likely these were men he had kidnapped intending to sell them into slavery. The coastal Amerindians had a folk-memory of such behaviour by English mariners.

In fact, there could have been a much more recent behavioural justification. It was suggested that after hostilities had broken out, it was Sassacus himself who had led the attack on Stone, believing him to be Dutch. Thus, by the laws of revenge, the killing was a proportionate and appropriate response to the murder of Tatobem.

Be that as it may, war, both inter-tribal and inter-cultural, now seemed likely if the rival land claims in the Connecticut Valley were to be resolved. All that was needed was an excuse for its justification.

At the time, there had been little response to the death of a piratical Virginian outside the territorial governance of the established settlements. Indeed, the first response from Massachusetts was a feeling of good riddance to an unpleasant dodgy trader.[2] Shortly, it would prove to be one of those useful justifications. However, right up to the time war broke out, peaceful coexistence was both evident and possible. Indeed, Massachusetts had viewed Stone as a trouble making, immoral drunk whose loss would not be grieved.

In 1634, a Pequot delegation visited Boston to discuss a trade deal which would also include the English negotiating a peace treaty between the Pequot and the Narragansetts. In return, the Pequot offered the Bay 'all their rights

---

[2] Roger Clap records: 'There was also one Capt. Stone about the year 1633 or 1634, who carried himself very proudly, and spake contemptuously of our magistrates, and carried it lewdly in his conversation. For his misdemeanour, his ship was stayed; but he fled, and would not obey authority; and there came warrants to Dorchester to take him dead or alive. So all our soldiers were in arms, and sentinels were set in divers places; and at length he was found in a great cornfield, where we took him and carried him to Boston; but for want of one witness, when he came to his trial, he escaped with his life. He was said to be a man of great relation, and had great favour in England; and he gave out threatening speeches. Though he escaped with his life, not being hanged for adultery, there being but one witness, yet for other crimes he was fined, and payed it; and being dismissed, he went towards Virginia. But by the way putting into the Pequot country, to trade with them, the Pequots cut off both him and his men, took his goods, and burnt his ship. Some of the Amerindians reported that they roasted him alive. Thus did God destroy him that so proudly threatened to ruin us, by complaining against us when he came to England. Thus God destroyed him, and delivered us at that time also'.

at Connecticut … if we would settle a plantation there'.[3] This mutually acceptable arrangement floundered on the rock of greed. To seal the treaty, the Pequot ambassadors had brought with them a gift (not a tribute) of two bushels of *wampum* plus an offer of a number of beaver and otter skins. In response, the Bay negotiators demanded 400 fathoms of *wampum*, 40 beaver skins and 30 otter skins, which in value would have equalled about half the Bay's annual tax revenue. The ambassadors balked and were further dismayed when told that they must also deliver up Captain Stone's killers. They explained that not only were the killers not Pequot but that the *sachem* involved had been killed by the Dutch while all but two of the guilty group were by now dead of the pox. In the end, both sides informally recognised a sort of heads of agreement without ratifying a flawed and contentious treaty. It brought peace, for a year.

At the very end of May 1636, Thomas Hooker a minister in Cambridge, Massachusetts, having decided to move away from the oppressive control of the Massachusetts church, led his 100 strong congregation (together with a farm's worth of cattle, goats and pigs), on a two-week journey west along the Connecticut Path. This was an old Amerindian track that linked central Connecticut with Massachusetts Bay. It is pertinent to note that their route led them from native village to native village until they finally emerged on the riverbank opposite present Hartford; yet, in all that time, this vulnerable procession of interlopers, had neither their path blocked, nor their way challenged, nor were they offered any form of violence. Theirs was thus a peaceful passage – but peace was not fit for the purposes of the governors of Massachusetts Bay and Connecticut.

There were no significant issues with the established settlements as Hooker had cleverly agreed to be under the jurisdiction of both the Bay and Fort Saybrook. This being the new settlement established at the mouth of the Connecticut River by two the indolent parliamentarians, Lord Saye and Brook. At one time, they had planned this site as a bolthole for important puritans such as Oliver Cromwell should his fighting or his finances go awry. In 1635, a military engineer Lieutenant Lion Gardener, had arrived at the site determined to build the most well-defended fort in New England.

Charles Stanley Reinhart, watercolour, 1890. The fight at Block Island exaggerates the achievements of Captain Endicott and his men. (Public domain)

---

3   J. Winthrop, *Journal, 1630–1649* R.S. Dunn, J. Savage, and L. Yeandle, (ed.).

NEW WORLDS, OLD WARS

Fort Saybrook. An artist's impression of the small but well-defended fort at the mouth of the Connecticut River. (New York Public Library)

Construction was finished just in time as in September 1636, the Pequot would arrive as an armed and aggrieved body of warriors.

Shortly after Hooker's small group had exited onto the Connecticut River, Jonathan Brewster, a trader at the Plymouth trading settlement on the river, sent a warning down to Fort Saybrook. It stated, 'the Pequot have some mistrust, that the English will shortly come against them', and were therefore planning a pre-emptive strike against both the settlers and their native allies. The source of this falsehood is, however, suspect. It is believed to have been voiced by Uncas, the *sachem* of the Mohegan, for there is no doubt that Uncas had ambitions to return in triumph as the grand *sachem* of the Pequot; their defeat by the English with him as their ally, could only benefit his plan.

Events now gathered momentum. At the beginning of July, the new Standing Council of Massachusetts sent a note to the governor of Fort Saybrook, conveniently John Winthrop Jr. – the son of the deputy governor of Massachusetts. It required him to summon the Pequot and demand that they either comply with the terms of the 1634 treaty or suffer the consequences.

The Pequot believed they had kept their side of the bargain. They had handed over a significant 'present' to the English and professed their innocence in the Stone affair. In rejecting this response, John Winthrop seemed to side with the Western Niantics – Stone's killers – accepting a large area of their territory as a gift from their *sachem*, Sassious. This intransigent attitude appalled Gardener who recognised it would be his settlement that would suffer the consequences. He told Winthrop: 'I know that you will keep yourself safe … in the Bay, but myself, with these few you will leave at the stake to be roasted, or for hunger to be starved'. These reasonable fears, and Gardener's plea for time to put his fort in order, were ignored. The Bay meant business … then there was another death.

Block Island lies 13 miles off the coast of New England, due South of Narragansett Bay – the home of the eponymous tribe, a subset of whom dwelt on the Island. Among this tribe, Captain John Oldham was a welcome trader. Banished from Plymouth for drawing a knife on Miles Standish (as well as other disharmonious behaviour), he moved to Massachusetts Bay where he became the overseer of shot and powder whilst also making a living as a trusted trader with the coastal Amerindians. They admired him sufficiently to give him a gift of 500 bushels of corn and the offer of an island home.

Oldham had also established a settlement at Wethersfield on the Connecticut River, taking the old Amerindian path in 1634 two years before Thomas Hooker. He was thus a man who travelled comfortably amongst the native inhabitants. In July 1636, things went horribly wrong.

Oldham had sailed to Block Island to trade; he had a crew of five plus his two young nephews, who he presumably would not have embarked should he have considered this to be a dangerous voyage. At some point, a fishing boat skippered by John Gallop, came across Oldham's vessel behaving in an un-seamanlike manner and closed to investigate. Having made an unopposed boarding, he found it had been seized by Block Island Amerindians who had murdered the crew and taken the nephews prisoner. The evidence pointed to the atrocity being carried out by local Narragansetts – for what reason it was difficult to decide.

This was the position taken by the newly arrived and elected governor of Massachusetts, the young aristocratic Sir Henry Vane. As if to avoid a reprisal, Miantonimo, a *sachem* of the Narragansett, took a war party of 17 canoes and 200 men to punish the guilty islanders and organised for Oldham's nephews to be released. Given the fact that the aim of both Massachusetts and Connecticut was the destruction of the Pequot, in which they desired the Narragansett to be their allies, the tribe of Oldham's murderers was an embarrassment. This was solved by the simple expedient of stating that the perpetrators had fled and taken refuge with the Pequot who, 'therefore justly brought the revenge of the English upon them'. Vane was content to go along with this sleight of hand.

Before the main act, it was considered that a side-show of strength was needed. In late August 1636, Captain John Endicott was despatched to sail from Boston to Block Island with 90 troops. Their role was to carry out a raid whose rules of engagement required them 'to put to death the men of Block Island but to spare the women and children', who would have been taken into servitude or sold into slavery in the West Indies. After this, Endicott was instructed to meet with the Pequot and demand 1,000 fathoms of *wampum* and to take some of their children as hostages for good behaviour. It did not work out as planned.

Endicott's landing met with a half-hearted opposition. Following this, the Amerindians retreated into the wooded interior from where they saw their homes and crops being torched but they remained safe. Endicott then sailed to the mouth of the Pequot (Thames) River to challenge the tribe to combat. Fortunately, the tribe had more sense than to await his arrival and left Endicott and his troops to wander hot and flustered through the forest margins. Frustrated at his inability to hold a parley, Endicott set fire to a large Pequot village before the embarrassed expedition returned to Boston empty handed. There, the volunteers who had enlisted in the hope of loot, had to be compensated for their losses.

With Endicott back in the Bay, the Pequot exercised their just anger caused by Endicott's behaviour by besieging the garrison at Fort Saybrook. At the same time, realising that they could not defeat the colonists by themselves, the Pequot sought to make an alliance with their previous adversaries, the Narragansett. If this was successful, all the outlying settlements beyond

Plymouth and Boston would have been far from safe. One man managed to prevent what would be for the English a catastrophic alliance, taking place.

John Williams had been banished from Boston for both his heterodoxic views and for stating his firm belief that land could only be acquired from the Amerindian owners by legal purchase –not through royal patent or local magisterial approval. He had found it safer to live alongside the 'savages' than the 'saints'. Nevertheless, when rumour of the proposed Amerindian alliance reached the Bay, they invited Williams to attend the discussions. Here, an alternative proposal was put to the Narragansett, that they should ally themselves to Massachusetts.

Williams's intervention was successful; the third major impediment to Pequot success was now in place. By the time hostilities broke out the Narragansett *sachem* Miantonomi, whose preference had been for neutrality, was firmly committed to the English cause. He also sensed opportunity, proposing that any attack on the Pequot should be launched by the Narragansett alone with the English providing logistic support. The plan was rejected; it would have been fortunate for the Pequot if it had not been.

Meanwhile, the Pequot continued with their show of dissatisfaction before Fort Saybrook where the siege would last until March 1637. Any defenders who ventured out were attacked while, in a like-for-like action, the Pequot set fire to English fields and killed their cattle.

The siege was as unthreatening as a siege could be, with the defenders never in any great peril and the attackers refraining from an assault on the walls. Much more significant is the record of a conversation during a parley. It began with the Amerindians asking Gardener if he had, 'fought enough', that is, if honour had been satisfied and normal relations could be restored. The commander's noncommittal reply brought forth another question – did the English kill women and children? Again, Gardener was elusive. There was a long silence after which the Pequot said:

> We are Pequots and have killed Englishmen and can kill them as mosquitoes and we will go to Connecticut and kill men women and children and we will take away your horses and cows and hoggs.

This is exactly what they did at Wethersfield on 23 April 1637 but perhaps, with cause. The settlers at this small steading on the Connecticut River had seized land from the local *sachem*, Sowheag, contrary to an agreement he had reached with them. He in turn, complained to the Pequot who attacked the settlement killing six men and three women and took two 'maids' as hostages. Thanks to Dutch intermediaries, the maids were released unharmed and with their maidenhood *in tacto* – much to the surprise of their prurient debriefers.

Connecticut had got the excuse it needed and on 1 May, its General Court met at Hartford and:

> … ordered that there shall be an offensive war against the Pequot and that there shall be 90 men levied out of the 3 plantations, Hartford, Weathersfeild [*sic*],

NEW ENGLAND THE PEQUOT WAR MASSACRE AT MYSTIC

& Windsor (*viz*) out of Hertford 42, Windsor 30, Weathersfeild 18; under the command of Captaine Jo. Mason'

The key word here was 'offensive'. The yet to be confirmed, new colony of Connecticut, had been forbidden by the Bay to engage in 'offensive' war. By doing so, it could claim Pequot land through right of conquest, thereby foiling the latter's aggrandisement desires. However, to retain the initiative, they needed to act fast before troops arrived from Massachusetts. Thus, despite the reservations of both Gardiner and Captain Underhill, Massachusetts's man at Saybrook, Mason sallied forth to war. He took with him 70 Mohegans led by Uncas who, in a test of his loyalty, had been despatched from the fort to bring back some Pequot heads; four seemed sufficient for him to pass.

Mason might have acted impetuously but he did not act without a plan. Realising that a direct assault of the major Pequot stronghold of Weinshaucks might not succeed nor might a landing nearby that gave away his intentions, he decided to attack the lesser village on the Mystic River. He chose to approach it overland from the east rather than disembark at the river's mouth so he sailed past the Mystic River and disembarked well to the east on the shores of Narragansett Bay. From there, with an escort of 500 Narragansett warriors, he set off to trudge back almost 30 miles towards the Pequot village.

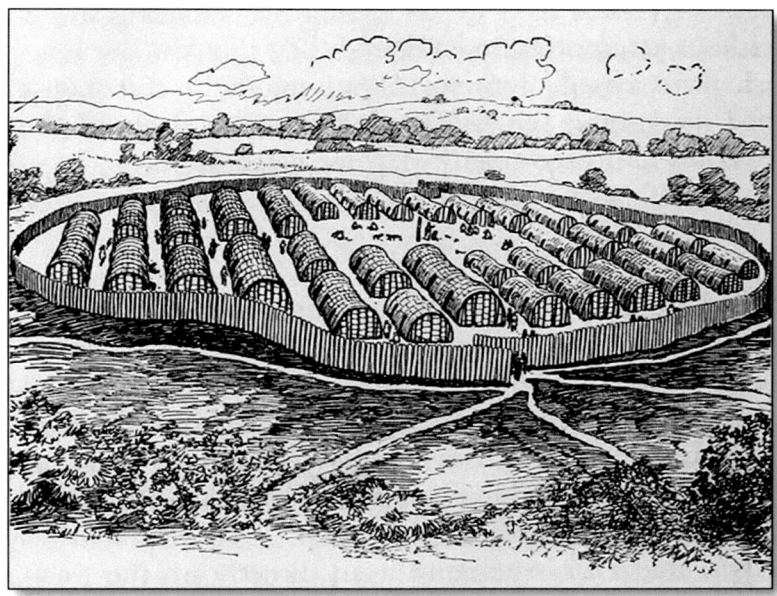

Artist's impression of the Pequot village at Mystic. (Public domain)

Now here is a mystery. For such a force to have moved through the woodland undetected seems improbable. Fennimore Cooper, writing many years later, but with some accuracy stated:

> It is unusual to find an encampment of the natives, lie those of the more instructed whites, guarded by the presence of armed men. Well informed of the approach of every danger, while it is yet at a distance, the Indian generally rests secure under his knowledge of the signs of the forest, and the long and difficult paths that separate him from those he has most reason to dread. But the enemy who, by any lucky concurrence of accidents, has found means to elude the vigilance of the scouts, will seldom meet with sentinels nearer the home to sound the alarm.[4]

---

4   J. F. Cooper, *The Last of the Mohicans* (H. C. Carey & I. Lea, 1826).

Nevertheless, without causing alarm, Mason, Underhill and their men were guided by the Narragansett to within two miles of the target village; they planned the assault to go in towards dawn while the moon was still bright. Before moving forward, the leaders invited their embedded priest to give their plans his blessing. Thus these:

> Christian heroes gathered around their chaplain, the Reverend Mr. Stone, and, with uncovered heads, united with him in fervent prayer that God would bless their enterprise. They were not going into the battle inspired by ambition, or the love of conquest, or the greed of gain. They were contending only to protect their wives and their children from the vengeance of a savage and a merciless foe.[5]

The English plan was to surround the palisade and pour in fire from every direction while their Amerindian colleagues were to form an outer ring to prevent anyone escaping. This was not to be an attack for either the squeamish or those with scruples, as Mason stated: 'We had formerly concluded to destroy them by the Sword and save the Plunder'.

It was obvious that by 'them' he did not intend to exclude women and children. His Narragansett allies, understanding this, demurred only to be told by Mason that: 'We ask no aid from you. You may stand at any distance you please, and look on, and see how Englishmen can fight'.

When it came, the volley of fire delighted Underhill who described it as being one of 'flint and match' thus indicating the change of weaponry from matchlock to flintlock was underway.

Moments before this fusillade, the attackers were detected; a dog barked and a frantic call of 'Englishmen! Englishmen!' was heard. It was too late for the still sleepy Pequot to prevent those English from tearing down the bushes blocking the two entrances and entering the village from opposite ends. Resistance now stiffened and the assailants started to take casualties. Mason, entering a wigwam, seized a firebrand and ordered his men to torch the place. As he gave the order, he was almost shot at close-range but his sergeant, Davis, cut the assailant's bowstring with his cutlass and seconds after, the attacker. Underhill followed Mason's example and set fire to the tinder dry mats which covered the crowded wigwams. Soon all was ablaze.

Moving away from the fire, the troops reformed their ring and watched as the Pequot fell in the flames. Several were reported to have been firing back until the heat melted their bowstrings. Others scrambled up the palisades only to be shot as they tried to jump to safety. A handful broke free and in Underhill's words:

> … came in troops to the Indians, twenty and thirty at a time, which our soldiers received and entertained with the point of the sword. Down fell men, women, and children; those that scaped us, fell into the hands of the Indians that were in the

---

5   C. Orr, (ed.), *History of Pequot War, The Contemporary accounts of Mason, Underhill, Vincent and Gardiner* (Cleveland: 1897).

rear of us. It is reported that there were about four hundred souls in this fort, and not above five of them escaped out of our hands.⁶

The outer circle of Narragansetts were astounded at what they had witnessed, 'It is too furious', they cried, 'and slays too many men'.

The Amerindian dismay was understandable. Even though instances of slaughter existed in their history (such as when in 1607, the Powhatan feeling threated by the Chesapeake who lived around present day Norfolk and Virginia descended on them and exterminated 'all the inhabitants, the *weroance* and his subjects', which may have included the last remnants of the lost colony of Roanoke ⁷); mainly, 'they seldom make war for lands or goods, but for women and children' whom they would abduct and bring up as their own thus increasing their cohort while insulting the prowess of their enemy. The war of rude words was a powerful, non-lethal weapon.

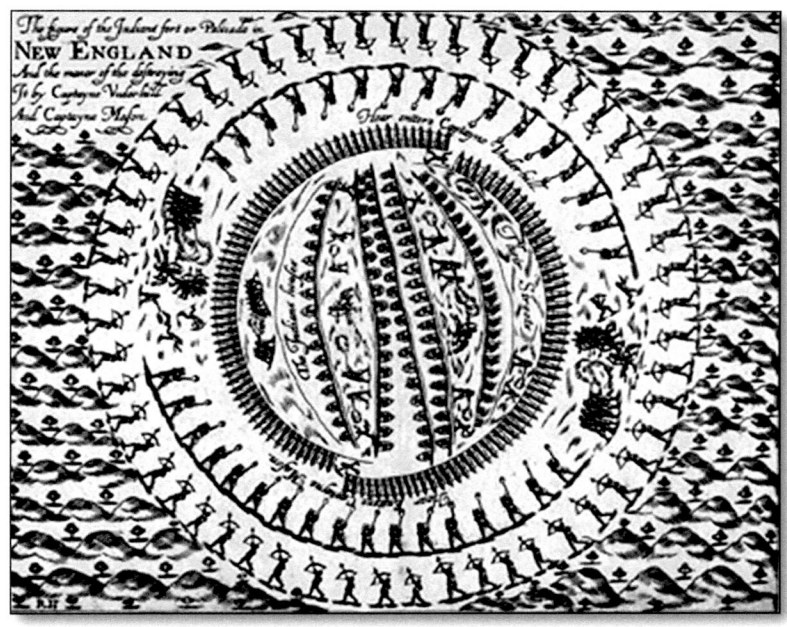

Massacre at Mystic. An engraving from John Underhill's account of 1638, *Newes from America*. Note that the outer ring of Narragansett are all armed with bows and arrows with not one firearm between them. (Public domain)

Furious as the attack may have been, there is no evidence that Mason, as Jennings would have us believe, marched on Mystic determined to commit a massacre.⁸ For a start, he had carried out no reconnaissance and did not know the layout of the village, how crowded it was, nor how many warriors might have been present. Surrounding the site while the occupants slept was a sound tactic and the firebrand which started the conflagration, was not prepared earlier but one that was fortuitously available when the assault seemed to be foundering. The work was soon completed, as Bradford described:

> Those yᵗ scaped yᵉ fire were slaine with yᵉ sword; some hewed to peeces, others rune throw with their rapiers, so as they were quickly dispatchte, and very few escaped. It was conceived they thus destroyed about 400. at this time. It was a fearfull sight to see them thus frying in yᵉ fyer, and yᵉ streams of blood [426] quenching yᵉ same, and horrible was yᵉ stinck & sente ther of; but yᵉ victory seemed a sweete sacrifice, and they gave the prays therof to God, who had wrought so wonderfuly

---

6   W. Underhill, *Newes from America* (London: 1638) <www.digitalcommons>
7   H. C. Rountree, *The Powhatan Amerindians of Virginia* (University of Oklahoma Press, 1989).
8   F. Jennings, *The Invasion of America*, Institute of Early American history (University of North Carolina, 1975).

for them, thus to inclose their enimise in their hands, and give them so speedy a victory over so proud & insulting an enimie. The Narigansett Indeans, all this while, stood round aboute, but aloofe from all danger, and left ye whole [224] execution to ye English, exept it were ye stoping of any y^t broke away, insulting over their enimies in this their ruine & miserie, when they saw them dancing in ye flames, calling them by a word in their owne language, signifing, O brave Pequents![9]

The figure of '400' slain is disputed. What is not in dispute is the extremely high number of non-combatants this included. Job completed; the attackers now needed to leave with alacrity for they knew the noise of their assault would have reached the warriors waking at Weinshaucks who would now be racing along the five-mile track that linked the two settlements. It is recorded:

> As soon as the savages came in sight of the fort, and saw its utter destruction, they stopped a moment, as if aghast with rage and despair. They howled and tore out their hair, and, by their phrensied gestures, appeared to be in a delirium of fury. They then made a simultaneous rush upon the English, resolved to take revenge at whatever sacrifice of their own lives. There were now but forty-four Englishmen in a condition to fight. Three hundred savages – seven to one – rushed upon them in demoniac rage. But European weapons, and the courage and discipline of civilised life, were equal to the emergency. These intrepid colonists, with cool, unerring aim, wasted not a bullet. Every report of the musket was the death of an Indian. The savages, thus repulsed, took refuge behind trees and rocks, and with great bravery pressed and harassed the English with every missile of savage warfare.[10]

Mason ordered a retreat towards the river where they presumed their pinnaces would be waiting for them. Carrying their wounded, they forced their way through the woods entrusting their defence to a rearguard of Narragansett for the strange reason that Underhill:

> … requested our Indians for to entertain fight with them. Our end was that we might see the nature of Indian war; which they granted us, and fell out, the Pequot, Narragansett and Mohegan, exchanging a few arrows together after such a manner, as I dare boldly affirm, they might fight seven years and not kill seven men. They came not near one another, but shot remote, and not point-blank … and then they gaze up in the sky to see where their arrows fall, and not until it is fallen do they shoot again. This fight is more for pastime than to conquer or subdue enemies.

This seems a strange interpretation given the woe that had just been wrought on the Pequot. Indeed, the Narragansett soon sought shelter from the furious Pequot by closing ranks with the retiring English. It was to be a stiff

---

9   W. Bradford, *Of Plymouth Plantation* (Boston: The Massachusetts Historical Society, 1912).

10   C. Orr, (ed.), *History of Pequot War. The Contemporary accounts of Mason, Underhill, Vincent and Gardiner* (Cleveland: 1897).

Destruction of the Pequot, nineteenth-century poster. Men, women and children all being put to the sword. (Public domain)

rearguard action during which the Amerindians sent, 'parties in advance to form ambushes in the thickets, and shooting their barbed and poisoned arrows from behind every rock and tree'.

It is pertinent to note that at no time, did either Underhill or Mason mention being fired upon by Amerindian musketry. Their possession of these weapons which would influence future campaigns, seems not yet to have taken place. Nonetheless, they attacked ferociously even though the English 'bullets outreached their arrows'. Underhill estimated that more Pequot warriors were killed during this fighting retreat than had died at Mystic, suggesting the burnt village was occupied mainly by women and children.

The attacks appear to have died away as the English reached the river bank. From here, Underhill embarked to sail over to Saybrook while Mason led his men to the Connecticut River. From there, they were ferried back to the fort but not before burning several Western Niantic settlements and killing some of their occupants. They left behind them a broken and grieving nation, no longer cohesive; its survivors fleeing in small groups in several directions but finding nowhere to rest that was free from danger. If they had so desired, the victors could, in accordance with Psalm 60, have made the Pequot, like Moab, their wash pot. They could have sought out Sassacus, the discredited *sachem*, and made him sign a peace treaty advantageous to the English, for he had nothing left with which to bargain. But the English were not going to be satisfied with anything other than total eradication – as this soon became clear.

Some 200 Pequot surrendered to their old enemy the Narragansett from whose *sachem*, Miantonom, they hoped to have received fair treatment in accordance with the norms of tribal warfare. This position was summarised by Roger Williams who wrote they expected: '… to be used kindly, have houses and goods and fields given to them: because they chose to come to them'.

However, this was not what the colonists wanted. A body of troops from Massachusetts, under the leadership of Captain Stoughton, demanded that the captives be handed over to them to be escorted back to where John Gallop (a captain after the Block Island fight), awaited their arrival. At that point, the men – only some 30 strong for this was a group of refugees not warriors – were killed while 33 of the women and children were divided between the Narragansett and Mohegans. The rest were despatched to Boston where many were sold into Caribbean slavery.

It is relevant to quote how Hubbard reported this killing, for he states that the men 'were turned presently into Charon's ferryboat, under the command of skipper Gallop'. It seems a writer who spent pages using biblical references to justify the colonists' war against the Pequot, had to turn to mythology to light-heartedly report this slaughter.

The only hope the Pequot had for survival as a people was either to join up with Uncas and their kin, his Mohegans; flee towards the Dutch or New York settlements or to seek shelter with the Mohawks.

Sassacus, carrying the tribal *wampum* with him, at first headed towards the Dutch. The English, following close behind, landed at Quinnipiack (present New Haven) where the Pequot were reported to have taken temporary refuge. Warned just in time, the *sachem* fled but many of his followers were not so swift and they were duly killed, including two *sachems* who despite being promised clemency, were beheaded.

The refugees continued their weary rout. On 13 July, they took shelter within the Munnacommock Swamp, an area small enough for the English, under the command of Captains Mason and Patrick, to surround with troops just 12 feet apart.[11] The more head-strong of these troops charged on in, only to be repulsed by the enemy's arrows which 'flew very thick' but only wounded and not lethally:

> as they pierced their hatte brimes, & their sleeves, & stockins, & other parts of their cloaths, yet so miraculously did the Lord preserve them as not one of them was wounded, save those 3. who rashly went into ye swampe.

A parley was arranged which resulted in many of the women and children being sent forth under promise of fair treatment. However, the warriors remained – foolishly, in Hubbard's view [as] 'they were possessed with such a spirit of stupidity and sullenness that they resolved rather to sell their lives for what they could get there'. Given the fact the English tended to slaughter or sell into slavery those they captured, the decision to fight to the death displayed qualities of greatness the English so admired in defenders during many a European siege.

The English began to cut a way through the swamp thereby forcing the defenders into a smaller and smaller area and importantly, a circumference they could easily control. Very soon, the soldiers were positioned just 12 feet apart all the way around with the enemy so-close that individuals could be

---

11   <www.fairfieldhistory.org>

picked off by musket shot if they inadvertently exposed themselves. Towards dawn, the elements intervened as a dense fog arose from the swamp. Taking advantage of this, some 20 to 30 Pequot broke free. As for the rest, the English moved into the swamp with gun and sword where they found:

> … several heaps of them sitting close together, upon whom they discharged their pieces laden with ten or twelve pistol bullets at a time, putting the muzzles of their pieces under the boughs within a few yards of them; so, besides those that were found dead, many more were killed and sunk into the mire.[12]

As for the survivors, the male children were sent as slaves to Bermuda while the women were either taken into servitude or handed to the allied tribes. One lady, the wife of *sachem* Mononotto, whose intervention it was claimed had saved the lives of the two maids captured at Weathersfield, ended up in the household of Governor Winthrop.

The selling into slavery or servitude is an important outcome. How could the English ever treat as equals a race whose men, women and children they were prepared to treat in such a manner? Years later, when it was the turn of the Narragansetts to expect colonial wrath, Winthrop was to receive a letter from his brother-in-law, Emanuel Downing, in which the latter outlined a policy which suggested:

> If upon a just war the Lord should deliver them into our hands, we might easily have men, women and children enough to exchange for Moors … for I do not see how we can thrive until we get into a stock of slaves sufficient to do all our business.[13]

Sassacus, his chief general Mononotto and the few who escaped, trudged on towards the Hudson River. Here they intended to seek sanctuary among the fierce Mohawks in return for gifting them the tribal *wampum*. It did not work; possibly aware of the advantages of pleasing the English, the Mohawks slaughtered them.

The following year an agreement was drawn up at Hartford which not only confirmed the destruction of the Pequot as a people, banning them from returning from exile, but demanded that there should be no inter-tribal conflicts without permission from the English. This was an agreement that meant business.

Massachusetts also realised that such conflicts might not be occasional in their occurrence so in 1636, the colony became the first English government to raise a permanent regiment based on county lines – pre-dating the first English regular regiment by six years. However, in 1638, the same government objected to the creation of an Artillery Company of Massachusetts Bay on the grounds that a professional force might mount a challenge to the civilian government. This concern was paramount in the abiding American idea of both the need for a militia and the need and right of everyman to bear arms.

---

12 C. Orr, (ed.), *History of Pequot War*.
13 J. Winthrop, *Journal, 1630–1649*.

In 1638 a group of exiled Pequot tried to create a new village on Pawcatuck Bay, near the border of Rhode Island. On discovering this Captain Mason, with 40 troops and 100 Mohegans landed on the shore, looted and burnt the village, and handed the survivors over to Uncas and his Mohegans.

The conflict had made Uncas a powerful man. He was strong enough to compete for hegemony over the Connecticut Valley with Miantonomi and his Narragansetts who, in 1643, having sought permission from the governor of Connecticut, invaded Mohegan territory with a force of 1000 braves. Despite being outnumbered, the Mohegans defeated their enemy and captured Miantonomi who Uncas handed over to Massachusetts for trial of treaty violation.

The Bay had neither justice or justification for trying the *sachem* for this offence, so they accused him of plotting against the English and, being 'of the opinion that it would not be safe to set him at liberty' nor having 'sufficient ground for us to put him to death', they solved their moral dilemma by handing him back to Uncas. They expected him to carry out their preferred sentence but only once he had escorted his prisoner beyond their boundaries. Having done so, Uncas, personally, brained Miantonomi with a tomahawk. In such manner did Christian counsellors salve their consciences while creating a recipe for future conflict.

Jennings saw the strategy employed by the English against the Pequot and in future Anglo-Amerindian conflicts, had European antecedents, especially in the campaigns waged against Scotland and Ireland.[14] These were:

1.   A deliberate policy of inciting competition between the tribes – divide and rule.
2.   A disregard for pledges and promises made to natives.
3.   Extermination as a weapon to terrify others.
4.   Falsification and faith to justify the waging of total war.

Since the first Europeans had come ashore in America various fatal epidemics had wreaked havoc on native societies. Some diseases introduced were however, social ones. Massacre is the malaria of society which, once infected, although it may lie dormant for decades, will erupt again with all its old ferocity. It is true that the first massacre recorded in the age of English settlement was carried out by the Amerindians in Virginia in 1622 but if one were able to grade massacres as the law does murders, this was an act of war. It was a defensive act and one that was executed in the traditional way that Amerindians had always fought and avoided the European fashion of meeting on a battlefield – this would have been suicidal. It was certainly not the onslaught of a sleeping community as happened at Mystic.

The Pequot War might have been nasty, brutish and short, but it gave those involved an experience they would not have gained in peaceful England. As a result, when civil war broke out in the homeland in 1642, there were Bay Colony individuals whose presence in England was either invited or self-

---

14   F. Jennings, *The Invasion of America*.

desired. Among these was Sir Henry Vane, whose time in Massachusetts had been cut short by his unacceptable support of religious tolerance in the Antinomian Controversy. This resulted in an obtuse, highly emotional religious dispute that led to blows and banishments. Vane was to serve both King and Parliament before and during the Civil War but, after a show-trial for treason, Charles II signed his death warrant and he was executed in 1662.

The well-trained Massachusetts Artillery Company sent several of its members back to England. Included was its sergeant major general, Israel Stoughton who, along with Captain John Leverett, joined Thomas Rainborowe's Earl of Manchester's Eastern Association Army. Stoughton was to die in May 1644 during the siege of Lincoln. The next year, no longer liking the organisation in which they were serving, most of the Massachusetts men sailed back to New England. Yet still others came over. Stephen Winthrop, son of Governor Winthrop, joined Rainborowe in 1646 while George Cooke took command of Rainborowe's regiment when its founder died in 1648. He went on to fight in Cromwell's Irish campaign of 1649 to 1650, taking part in the siege and sacking of Wexford – a European assault that mirrored the one at Mystic. Still fighting, Cooke died on campaign in 1652.

The slaying of Anne Hutchinson, New York, August 1643. Forced out of Boston because of her beliefs, Anne Hutchinson moved to New York, dying during one the colony's several conflicts with local tribes. (Public domain)

It was not just soldiers that the colonies could provide. Several surgeons and preachers, such as Hugh Peter and Harvard graduate, George Downing, also sailed back to support the parliamentary cause while seamen crossed the Atlantic to join the Protectorate navy either at sea or as Navy Commissioners.

The destruction of the Pequot reinforced the colonists view of the righteousness of their cause and, indeed their 'manifest destiny'. At a meeting in New England in 1640, the following motions were adopted:

1. The earth is the Lord's and the fullness thereof.
2. The Lord may give the earth or any part of it to his chosen people.
3. We are his chosen people.[15]

Back in America, Mystic's poisonous tendrils continued to creep across the land. First, in the almost identical assault of the Narragansett in the Great Swamp Fight of 1675 and then, crossing the continent, culminating in the massacre at Wounded Knee which brought the centuries of Amerindian wars to a close. That final slaughter took place in December 1890 with the killing of 146 Lakotas – 82 men and 64 women and children. The cultural contagion would continue westward until the shame of My Lai in Vietnam when on 16 March 1968, some 500 unarmed villagers, including men, women and children were killed by U.S. Army soldiers. Some of the women were gang-raped before being killed. Twenty-six soldiers were charged with criminal offences, but only Lieutenant William Calley was convicted and he served just three and a half years of a life sentence.

An eyewitness account of the My Lai massacre reads as if it is a direct descendant from the assault on Mystic:

> I walked up and saw these guys doing strange things ... Setting fire to the hootches and huts and waiting for people to come out and then shooting them ... going into the hootches and shooting them up ... gathering people in groups and shooting them ... As I walked in you could see piles of people all through the village ... all over. They were gathered up into large groups. I saw them shoot an M79 grenade launcher into a group of people who were still alive. But it was mostly done with a machine gun. They were shooting women and children just like anybody else. We met no resistance and I only saw three captured weapons. We had no casualties. It was just like any other Vietnamese village – old papa-sans, women and kids. As a matter of fact, I don't remember seeing one military-age male in the entire place, dead or alive.[16]

Such behaviour through the centuries, must be challenged. The question should be asked how could an otherwise civilised society, treat ethnically different people in a way that defied all the social mores that they considered necessary within their culture?

---

15 V. Coleman, *Rogue Nation* (Blue Books, 2002).
16 S. M. Hersh, *Eyewitness accounts of the My Lai massacre* (The Plain Dealer: 20 November 1969).

7

King Philip's War: Part 1

Ambushing Amateurs 1675

'Many men lost by not taking heed to the ambushments of the enemy nor observing their methods'. – Governor John Leverett, of Massachusetts, 24 September 1675.

'Colonial soldiers could see no enemy to shoot at, but felt their bullets out of the thick bushes where they lay in ambushments'. – Daniel Gookin

Plymouth Colony played a very minor role in the Pequot War. One would like to think it was holding true to its earlier open attitude to its native neighbours but, sadly, it was mainly because it was in a sulk with the Bay over the latter's bullying ways in Maine and elsewhere.

When they landed in 1620, the Pilgrims were suspicious and afeared of the local people whom they sighted but seldom met. After all, they had no idea of the size of the indigenous population, how warlike they were, or how well they were armed. Nevertheless, thanks to Squanto the go-between, by March 1621, they had signed a treaty formalising the desire for peaceful coexistence with the neighbouring Wampanoag. Shortly afterwards, they agreed terms with the more warlike Canonicus and his Narragansett tribe. Even so, for the Pilgrims, peaceful coexistence meant a separate development for they and the Puritans, who arrived in large numbers after 1630, wished to practice self-advantageous apartheid. Before that numerically superior group arrived, the Pilgrims were prepared to turn to the sword if it suited their purpose.

When a rival hippie-like group settled, not just alongside but amongst the Massachusetts at nearby Wessagussett, Miles Standish (Plymouth's equivalent of John Smith), on a pretext, marched on the village. He slew a number of natives, spiking the head of their leader, Wituwamat, on a pole above the fort at Plymouth. Not surprisingly, the English settlers at Wessagussett fled, as did many of the locals, convinced more massacres were planned. Peace was to a certain extent, imposed and the rivals rid.

NEW WORLDS, OLD WARS

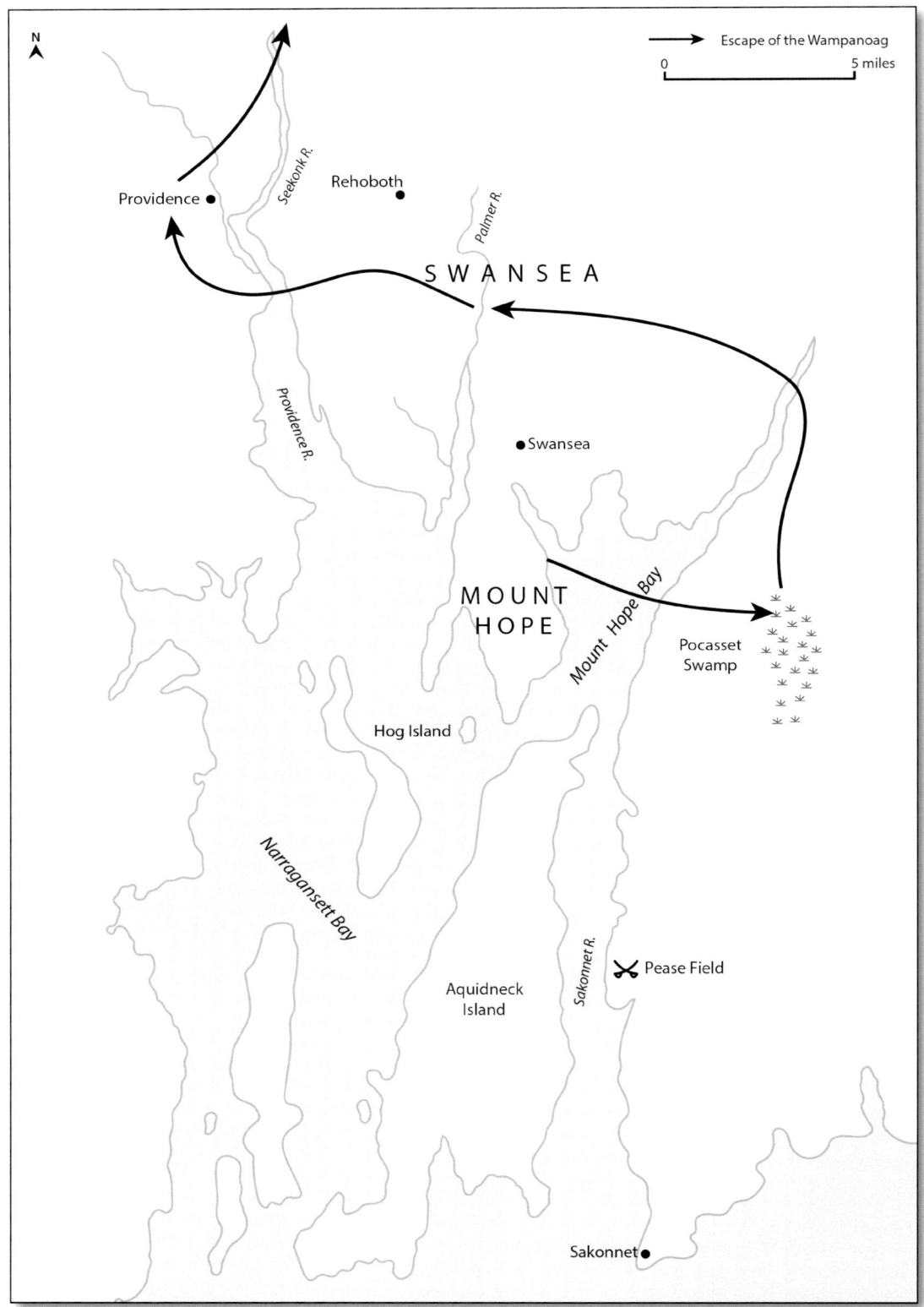

The escape of the Wampanoag

The Wampanoag leader Massasoit was about 40 years old when the treaty was signed and it lasted, not without challenges, until his death in 1661. This was partly due to the mutual respect between the *sachem* and the Pilgrim's leader, Edward Winslow. Massasoit had saved the Pilgrims from starvation and his own life had been restored by Edward Winslow's nursing in 1623. It was also because a variety of resentments had not yet reached boiling point. The two nations found themselves as awkward neighbours with the parvenus more and more imposing their trading terms, ethics, religion and land lust, on the tribes. The tribes could see their own way of life and mores being threatened and undermined often by means they found incomprehensible, questionable, unfair, unkind and often accompanied by an infusion of that alien liquid, alcohol.

However, of all the demons waiting to cry havoc, one dominated all the rest; the arrivistes desire for more and more land – a desire complicated by inter-colonial rivalry that saw tribal lands both as an impediment to expansion and a bargaining chip amongst rival settlers. The early treaty enabled the colonists to procure lands using legal trickery as a substitute for violence but when it became necessary for their own ends, the colonists would have no qualms in seizing land by force.

The Narragansett *sachem* Canonicus, died in 1647 but not before making a formal peace treaty with King Charles in 1644. There was no immediate reason why the deaths of these wise leaders should have brought the alliances between Amerindians and incomers to an end – except that both Massachusetts Bay and Plymouth had altered and expanded greatly. Instead of being nuclear settlements surrounded by quiescent or unapproachable tribes, townships were springing up along an open border many miles from the original settlements. Meanwhile, both Connecticut and Rhode Island were now nascent colonies and Maine had been incorporated into Massachusetts Bay.

Massasoit the Wampanoag leader with whom the Pilgrims agreed a peace treaty that lasted for 40 years. (Author's collection)

It was also significant that a few villages were founded as centres for Amerindians who had converted to Christianity, referred to as Praying Towns. The inhabitants of these, felt a duty to serve God, King and colony, although their naïve trust was not reciprocated by their wary white neighbours. These neighbours were moving away from the idea that 'fighting with Indians about horses and hogs' was a matter 'too low to shed blood', to one where seized land should be defended by well-armed settlers whatever the consequences. Good, fertile land was at a premium and very much in demand.

By 1670, the English population of New England numbered tens of thousands, greatly exceeding the disease-reduced native population by about 20 to one; yet the latter still appeared to own vast uncultivated acres of wilderness. Not surprisingly, land, its leasing and ownership, was to be the source of strife.

Massasoit was succeeded by his son, Metacomet, who had adopted the classical name of Alexander while his younger brother was now referred to as Philip. In 1662, Plymouth Colony, feeling concern over Alexander's land deals, summoned him to appear for questioning, threatening his person when he appeared to cavil at the idea. Whatever his treatment, a short while later he took ill and died. This understandably led to suspicions of poisoning.

Philip, now the grand *sachem*, also had to endure arbitrary summonses in which his loyalty was questioned and his followers' arms seized. The pressure and humiliation continued with court appearances and signed surrenders of authority and weapons. Nor did the English pay much regard to Metacomet's powerful and influential widow, Weetamoo, not believing that a *sunksqua* or *squaw sachem* could hold property, manage affairs and command a community; after all English wives had no such rights. The results were indignant, hostile *sachems*, busily conspiring to form sufficient alliances should need and opportunity arise, to strike a fatal blow against the hated intruders.

It was the English who provided the excuse. On 29 January 1675, a Christian Amerindian, John Sassamon, who occasionally served as Phillip's secretary, was murdered beside a frozen body of water known as Assawompsett Pond. His body was pushed through a hole in the ice to make it seem as if he had fallen in. Buried but exhumed on suspicion of foul play, the Massachusetts authorities soon arrested three suspects whom they considered had a reason to murder Sassamon. It would seem, he had been acting as a double agent, both misinterpreting documents laid before Phillip and informing the authorities of the *sachem*'s plans for an uprising. He had received an education at Harvard and several documents regarding the sale of land indicate that his sympathies lay with the English. There was reason enough for suspecting the murderers were Phillip's agents and a confession was procured from one of them before he was hanged alongside his two companions.

Guilty or innocent, Phillip would have expected to have exercised jurisdiction over his own. Massachusetts's action was a direct challenge to his authority over his people. For him, this was one more indication as to the disdain which the incomers felt for both his person and his property, the land on which they dwelt. At the time, it was generally agreed that the English 'had begun a war by the execution of three Amerindians for murder' but that was merely the source of the spark, the explosives had been piled up for many a year.

Adding to the insults he experienced, Philip also believed, somewhat forlornly, that as a king himself he was answerable only to his fellow king, Charles II of England. This was not too outlandish a position for him to take. His neighbours, the Narragansett had petitioned a sympathetic king in April 1644, when the *sachems* Canonicus and Pessacus, had submitted their land and possessions to the king on the understanding that he would grant them 'royal protection' against their enemies. By this, they did not mean their fellow Amerindians but 'His Majesty's pretended subjects', the

Massachusetts colonists – the barbed 'pretended' inferring the illegality of the independently minded colony.

Armed with a successful submission, the Narragansett were able to inform Massachusetts that they shared an equality of status with the incomers 'being subject now unto the same king and state as you yourselves are'. This entitled them to approach the king of England to arbitrate in any dispute between Amerindians and English, including complaining of 'violence and injustice from the Massachusetts … that had caused them to be fined, and then took their whole country in mortgage'.

Such a position of equality would have been assumed by Philip, who would have felt that rather than acting with a 'mutinous temper', he was defending his people against the treachery of Massachusetts. Indeed, along with the Narragansett he might have considered his land rights de jure but none of the colonies, except for Rhode Island, were ever likely to consider them de facto.

The death of Sassamon. The investigation, the trail and execution of the suspects led to the outbreak of King Philip's War. (Author's collection)

Philip was too trusting or naïve to consider where the road he was treading, would lead. Warned by the reconciliatory Easton that the Wampanoag should avoid war at all costs (because the English 'were too strong for them'), Philip replied that in this case, 'the English should do to them as they did when they were too strong for the English'.[1]

---

1   L. Brooks, *Our Beloved Kin* (Yale University Press, 2019).

With the prospect of war looking more likely, the English endeavoured to wean tribal support from Philip. In June 1675, messengers were sent to the Nipmucks, Narragansett, Quaboag and a number of tribal towns, to organise treaties ensuring they would not support Philip. All agreed to remain faithful, even in subjection, to Massachusetts. However, four of the tribes' *sachems* were later reported to be at the Amerindian rendezvous site of Menameset in July.

In mid June, Benjamin Church, a pioneer adventurer and friend of Awashonks (the squaw *sachem* of the Sakonnet, one of Philip's subordinate tribes), was invited by her to a dance. Here he witnessed six Wampanoag braves, their faces decorated with war paint, trying to persuade Awashonks to join in a struggle against the English. Bravely, and on Church's advice, she declined and he, perhaps surprisingly, was able to depart unharmed or unhindered.

Two days later, the Rhode Island's lieutenant governor John Easton, met Philip and unsuccessfully proposed arbitration. The unlikelihood of this was made more obvious when Church met Peter Nunnuit, Weetamoo's current husband, who informed him that Philip's young men intended burning English villages and slaughtering cattle. Armed with this alarming news, Church rushed post-haste to report what he had witnessed to Governor Winslow. The governor had made a similar approach to Weetamoo suggesting that if should she renounce Philip, she 'shall assuredly reap the fruits to your comfort when he by his pride and treachery has wrought his own ruin'.

Meanwhile in Swansea, the boil was about to burst just where poisonous relationships were most apparent. By 1675, the land that Philip could truly call his own was almost limited to the peninsula of Mount Hope. This was a triangle of land, about seven miles long and four miles wide at its widest, accessed by an isthmus of land less than a mile across at its narrowest. North of this domain lay the dispersed settlement of Swansea – like an alien hand throttling and containing the Wampanoag.

Here, the inhabitants had nervously become aware of armed tribal movements during the previous days. A rider was despatched to plead with the governor for support. As the sounds of drums and the movement of warriors increased, the houses nearest the isthmus were abandoned only to be sacked by the watching Amerindians once their residents had taken up shelter in the local garrisons. When some colonists, returning to their empty houses surprised intruders, one of them, John Salisbury, opened fire and killed a Wampanoag.

By the evening of 21 June, reinforcements under the command of Captain Cudworth, had arrived at the Swansea garrison, their vanguard being led by the enthusiastic Benjamin Church. A day later, Winslow received assurances from his fellow governors (Leverett, of Massachusetts and Coddington of Rhode Island), that the former would furnish troops and ammunition while the latter would mount boat patrols around the Mount Hope peninsula – Philip and his men could be hemmed in. At the same time, missions were despatched to the Nipmuck and Narragansett to discourage them from making a disastrous decision to link up with Philip

On 24 June, the Wampanoag took revenge for the death of their brave. Warriors descended on Swansea, burning, looting and slaying nine settlers, including John Salisbury. Their rampage was made easier as the villagers and their reinforcements had chosen to hunker down in a few fortified dwellings rather than mount patrols. The war had begun.

At this moment, another rider was despatched from Swansea to raise the alarm. Simultaneously, the Wampanoag fearing the worst, sent many of their women and children to seek safety with the Narragansett. Their view being that a fight would break out because the 'English were as afraid of Philip as he was afraid of the English'.

The next day, a last-minute approach to Philip was abandoned when the parleying party stumbled across the mutilated bodies of two Englishmen lying on the track. The two men had been messengers sent to seek medical help after the previous Amerindian attack.

Armchair generals seldom make strategic or tactical errors but with hindsight, it is difficult to see what Cudworth had achieved in the days leading up to the killings of 24 June. Even with the troops he had at his disposal, he could have placed a cordon before Mount Hope to coop-up the violent Amerindians who might even have been acting independently from Philip's more cautious approach.

By 28 June, with the arrival of the Massachusetts troops, the combined force of the colonies numbered over 350 including 50 cavalrymen and some friendly Amerindians. There was certainly sufficient to mount a significant assault on Philip's territory, undefended as it was by any fortifications.

However, instead of a planned attack, some hot-heads rode over the bridge separating the two forces and were met with a fusillade fired by ambushing Amerindians which killed one man and scared many who rapidly retreated. The following day, a better organised advance was made but they came across the heads of the Englishmen killed on the 24th, mounted on bloody poles. Of Philip and his people there was no sign – just an abandoned village.

This botched operation could not be better, although it was inaccurately summarised in a letter from William Harris, 'a weary traveller for the space of almost forty years in the wilderness of New England'. Writing to Sir Joseph Williamson, the English Secretary of State for the Northern Department, he recorded the troops:

> … marched after Philip in a few files some miles long and shot at the green shrubs when they saw not the enemy, so the Indians, hearing their guns, had room to slide by them; at the last they found Philip in a swamp, but could not draw him out, so they marched back again'.[2]

The foe, having been given ample time to prepare, had already fled. Paddling over the water eastwards to seek shelter in the swamps of Pocasset Country, they were undisturbed and able to persuade *sachem* Weetamoo to join their cause. They had chosen well the place to go to ground, as one observer noted:

---

[2]   *CSP Colonial*, Vol. 9, 1676–1677, 1021 12 August 1676.

> This Pocassit Swamp is judged about seven or eight miles long and so full of bushes and trees that a parcel of Amerindians may be within the length of a pike of a man, and he cannot discover them; and besides, this as well as all other swamps is so soft ground, that an Englishman can neither go nor stand theron, and yet these bloody Savages will run along over it, holding their guns cross their arms.[3]

The technique was to bend at the knees using the shins as swamp-shoes. Outside the swamp any wandering Amerindian was now in mortal danger for:

> It shall be lawful for any person ... that shall find any Amerindians travelling or skulking [outside closely proscribed limits] to command them under their guard ... or to kill and destroy them as they best may or can.[4]

With Philip confined to swampy Pocasset and his warriors' options inhibited by the presence of their remaining wives and children, an encircling and tightening noose by the combined forces of Plymouth and The Bay could have brought the war to an early, even negotiated, conclusion. Yet, while the pursuit of Philip was being planned but not pursued, Massachusetts decided it was more important for its wellbeing to put pressure on the untrusted Narragansett. The tribe had been their significant allies in the Pequot War but for many years had become too strong and stroppy for Massachusetts's liking, even claiming an equality through their being 'subjects under the same king'. In 1653, during the Dutch war, an expedition was prepared against them for supposedly, siding with the Dutch but peace in Europe meant it had to be cancelled.

On 5 July, Massachusetts ordered its forces in Swansea to move towards Narragansett. They were to provide threatening support to the mission led by Captain Edward Hutchinson, to pressurise the Narragansett in remaining neutral. The captain was to ignore the tribes' marriage links with the Wampanoag and the Pocasset. This included the widowed Weetamoo who had abandoned Petonowit (husband number four) when he allied with the English; that August, Weetamoo was to marry the Narragansett warrior Quinnapin.

The captain also took no notice of the Amerindian tradition of offering shelter to refugees. Amongst other things, Hutchinson was to demand the tribe surrender any Wampanoag they held – dead or alive – a payment being made for any captives or heads handed over. In addition, the tribe was expected to send hostages to Boston to guarantee their compliance. If the tribe's negotiators refused or cavilled at the terms, then Hutchinson was to be ready to use force.

This threatening posture was modified on 9 July when Captain Wait Winthrop arrived from Connecticut. True to his unusual Christian name, he proposed delaying the use of force while in his governor's words, 'It is best to keep and promote peace with them' even if it meant 'bearing some of their

---

3   N. Saltonstall, *The Present State of New England with respect to the Amerindian War*, 1675.
4   *Ibid*.

ill manners and conniving at some irregularities'. Besides which, woodland warfare was best carried out when the leaves were off the trees, the ground was hard and supplies for the enemy would be in short supply.

The Connecticut argument held for the meantime. Under duress, the Narragansett negotiators, none of whom were senior *sachems*, accepted most of Massachusetts demands, reluctantly and certainly with seething resentment. Ten days had been spent on this expedition, days in which the war against Philip could have been concluded but only if a coordinated and concerted attack had been made. It was not.

Meanwhile that July, a small and inadequate group of soldiers led by Captain Fuller supported by Benjamin Church, rowed over from Aquidneck Island and disembarked on the Pocasset shore. There they spent an uncomfortable night not helped by the fact that they had left their rations behind. The next morning, they divided into two parties and wandered along the beach hoping to attract Amerindians. On doing so, Fuller's force took fright and hastily re-embarked. However, Church's group (made of sterner stuff) when attacked by a larger, well-armed group, retreated through a 'pease field' and took shelter behind some rocks to await rescue from the sea. Thereby, conserving their own powder throughout the afternoon and early evening.

Their rescue was a tortuous affair. The skipper of the rescue boat did not dare to get close to within enemy fire, so he let a canoe, attached by a line, drift down to the desperate defenders. They embarked two-by-two and were hauled back to safety while those onboard and ashore kept up a protective fire. Church, relishing his role, was the last to embark; there were no casualties. As an example of the adventures of an amateur army, this escapade would be hard to beat. They would need to do better than this if they were to triumph – but for a long time, they did not.

The catalogue of clumsy errors continued with the incomplete encirclement of the Amerindians sheltered in the swamps. A fort was erected to apprehend any attempting to return to Mount Hope, but aggressive inroads were not made into the swamp itself. Nor was a watch kept over the northern exit, from which Philip and Weetamoo led their peoples on 29 July; he heading to join the war-ready Nipmuck, she taking her people towards the hospitable Narragansett. The English with their Mohegan allies pursued but only managed to bruise the heels after which they were snapping.

One night, a small force from Rehoboth reinforced by 50 Mohegan, discovered Weetamoo's overnight encampment. Before they could launch a devastating attack, some of Philip's men arrived to alter the odds and give the Pocasset a chance to flee. They did so, leaving behind sufficient belongings for the Mohegan to chose plunder over pursuit. Those captured were promised clemency by Church but then sold into slavery.

The failure to catch-up is not surprising when the burden carried by the pursuing soldier is noted. Ellis describes that:

> The infantry were armed with muskets and long knives fitted with handles to fix to the muzzles, and carried a knapsack, six feet of fuse, a pound of powder, a bandoleer passing under the left arm and containing a dozen or more cylinders

holding a measured charge of powder, a bag containing another three pounds of bullets and a horn of priming powder. The troopers were equipped with a sword and either two pistols or a carbine. All carried in addition a few articles of wearing apparel, a day's provisions and a pound of tobacco.[5]

The majority carried matchlocks so they also needed to carry a rest on which to place their muzzle when firing. The breech cloth warriors, light-footed in their moccasins, even encumbered by their families, could move much faster along familiar tracks. In a few days, the escapees were ready to recommence hostilities. Everything was in place for an autumn of ambushes and unannounced assaults.

The Wampanoag trek had brought them close to the isolated hamlet of Brookfield whose very survival depended on the 20 families located there continuing to believe they had good relations with their Amerindian neighbours. This belief, along with its location, made it a good centre from which to launch reconnaissance and punitive patrols. One such group led by Captain Hutchinson and guided by Brookfield men, rode out on 2 August, without flankers and against the advice of their scouts. They bravely rode into a gulley surrounded by scrub only for the scrub to erupt with musket fire from ambushing Nipmuck. The only way out was up the steep bank and many tumbled from their mounts as they tried to urge them on and back towards Brookfield. They left eight dead or dying behind them.

A nineteenth-century impression of the attack at Bloody Brook in September 1675 when the Nipmuck, under their sachem Muttawmp, killed some 67 militia and civilians. (Public domain)

---

5   G. Ellis & J. Morris, *King Philip's War*, (Grafton Press, 1906).

KING PHILIP'S WAR: PART 1

Back at Brookfield there was panic. The community, about 80 strong, rushed into the stoutest house and prepared for a siege. The two men despatched to raise the alarm were driven back by the approaching horde who soon had the garrison surrounded and peppered with close-range shot – although only two men died in the first hours of the assault. Flaming arrows fired onto the roof also failed when the defenders cut holes through the shingles and extinguished the flames. Casting around for another options. the Nipmuck lit a fire against the wall only for a few brave defenders to dash out and douse the flames. Finally, the attackers constructed a rickety two wheeled cart loaded with flaming straw which they pushed towards the building using several lengths of pole to keep out of musket range. This was a miracle moment for Brookfield as a sudden rain shower dampened the fire.

By this time. the siege had lasted almost 48 hours and it is unlikely that the defenders could have held out much longer. However, into the village charged Major Simon Willard with his troops and with their timely arrival, the Nipmuck drifted away – but so did the besieged. After a few weeks of assessing the odds of its survival against another attack, the town was abandoned; the Nipmuck had won. The evidence from Bodge states:

> Skill and bravery could avail but little against the tactics of a skulking foe who came when and where least expected nearly always striking those least prepared,

In their attack on Brookfield in August 1675 the Nipmuck used a fire-wagon in an attempt to drive the settlers out of their blockhouse. (Public domain)

applying the torch, shooting from the safe covert of the woods and, before effective resistance could be offered, vanishing.[6]

In the Connecticut Valley, English demands that the hitherto peaceful River tribes surrender their arms, created another enemy who could turn their fieldcraft to advantage. Following the killing of several English settlers, a decision was made to evacuate the lonely settlement of Squakeag (Northfield, Massachusetts) on the upper Connecticut. Captain Beers and 36 men were despatched northwards to assist in this work. On 4 September, just two miles short of the township, they were ambushed with the appalling loss of Beers and some 20 of his men.

The triumphant Amerindians now concentrated their efforts on the next settlement downstream – Deerfield. This vicinity had been reinforced by the presence of the gimlet-keen and skilled soldier, Captain Samuel Moseley and his company. Nevertheless, the decision was made to also evacuate Deerfield.

On 18 September, burdened with numerous carts laden with desperately needed grain gleaned from the already abandoned town, Captain Lathrop and his company were ambushed five miles south of the town at a site forever known afterwards as Bloody Brook. There was little chance of escape and had it not been for the arrival of Moseley and his men, all may have been slaughtered. As it was, when the English returned the next day to bury their dead, they interred 64 of their comrades, 'the very Flower of the County of Essex … none of whom were ashamed to speak with the Enemy at the Gate'.[7]

Amerindian rejoicing was very evident, taunting their hapless foes with bloody tokens of their triumphs. An equal and opposite reaction was felt far from the front as militia committees and their executive constable struggled to fill their quotas of impressed men who were urged on by propaganda such as: 'It would therefore be in vain to … enumerate the horrid massacres, murders, savage cruelties, cowardice, ungrateful and perfidious dealings of blood-thirsty barbarians'.[8]

This was certainly the opinion that drove Moseley, 'an excellent soldier and an undaunted spirit'. He was an ex-sea captain whose volunteer company consisted of captured Dutch pirates, mercenary minded ne'er-do-wells and local rogues. Moseley, albeit an Amerindian-hater, was also responsible for one of the few light-hearted, farcical, moments in this brutal war. In August he met with a group of 300 Amerindians in open land and prepared for battle:

> All being ready … Captain Moseley plucked off his Periwig, and put it into his breeces, because it should not hinder him in fighting. As soon as the indians saw that, they fell a Howling and Yelling most hideously, and said, Umh, Umh, me no stawmerre fight Engismon, Engismon got two Hed,; if me cut off un Hed, he got noder, a put on beder as dis.[9]

---

6   G. M. Bodge, *Soldiers in King Philip's War* (Boston: 1906, Clearfield: 2009).
7   W. Hubbard, *The Present State of New England* 1676 (Public domain).
8   J. Foster, *Chronology of some memorable Occurrences happening in New England*, 1676.
9   <www.warpaths2peacepipes.com>

The initial surge of support from Massachusetts was tardily followed up. It was not until October that the General Court for the Bay realised that a more serious response would be necessary to overcome the Amerindian aggression. This meant placing the whole colony on a war footing. Therefore, they passed their 'Lawes and ordinances of War … for the better regulating their forces and keeping their soldiers to their duty'.[10]

Being a Puritan people, for whom guilt and backsliding were facts of faith, they required their troops to be both physically and morally well-equipped. They were to don the full armour of God in their struggle against the forces of evil, with the breastplate of righteousness and the shield of faith to quench all the fiery darts of the wicked.[11] This was important for an army that would be raised as much through impressment as by volunteering.

To encourage high morality (and morale?), blasphemers were to have their tongues bored with a hot iron and with equally unpleasant punishments for swearing and derogatory acts.

Death was also deemed suitable for striking an officer, desertion, sedition or mutinous behaviour, or even for failing to report such mutterings. Capital punishment on active service was available against 'rapes, ravishments, unnaturall abuses and adultery'. Lesser crimes warranted other 'grevious punishments'.[12]

As Puritans, there were some farcical interpretations. In unsuccessfully seeking an annulment of his fine, one Jonathan Adderton stated: 'Captain Henchman wrongfully accused him of profanation of the sabbath when his only offence was cutting up an old hat and putting the pieces in his shoes to relieve his galled feet'.

There were also practical rules governing the care of weapons, bullets and powder. The court was well-aware how limited and precarious their logistic supply and support was: a concern the Amerindians, all too worryingly for them, shared.

Civilians whose towns and homesteads were threatened, were expected to comply with the orders of their local committees of militia, including gathering:

> … into one or more garrisons … upon penalty of five shillings per day, being herby obligated to labour in and provide such fortification or fortifications as they [the committee] shall agree upon … and all inhabitants to attend their places in such fortifications or garrison as they are appointed unto, and in case of alarm or invasion, to appear at and for the defence of such places …

In these few lines, the General Court created the strategy that did more to ensure the safety and survival of its widely dispersed colonists than in any other directive. The other important strategic aim of the united colonies was

---

10   N. Shurtleff, (ed.), *Records of the Governor and Company of the Massachusetts Bay in New England,* (Boston, 1854).
11   *Ephesians* 6:10–19.
12   N. Shurtleff, (ed.), *Records of the Governor and Company of the Massachusetts Bay in New England,*

NEW WORLDS, OLD WARS

An attack on a township. After many such raids with houses set on fire, crops burnt and livestock driven away, the order went out to evacuate the isolated settlements. (Public domain)

'better for us to find them at their homes than for them to find us at ours'. In the end, it was the successful pursuit of this objective that would win the war. Yet there was still a long trail to trek, including learning lessons from their foes. Bodge reflects:

> Elated by recent success the Indians pressed more closely about the western towns, watching warily that no opportunity might pass to strike a safe and telling blow. Their leaders constantly outgeneralled our officers, and in every engagement took care to have the odds in numbers, position and method of attack on their side.[13]

The colonial governments thus responded well to the threat they were facing. However, the issue of orders and the provision of support did not mean the inexperienced troops in the field could change rules of behaviour into successful rules of engagement. One major change was vital; to reduce the number of forays despatched to hunt down Amerindians in the forest and swamps. Effort needed to be put into garrisoning and protecting the remaining towns such as Springfield. Here, 30 homes were smouldering

---

13   G. M. Bodge, *Soldiers in King Philip's War* (Boston:1906, Clearfield: 2009).

ruins from an attack by the local, trusted Amerindians under their *sachem*, Wequogan.

Defences were now being built throughout the threatened territory. These included strengthened garrison houses, defensive walls of stone and timber, watch-towers and other fortifications. Those at Bridgewater were to 'be made with half trees seven-foot high above the ground, 6 rods long (33 feet) and 4 rods wide …'

Meeting in Boston, the Commissioners of the United Colonies had another idea. From the start of hostilities, more and more tribes had either decided, or been driven to, take up arms in support of Philip. Two of the greatest had not yet done so. Of these, the Mohegan under their *sachem* Uncas, had remained loyal to the English cause. The other, the Narragansett, had given sympathy and shelter to the refugees but not lifted a finger to assist them. Before they did so, the Commission decided to neutralise the threat.

There had to be justification for this assault – the flaky nature of which might best be summed up in a letter from William Harris to Sir Joseph Williamson back in England:

> The war was also just with the Narragansetts, many of whom were with Philip in the first fight about Mounthope, and on Philip's flight thence were received back with a great woman of Philip's party and her men; the Narragansetts, at the demand of the English, entered into articles to deliver them but did not, making large pretences of peace so as to delay the war till after their harvest, and receiving rewards from the English for the heads of persons said to be of Philip's party, but all in deceit, the heads being those of men killed by the English or of Narragansett deserters, or of certain of Philip's men against whom they had a grudge. This grudge arose out of a trial in Rhode Island, when a man (related to Philip) having killed his wife and her adulterer (of the Narragansetts) was condemned to death, but the sachems would have two (of Philip's party) condemned, but the court would not admit it, whereupon the Narragansetts were indignant, and said that before the English came they could do what they list with Philip's party. The Narragansetts had then many of Philip's men whom they did not deliver up, and all about Hadley and Deerfield they aided Philip's men against the English.[14]

Of course, some assaults of isolated settlers could be blamed on the Narragansett but these were probably the acts of the usual young hot-heads caring little for the orders of their seniors. In fact, there was nothing in the November 'declaration of war' or the order for an advance on Narragansett territory, that could be called a legitimate *casus belli*. It included such feeble statements such as the United Colonies felt justified because the Narragansett, 'did in a very reproachful and blasphemous manner, triumph and rejoice' over the English defeat at Hadley.

In addition, to overcome their unease at assaulting a reasonably blameless foe, Massachusetts declared 2 December to be a day of humiliation and public prayer. They blamed the Amerindians' predicament on their own

---

14   *CSP Colonial America*, Vol. 9, 1021, 12 August 1676.

The Great Swamp Fight of December 1675 when the Narragansett fort was set alight. Contemporary drawings of the event are of a uniformly poor quality. (Author's collection)

backsliding, their over-fussy dressing and 'their long-haired and occasionally bare-breasted ladies and excessive drinking and the sin of idleness' for which God was exacting a punishment in the shape of the savages.

The sins of its own society, with its biased views, were sufficient for the largest army ever assembled in New England to be mustered to march against a tribe who had up until then, been either friendly or neutral in the war. There was also worrying evidence that the king in England was likely to support the Narraganset in any legal dispute over land they had with Massachusetts. This was important as the colonists needed to convert more land to pasture for beef cattle so that they could supply meat to the West Amerindian planters. The planters were loath to grow anything other than wealth-creating sugar cane on their acres – including food for their slaves.

The force's preparation for a winter campaign showed that the colonies had learnt about the logistic effort necessary to support several men in the field. Here, the men would be required to bivouac in the open and tramp through snowdrifts and frozen or freezing marshes.

Anger grew that the Narragansett were not beheading or delivering up to the English for decapitation or enslavement, the numerous refugees who were seeking shelter with them, but were instead 'relieving and succouring Wampanoag women and children and wounded men'. It never seemed to have occurred to the Bible-quoting, church-controlled colonists' leaders and opinion influencers, that the Narragansett – in their hospitality – were simply obeying two important Christian texts. Firstly, Christ's differentiation between the sheep and the goats:

> For I was an hungered, and ye gave me meat: I was thirsty, and ye gave me drink: I was a stranger, and ye took me in. Naked, and ye clothed me: was sick and ye visited me.[15]

Or Saint James's statement that:

> Pure religion and undefiled before God and the Father is this, To visit the fatherless and widows in their affliction.[16]

It could be argued that the Narragansett, who had aided the colonies in their war against the Pequot, had every reason to be aggrieved with their English neighbours. The same neighbours who had so recently and unjustly, supported the Mohegans in their inter-tribal war and authorised the judicial slaying of their revered *sachem*, Miantonomi, by Uncas. Yet, they had held fire. The English were not going to do so: many of them either remembered or had been told of the successful destruction of the Pequot village at Mystic in 1637 – now they had an opportunity to emulate their fathers.

The strategic wisdom of such a move was questionable. Given the trouble the troops were having in containing the attacks by minor and uncoordinated tribes, the provocation of the largest and most warlike would seem to be irresponsible and irrational.

A glance at a map might answer the question of irrationality. Whereas Philip was lord over a few hectares of the Mount Hope peninsula which could be seized in his absence without much effort, the Narragansett owned lands coveted by all three of the united colonies. The war with the Wampanoag had gifted the land-lusting English with an opportunity of acquiring Narragansett land by 'right of conquest'. A hint of this objective might be indicated in the words of the proclamation read out to the Massachusetts men who were told: 'if they played the man, took the Fort, and drove the enemy out of Narragansett Country … they should have a gratuity in land besides their wages'.[17]

The intention was to raise up a mighty army which would fall upon the unprepared enemy who were sheltering and unthreatening with their families, in a fort in a swamp to the west of Narragansett Bay. To this settlement, the English were drawn like Joshua to Makkedah with a similar objective and outcome.[18] The 1,000-man army was to be led by the elderly soldier Josiah Winslow, the governor of Plymouth Colony. The now experienced Major Appleton of Essex County would command the largest contingent, that of Massachusetts. In amongst the men of 'strength, corrage and activity' was the tireless Benjamin Church and his rival the blood-thirsty Captain Moseley.

Problems arose in the enlisting of sufficient men to make up the force. Many towns had lost young men in the fighting and their peers and families

---

15 *Matthew* 25:35, 36.
16 *1 James* 1:27.
17 K. F. Zelner, *A Rabble in Arms: Massachusetts Towns and Militiamen during King Philip's War* (New York University Press, 2009).
18 *Joshua* 10: 28–30.

were loath to allow others to be impressed. Draft dodging meant that several failed to respond to the summons while many slipped away. Eventually, the required number arrived at the colonial rendezvouses of Dedham, Rehoboth and New London. While they were making their way there, the necessary logistics to supply the force with food, arms and ammunition for a two-month winter operation was also being arranged, including ensuring all troops were directed to wrap up warm.

Autumn had turned into a fierce winter by the time the troops had been mustered, briefed and despatched to Smith's garrison at Wickford on the western shores of Narragansett Bay. Massachusetts and Plymouth sent their men by boat but the Connecticut companies marched along the old Pequot route from New London to Wickford. This took them through the territory of the Niantics, a sub-group of the Narragansett whose sage *sachem* Ninigret, had lobbied both his fellows and the English in favour of a peaceful settlement with himself as the broker. He was ignored but remained true to the agreement reached with the English in July. As a result of this, the Connecticut contingent marched unmolested.

Even the Narragansett, aware of the build-up of forces on their boundary, responded with a less than powerful repulse. The garrison house and rendezvous site of Pettaquamscut was torched resulting in many fatalities but very few other disruptive attempts were made.

Thus, on 18 December, the army united shelter-less at Pettaquamscut. Their discomfort was increased by a lack of provisions and too few tents to camp out comfortably in the bitter weather – mostly problems of their own making. However, they had managed to capture a few of their enemy, among whom was a warrior named Peter. He agreed to turn traitor and led the troops along a hidden path right up to the Narragansett's main fortified village which lay within an impenetrable swamp. Forty-seven of the other captives were sold into slavery by Captain Davenport for 80 pounds but he would not live long enough to enjoy his profit.

The low temperatures and limited rations meant there was little time to lose and with the arrival of a grey dawn, a long line of weary soldiers was led on a ten-mile march through deep snow and into the woods and the swamps which soaked their feet and froze their fingers. Their only advantage was that the ponds and streams were frozen allowing them to slither, rather than wade, across the waterways.

At any moment, they might have been successfully ambushed but were not. It was gone midday before they had their first encounter with the enemy who withdrew rapidly after an exchange of fire. In pursuit, the troops soon realised that they had arrived at their objective. Tall and forbidding, a large fort built from thick stakes on firmer ground, confronted them. The surrounding trees and scrub had been felled creating an awkward approach over the killing ground while the fort itself had several blockhouses from which a raking fire could be directed against an advancing foe. Within the walls, some 100 wigwams were crowded together indicating that a great number of people were dwelling inside. It was also reported these wigwams were 'rendered bullet-proof by large quantities of grain in tubs and bags, placed along the sides'.

It seemed to be a formidable obstacle but the English had exited opposite what appeared to be a weakness in the incomplete walls. Passing through a gap in the structure lay a large tree trunk, inviting the onrushing English to press forward. Led by the impetuous Moseley, this is what they did, although it was his two fellow commanders, Johnson and Davenport, who first fell dead. Having forced an entry, this forlorn hope was at first repulsed, with significant losses, as the Amerindians fired on them from three sides. Another assault allowed the troops to gain and retain entry but without being able to press forward their advantage.

The attack, launched spontaneously without briefing or plan, had two tactical failings. Firstly, it had removed the advantage of surprise, creating a seething foe and, secondly, unlike at Mystic, it had failed to surround the fort first, thus allowing many to escape to fight again.

Benjamin Church had been aware of the latter problem and led a group of men in pursuit of the fleeing Amerindians – several of whom were intent on firing on the English from the bushes surrounding the fort. Creeping up on one group who were preparing to fire on the troops inside the fort, Church ordered his men to wait until the Amerindians stood up for a better aim before he gave them 'an unexpected clap on their backs'.

Some braves re-entered one of the blockhouses from which they continued the fight. One of them fired small shot into the approaching Church; one bullet burying itself in his mittens, one grazing his leg but the third passing through his thigh and striking his hipbone. Limping back to his leader, Church arrived just as, in his opinion, a disastrous decision was being made. Still faced with a stubborn foe and unwilling to make an entry into the gloomy wigwams to clear them one-by-one, Winslow had approved setting fire to the forts and the huts within which were crouched the cowering women and children.

For reasons other than compassion, Church advised against this move; firstly, evening was coming on and the English needed the shelter and warmth that the fort could provide and secondly, the huts contained stocks of corn and other foodstuffs on which the hungry host could well satiate itself. Moseley, Church's rival, argued otherwise, possibly suggesting that if the English remained much longer, the Narraganset could regroup and ambush them on the long walk out. Winslow agreed and the fort was torched. Hubbard made light of the incineration writing that the flames had made 'their cookrooms too hot for them at that time, when they and their mitchin fried together'.[19]

The precise number of fried Amerindians is not known but it has been estimated that between 300 and 600 died in the fort. One captive believed it to be 700. Dudley wrote:

> We generally suppose the enemy lost at least two hundred men … a captive woman … informing that there were three thousand five hundred men engaging us and about a mile distant a thousand in reserve.[20]

---

19 W. Hubbard, *The Present State of New England*, London, 1677.
20 G. M. Bodge, *Soldiers in King Philip's War*.

Whatever the number, the English had secured a major victory but against an unprepared and possibly unwilling, foe. Certainly, the day did not deserve the accolade that Bodge gave it when suggesting that 'if the whole history of the 19th day of December 1675, were known, no braver day would stand in our country's annals for heroic daring and suffering'.[21]

In the ashes of the fort, the English discovered the remains of a simple forge and equipment needed to repair muskets – a vital skill when every weapon, including the barrel, was a one-off with few parts inter-changeable. Its loss would be significant.

Materiel losses were just one aspect of the defeat; the Narragansett tribal structure had been shattered, families were fleeing, others taken captive and enslaved, still others wandering famished. Their plight was made worse by English foraging parties seeking out and destroying grain stores – yet there were significant survivors.

The *squaw sachem* Quiapen, had survived, ensconced in a different fort built amongst the rocks by the Amerindian architect Stonewall John. Its location was not discovered until many months later, by which time she had left to trek north into the arms of John Talcott and his Connecticut force who were to kill her and nearly 200 of her followers.

Leaving the heat and light of the burning fort behind, the English, carrying their many wounded with them, set off on the dark and icy journey back towards Wickford. The majority arrived there at two in the morning by which time about 20 of the injured had died of their wounds or hypothermia. At Wickford, surgeons struggled to save the remainder but over 30 were buried at the base. The final English death toll was probably about 80 including many of the company commanders who had led from the front. The Great Swamp Fight, as it became known, thus caused losses to both sides.

Although these were immediate and rectifiable for the English, for the Amerindians, the fight was an irrecoverable disaster. Not just because they finished as a fighting force but because the foodstuffs that had gone up in flames included all their winter reserves. From now on, they would have to wonder through the woods constantly fighting against famine. The one positive benefit was they were now being led by the young *sachems* Canonchet and Quinnapin, who had allied the Pocasset to his tribe by marrying their *squaw sachem* Weetamoo.

The recouping English under Winslow took their time to take advantage of the Amerindians' plight. The wounded were carried to Newport, Rhode Island, where the charitable care they received was tellingly contrasted with the way Massachusetts treated the Island's dissenters when they travelled to Boston. The fit stayed behind living off the meagre rations which showed how the inadequate had been the much-vaunted plan to provide the army with two months worth of rations.

During this time, peace feelers were extended by both sides but no progress was made. Peace was also not apparent amongst the colonial troops

---

21 *Ibid.*

with Connecticut arguing strongly for its surviving troops to be discharged. Eventually they were allowed to move down the coast to Stonington for rest and recuperation. Following pressure from the Bay, their own government ordered them back to Wickford where they arrived on 27 January – a fortnight after reinforcements had come from Massachusetts. That morning, the Amerindians had raided Pawtuxet setting buildings alight and driving off the livestock.

The next day, Winslow began what became known as the 'hungry march' – his tardy pursuit of the Narragansett. It was not a success. Not only had the English set off late but compared with the tribe, which was travelling light, the colony troops were weighed down.[22] Apart from a few sporadic exchanges of fire and the slaughter of some stragglers, the chase achieved little. The only memorable event involved – as could now be anticipated – Benjamin Church.

A refugee, hampered from flight by injury, was captured and after failing to divulge any intelligence after a vigorous interrogation, was handed over to the Mohegan for execution. The disapproving and injured Church withdrew into the evening shadows only for the captive to break loose and flee straight into his arms. A wrestling match followed, the captive broke free and set off again with Church in limping pursuit. This time, the short-sighted man crashed into a tree, enabling Church to grapple him again. He would have escaped had not the Mohegan executioner arrived, worked-out which man was which in the dark and brought his tomahawk down firmly on the head of the Narragansett. Moments later the delayed execution took place.

Such incidents were reported because of their rarity in an otherwise tardy pursuit of an escaping enemy. With nothing to show for their endeavours, Winslow was forced to abandon the exercise and head for home, reaching Boston with his exhausted men on 5 February 1676.

Following the massacre of the Narragansett, the hills, valleys and woods of New England witnessed groups of Amerindian men, women, children and the occasional hostage, wandering with no place to lay their heads that could be called a secure home. Unlike their pursuers, men under military command who were mostly provided with rations and supplies of ammunition from a secure base, these sojourners had to make do and mend, skirmish and scrounge for essential support.

Thus, they almost required to attack isolated English settlements, not only to glean deserted fields but also to divert their enemy from single-minded pursuit. They could neither embark on a long march to safety nor find refuge in an isolated valley forge. Nowhere could they revive, replenish, rest and recuperate; their territory was bounded by sea, wide rivers and high hills beyond which, lay enemy tribes. In this respect, they resembled deer – seemingly free to roam in a royal hunting forest but coming up against insurmountable barriers which they could not cross to escape to freedom.

---

22   G. Ellis & J. Morris, *King Philip's War* (Grafton Press, 1906).

Many would seek sanctuary with the Nipmuck who at first, treated them like suspected enemies not believing their alliance with the English could have ended in such a fashion. But it had and the English by their actions, had created a powerful enemy force of Wampanoag, Narragansett and Nipmuck – tribes eager to strike back.

8

King Philip's War: Part 2

The Slaying of the Sachems 1676

> The natives and colonists of New England had enough in common to form their own unique society. Fought among various groups of those Indians and English, King Philip's War was a civil war that destroyed that incarnation of New England.
> – James D. Drake, *King Philip's War*

Shortly after the return of Winslow's troops, the deputy governor of Massachusetts Samuel Symonds, wrote to the English government stating the 'pesky Indians':

> … leave their women and children in hideous swamps and inaccessible places, and themselves disperse in small parties all over the country, and by ambuscades and secret skulkings so infest the highways that many travellers have been cut off; then on a sudden, multitudes gathering together, fall on the out towns which lie dispersed a great distance from one another. Then having fired the deserted houses, barns, &c. they as suddenly disappear before any relief can come, so that many country towns and farms are destroyed in Plymouth, Connecticut, and Maine. Since the beginning of the war above 500 of the King's subjects have been slain, towns and villages ruined, houses not to be numbered burnt, people much distracted, husbandry and trading obstructed, and scarcity of bread, corn, and provisions to be feared.[1]

Away from Narragansett Country, the mid winter had been a time of quiet. For both sides, finding food came first with the Amerindians forced to forage

---

1   *CSP Colonial, America & West Indies, 1675–1676*, Vol. 9, 876, April 1676.

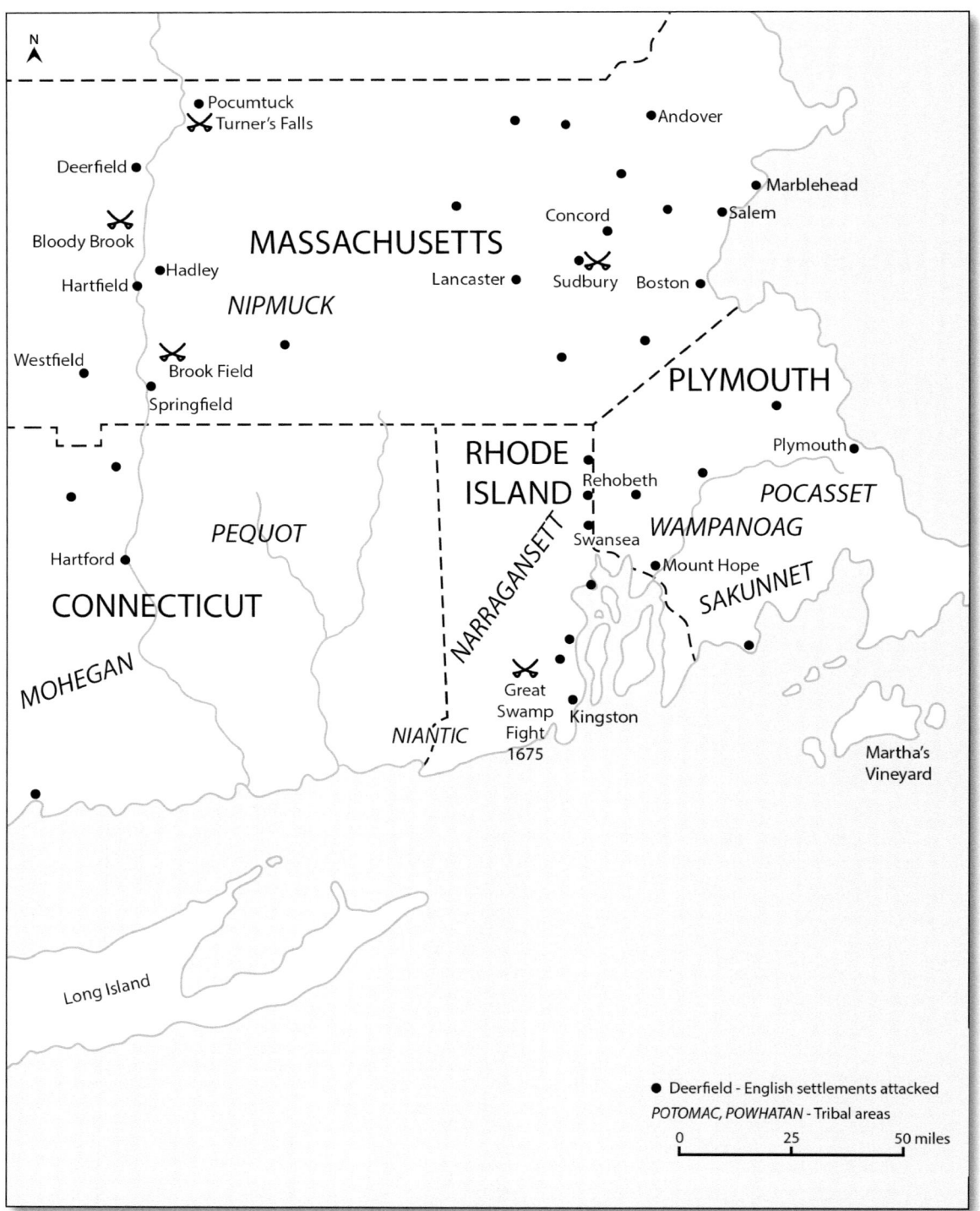

New England in King Philip's War

as most of their winter supplies lay behind enemy lines. It was not until the beginning of February that the attacks on the settlements recommenced and did so with a widespread violence. The winter quarters of the groups launching these attacks cannot be known with certainty although, from their targets it can be assumed that they were well dispersed. Some of the Nipmucks were in the upper Connecticut, near Northfield; others, soon to be joined by the refugee Narragansett, at Menameset, north of Brookfield; another group over-wintered near Mount Wachusett, not far from Lancaster. All were well placed for rapid raids on the nearby towns.

Meanwhile, Philip and the Wampanoag had crossed the Hudson River, perhaps hoping that royalist New York would succour fellow subjects of the same king. Possibly, he hoped to return to the fray becoming allied with the ferocious Mohawks whose reputation would add additional fear for the isolated English families. Instead, his plans went woefully awry. The Mohawks, possibly encouraged by their English allies, turned upon their unwelcome visitors and slew hundreds of them. Philip escaped unharmed but crossed back into the Connecticut Valley, with a humbled and much-reduced company. It is doubtful what further hostile activity his braves could inflict independently. They also faced, as did the Narragansett, a major shortage of supplies – both food and weaponry of which powder was the most critical. They found caches of it in the towns they attacked and it is probable they got some from the French and Dutch but that would not have been freely given. Powder need purchasing and their reserve of *wampum* and their ability to deliver pelts were both much diminished.

Bereft of food in their current locations, both major groups knew that large caches of corn lay hidden back in their tribal territories. In due course, small parties would be despatched to gather and return with these supplies. It would be a dangerous mission and grievously, so it turned out to be … on several occasions.

Towards the end of January, an Amerindian spy reported that the Nipmuck were planning an attack on Lancaster which they had visited in August, killing seven men. Unfortunately, Massachusetts ignored the first warning and did not respond in a timely fashion to the second. By that time, the Amerindians were able to isolate their target from reinforcements by burning the connecting bridge by way of announcing their arrival on 10 February. Luckily, the defenders had heeded the warning and taken shelter in six garrison houses – of which five repulsed their attackers. What happened in the sixth is best described by one of its occupants, Mary Rowlandson, the wife of the pastor who had departed earlier to seek help:

> Some in our house were fighting for their lives, others wallowing in their blood, the hop use on fire over our heads, and the bloody heathen ready to knock us on the head, if we stirred out.
>
> Of 37 persons who were in this one house, none escaped either present death or a bitter captivity … there were twelve killed, some shot, some stab'd with spears, some knocked down with their hatchets. Such dreadful sights … our dear friends and realstions lie bleeding out their heart-blood upon the ground. There

wasv one who was chopped into the head with a hatchet, and stripped naked, and was yet crawling up and down.²

Mary, her badly injured and dying six-year-old child Sarah along with another son and daughter (soon to be separated off), were among those taken into captivity. She was to remain with the Amerindians for 11 weeks during which her captors moved camp 20 times, giving a clear indication as to what life was like for these, by now homeless and hunted wanderers.

Six years later Mary's account of her travails, interestingly sub-titled, *The Sovereignty and Goodness of God*, became an instant bestseller – the New World's first, and rightly so. It gave rise to the 'captivity' genre books and films, including Fennimore Cooper's, *The Last of the Mohicans* and, probably the greatest western film ever made, *The Searchers* ³. It is worth spending some time travelling with Mary as hers is the only account of the war as witnessed from the Amerindian side.

Mary was scathing in her criticism and disdain for her captors. For her, trudging sore-footed through snow and swamp, there was no Stockholm Syndrome, her captors remained throughout 'a savage, brutal and barbarous enemy' albeit she suffered no personal assault as she most certainly would have done if seized by soldiers in a European campaign. She was fed, watered, warmed and clothed, although required by her 'mistress', Weetamoo, to forage for food and firewood. However, while her dying child lived, she was carried comfortably on horseback. It was hard work but as Jennifer Potter concludes, writing of one of the women captives of the Powhatan in Virginia in 1622, the widowed Jane Dickenson:

> Jane remained with the Indians for ten months until she was redeemed with glass beads supplied by Dr. John Pott, who forced her to work for him to pay off her own debt and the remaining years of her husband's indenture, servitude she considered little different from her slavery with the Indians.⁴

It is noteworthy that in her remarkable account of her captivity, Mary Rowlandson, also made pithy condemnations as to the professionalism of the New England Army, writing:

> Of the fair opportunity lost in the long march, a little after the fort-fight, when our English army was so numerous, and in pursuit of the Enemy, and so near as to take several and destroy them: and the enemy in such distress for food, that our men might track them by their rooting in the earth for ground-nuts, while they were flying for their lives. I say, that our Army should want provision, and be forced to leave their pursuit and return homeward …

A few lines later:

---

2   M. Rowlandson, *Narrative of the Captivity of Mrs. Mary Rowlandson*.
3   Warner Brothers, 1956.
4   J. Potter, *The Jamestown Brides* (Atlantic Books, 2018).

> I cannot but remember how the Indians derided the slowness and dumbness of the English army, in its setting out … Thus, they did scoff at us, as if the English would be a quarter of a year getting ready.

It would only be possible to make an intelligent guess as to the conditions under which the refugee groups travelled were it not for a remarkable account penned by Mary Rowlandson. This peripatetic preamble, carrying their young, frail and elderly on their backs, should be set against the fact that, in peaceful times, many tribes would settle in a village for over 10 years before soil exhaustion and thinning-out of game required them to move to a new home which might take 18 months to create.[5]

The tribes found themselves unable to plant, let alone harvest, any crops. As they had found out at Turner's Falls when they came together for the seasonal fishing, the English would soon discover their whereabouts. Nevertheless, much of what Mary saw with her English eyes and discerned as wilderness, was to her captives, a familiar landscape with hidden pastures.

The discomforts of camp life and the constant search for a place by the fireside, are all made clear by Rowlandson but it is the constant search for sustenance of any and even squeamish description that truly indicates the parlous state of the 'savages'. At first, she found it difficult to swallow such fodder as boiled old horse leg finding 'it was very hard to get down their filthy trash'. By week three, her stomach became reconciled to eating 'that which a hog or dog would hardly touch', and it was the amount not the ingredients that became important.

Just as well, her descriptions could turn a reader's stomach let alone that of the diner:

> The chief and commonest food was ground-nuts; they also eat nuts and acorns, artichokes, lily roots, ground beans, and several other weeds and roots. They would pick up old bones, and cut them to pieces at the joints, and if they were full of worms and maggots, they would scaled them over the fire to make the vermin come out, and then boil them, and drink up the liquor, and then beat the great ends of them in a mortar and so eat them. They would eat horses' guts, and ears, and also … bear, venison, beaver, tortoise, frogs, squirrels, skunks, rattle-snakes; yea, the very bark of trees.

On one occasion, her master invited to her to dinner and gave her 'a pancake, as big as two fingers; it was made of parched wheat, beaten and fried in bear's grease, but I thought I never tasted pleasanter meat in my life'. Bits of bear and horse were frequently on the menu but one day she had to be content with six acorns and two chestnuts, on another it was bark of tree broth with a handful of peas and a few roasted ground-nuts:

> I cannot but think what a wolvish appetite persons have in a starving condition: for many times when they gave me that which was hot, I was so greedy, that I

---

5 Information supplied by Wandat, Québec, Canada.

should burn my mouth, that it would trouble me hours after, and yet I should quickly do the same again. And after I was thoroughly hungry, was never again satisfied. For though sometimes it fell out that I got enough, and did eat till I could eat no more, yet I was as unsatisfied as I was when I began.

The nadir was probably on her eighteenth removal when, much to her master's indignity, Mary scrounged some pieces of boiled horse's feet, so tough and sinewy that an English child could not digest it; at which Rowlandson took it out of his mouth and found it 'savoury to her taste'. Despite the terrible deprivation being endured by the fleeing Amerindians, she did not see 'one man, woman, or child, die with hunger', although she was present at the burial of her mistress's *papoose*.

Even such inedible food was often unavailable when the tribes were in the presence of their enemy and 'found such warm entertainment, that though they had kindled their fire, they durst not stay to roast their breakfast'.[6]

To the end of her stay, Rowlandson became one of the few English to actually meet with King Philip. She found him friendly and supportive, even offering her a great compliment of a few pipes of tobacco which she, a reformed smoker, had the strength to decline 'sucking a stinking tobacco-pipe'. It seemed he was instrumental in negotiating her release but invited her to give him two coats (i.e. lengths of cloth), 20 shillings, half a bushel of seed corn and some tobacco just to give her the good news (which she already knew) that her freedom had been negotiated for 20 pounds. In a short time, some 20 other captives were also released unharmed including Mary's son Joseph and her daughter Mary.

While these negotiations were taking place, she witnessed the only occasion of drunkenness amongst the Amerindians when her master, the *sachem* Quinnapin, was given alcohol by John Hoar the English negotiator. It showed just what a potent weapon drink was in the English arsenal and how well they knew how best it could be deployed. Mary is also witness to the power of that other great English weapon, 'faith' (she was married to the minister Joseph Rowlandson) and she used faith as a defensive not an offensive weapon.

Throughout her account she is sustained by drawing on biblical references and analogy. At no stage does she question her lot and is unshakeable in her trust in the Lord. However, the ethnocentricity of faith is also obvious; she believes the kindnesses she is shown is by favour of God – not the godless Amerindians. One most striking analogy of comparing her fleeing host to the

The cover of Mary Rowlandson's book, written in 1682, an immediate bestseller and the most accurate record we have of the war as experienced by native families.

---

6 C. H. Lincoln, (ed.), *Narratives of The Amerindian Wars* (New York: 1913).

KING PHILIP'S WAR: PART 2

children of Israel being pursued by the wrathful Egyptians, never occurs to her and is never accounted by her.

Additionally, she witnessed examples of the Amerindians' skills. While being hotly pursued, they came to the banks of Miller's River and swiftly felled trees to make rafts. They acted so efficiently that, Mary Rowlandson, 'did not wet my foot', and managed to have the whole host cross over to the other side before the English, under Major Savage, arrived and abandoned their pursuit.

The harrowing of homesteads and the blitz of garrisons was the primary experience of New Englanders who were forced to abandon one-third of their towns. The account of Mary Rowlandson and another about an anonymous family (related by John Abbott), forms a fair representation of them all. Abbott records:

Benjamin Church who adopted native tracking methods to hunt down the dispersed warriors and is rightly considered the founding father of The Rangers. (Public domain)

> The following scene, which occurred in a remote section of the country at a later period, will illustrate the horrible nature of this Indian warfare. Far away in the wilderness, a man had erected his log hut upon a small meadow, which had opened itself in the midst of a gigantic forest. The man's family consisted of himself, his wife, and several children, the eldest of whom was a daughter fifteen years of age. At midnight, the loud barking of his dog alarmed him. He stepped to the door to see what he could discover, and instantly there was a report of several muskets, and he fell upon the floor of his hut pierced with bullets, and with a broken leg and arm. The Indians, surrounding the house, now with frightful yells rushed to the door. The mother, frantic with terror, her children screaming around her, and her husband groaning and weltering in his blood, barred the door and seized an axe. The savages, with their hatchets, soon cut a hole through the door, and one of them crowded in. The heroic mother, with one blow of the axe, cleft his head to the shoulder, and he dropped dead upon the floor. Another of the assailants, supposing, in the darkness, that he had made good his entrance, followed him. He also fell by another well-directed stroke. Thus four were slain before the Indians discovered their mistake.
>
> They then clambered upon the house, and were soon heard descending through the capacious flue of the chimney. The wife still stood with the axe to guard the door. The father, bleeding and fainting, called upon one of the little children to roll the feather bed upon the fire. The burning feathers emitted such a suffocating smoke and smell that the Indians were almost smothered, and they tumbled down upon the embers. At the same moment, another one attempted to enter the door. The wounded husband and father had sufficient strength left to seize a billet of wood and despatch the half-smothered Indians. But the mother was now exhausted with terror and fatigue that her strength failed her, and she struck a feeble blow, which wounded, but did not kill her adversary. The savage

was so severely wounded, however, that he retreated, leaving all his comrades, six in number, dead in the house.[7]

As critical to the understanding of how the 'enemy' managed is Mary Rowlandson's account – away from her wanderings, the war continued briskly. Eleven days after Lancaster it was the turn of Medfield. Here the Amerindians tried out a new tactic. Instead of war-whooping their way in, they crept in at night and lay in wait for the inhabitants to stir, picking them off one-by-one when they did so before setting the outbuildings alight. Next, worryingly, coastal Weymouth was attacked. Given their winter successes, it is no wonder that observers were pressing for a positive response with Roger Williams advocating: 'we would pursue them with a Winter War, when they should not as Muskeetoes and Rattlesnakes in Warme Weather bite us'.

The Amerindian offensive continued from winter into spring. It was not only border towns but settlements close to Plymouth and Boston that were attacked by raiding groups who seemed to be able to range freely over the colonies' territories. On 12 March, the outskirts of Plymouth was raided; a garrison house was destroyed, its occupants slain and much-needed stores seized. The list of items taken gives an idea of what the Amerindians needed most to continue their campaign. It included: eight muskets, 30 pounds of powder, a large lump of lead for making bullets and some money.

Fear itself was most evident, as Abbott (not over dramatically) summarised the situation:

> No one could sleep at night without the fear of an attack from the Indians before the morning. In the silence of the wilderness, many a tragedy was enacted of terror, torture, and blood, which would cause the ear that hears of it to tingle.[8]

Many places were abandoned including the strategic settlement of Marlborough which having lost its civilian population, became a garrison base. In response, Plymouth Colony issued an order: 'none of the inhabitants within the jurisdiction of Plymouth Colony shall abandon their towns under the penalty of forfeiture of their personal estates'. The council's nightmare scenario was the colony being reduced to a coastal strip of settlement; its present boundaries either taken back by the natives or, possibly worse, seized by its more powerful colonial rivals.

Vigilance was the main defence with towns being told to mount guards and given permission to organise guard duties and send out patrols to both attack and give warning of potential assault. Such missions were not that successful as John Pynchon complained to the Massachusetts Bay governor: 'we are endeavoring to discover the enemy; daily send out scouts but little is effected; we sometimes discover a few indians and sometimes fires, but not the body of them, and have no indian friends'.[9]

---

7   J. S. C. Abbott, *The History of King Philip's War, 1857* (Harper & Brothers, 1901).
8   *Ibid.*
9   J. Winthrop, *Journal, 1630–1649*.

The apotheosis of the Amerindian's campaign occupied the period between the end of March and the end of April. Their first significant triumph was on 26 March when Captain Michael Pierce (a trained-band soldier) who was overnighting at Rehoboth, was informed the enemy were gathering on the banks of the nearby Pawtucket River. The previous day, Pierce appears to have had a very successful foray against the Amerindians for Rehoboth's minister, Noah Newman, recorded:

> Cap. Peirce went forth with a small party of his men & indians with him, & upon discovery of the enemy fought him without damage to himself, & Judged that he had Considerably damnifyed them. yet he being of no greater force Chose rather [to] rtrete & go out ye next morning with a recrute of men.[10]

Perhaps it was that success which led him to set out again the following morning. This time he went with a company of 65 soldiers from Plymouth Colony and some supporting Amerindians and took the added precaution of sending a messenger to Providence to request back-up. Sadly, it being a Sunday, the messenger delayed delivering the request until Morning Service was completed in Providence.

Meanwhile, Pierce led his men to the banks of the Pawtucket where he turned north keeping command of the high ground above the eastern bank and trekking through reasonably open countryside. They sighted a group of four or five Amerindians and the English gave chase. The fugitives, all showing signs of panic, dived into the deep, fast flowing river swollen from the spring melt and waded across. Their pursuers plunged in after them, the powder on their packhorses getting a soaking. They moved up the bank and then suddenly, from out of the bushes, came fire from the guns of some 500 Amerindians – commanded by Canonchet – with more arriving in support. Initially, the fierce English response held their foes back enabling Pierce to organise a retreat but this proved to be a temporary lull. The troops formed a circle, double distances between each man to limit the danger of one shot causing two casualties but it must have soon been evident this was a fight to the end. Few seemed to have run, perhaps loyalty to their injured leader kept them together until all hope was lost. Finally, conditions reached a point that the company's defence was no longer effective. 'Then the indians, perceiving this, ran upon them, killing some and seizing others. Others of the soldiers fought their way through the indians and, although struck by bullets, ran away and got home'.

Before two hours had passed, it was all over. The poet Benjamin Tompson summed up the final moments in his long poem *New England's Crisis*.[11]

> Foolhardy fortitude it had been sure
> Fierce storms of shot and arrow to endure
> Without all hopes of some requital to
> So numerous and pestilent a foe.

---

10   G. M. Bodge, *Soldiers in King Philip's War*.
11   B. Tompson, *New England Crisis*, Boston, 1894.

> Some musing a retreat and thence to run,
> Have in an instant all their business done,
> They sink and all their sorrows' ponderous weight
> Down at their feet they cast and tumble straight.
> Such who outlived the fate of others fly
> Into the Irish bogs of misery.

When a burial party arrived a few days later, they interred over 40 soldiers and friendly Amerindians – including Pierce.

The victory won something very important for the Amerindians and they had access to food and the stores of Rehoboth. Feeling themselves temporary immune from attack, Canonchet's marauders camped outside the town and looted at leisure. The surviving inhabitants, having taken shelter in five garrison houses, were left alone but all the outlying houses and barns were burnt and livestock were either slaughtered or driven away.

Inevitably, there were captives. Of their fate we have a single reference of torture with William Harris writing:

> Pierce's soldiers were very valiant, brave men, and slew many indians. But we have heard lately, from some indian captives taken by the English, that the indians took two of the 70 alive. They tied them to trees, and the indian women whipped them almost to death, and then cut off some of their flesh, and put hot embers in the wounds in a most cruel, barbarous manner.[12]

There has been much analysis by way of a Board of Enquiry into the disaster, perhaps best summarised by LaCroix:

> First, Pierce chose not to secure a conservative posture to defend Rehoboth. Instead he went on the offensive, a strategy for which the colonial forces in the latter half of the seventeenth-century were ill trained. Second, if Richard Bowen's argument is correct, the command departed for Pawtucket without waiting to be reinforced by Captain Mosely. Third, when Captain Pierce began his ill-fated march, he had to understand either his company would not be supported by Providence, or was unaware of the fate of his message for assistance, in which case the possibility of reinforcements was purely speculative. Fourth, despite the severity of the river crossing, and the resulting damage to the company's powder supply, the company continued to press the attack. Finally, the most serious matter of culpability was that Pierce, in defiance of even the most rudimentary rules of warfare, apparently made no adequate reconnaissance to discover the enemy's strength and position or the terrain over which they would be moving. Still, to place the full responsibility of the colonial defeat entirely on overconfidence is to lose sight of other prefatory factors that might have might have also played a significant role in the defeat. Most notable is the distinct possibility that Captain

---

12 W. Harris, 1902, Harris Papers, Clarence S. Brigman, (ed.), Collections of the Rhode Island Historical Society, Vol. 10. (Providence: Standard Printing Co, RI.)

Pierce, like many second-generation military leaders, was not adequately trained or have the experience to successfully command such an operation.[13]

The friction between the centre and the periphery of the colonies is well illustrated by a letter written on 19 April by the Reverend John Cotton of Plymouth, reflecting on the fate of Rehoboth:

Worthy Sir:

With refference to the transactions of the last weeke, I am exceedingly afflicted to think that wee should so reele and stagger in our counsels as drunken men, and that soe pretious a people as Rehoboth should be soe forsaken by us for our own selfish interests. If I were in your study alone, I would tell you how much blemish some have gotten for being so backward to maintain a garrison at Rehoboth. This morning the Govr (being much encouraged by Capt. Bradford and the treasurer thereunto) hath sent 2 men post to Rehoboth, to signify that if they will come off, an army from us shall guard them; but if they will stay and judge it neccessary for their safety, they shall have from us 40 or 50 men to keepe garrison with them, et cetera And truly, sir, if your southerne men shall faile in this, it will be just matter of reproach to them; however it is resolved helpe shall be sent them if they accept it. e hath who is the last in the nomination of the 18: Mr. Dudley hath 651. An Amerindian at Boston who was improved as a messenger to the enemy being returned affirms that Capt. Pierce and his killed scores of the Amerindians that Sabbath day. I must now conclude this letter having sundry things to transcribe for you which just now I recd from Boston. Our church hath set apart this following Wednesday for Humiliation and pr. I am much straitned for time, but my respect to you obliges me to transcribe the enclosed.

In the absence of friendly Amerindian scouts, ambush remained the most potent weapon for the 'skulking savages' who realised that a fight in the open would only have one result. This makes King Philip's War a conflict where skirmishing was more frequent than battles, indeed there were only two major engagement to which that word could be applied.

The preliminaries for the first of these began following a war dance near Mount Wachusett during which it was agreed to lay waste to isolated Sudbury, where a strong force of warriors arrived on the evening of 20 March. Whether or not Philip himself was in command

Modern reconstruction of a transitory Amerindian camp. (Author's collection)

---

13   L. K. La Croix, *Captain Pierce's Fight* (Masters Dissertation, University of Boston, 2011).

of this group is conjectural but contemporary accounts place the 'fiend' among the horde.

News of the next day's encirclement soon reached Concord, Watertown and Marlborough and relief was despatched from three directions. Of these, only the men from Watertown arrived safely. The small contribution from Concord were ambushed while wading across a water meadow. There was just one survivor. One small group of 18 troops heading from Brookfield to Boston were also ambushed, losing four men a few miles from Sudbury but remaining intact so as to render support to Sudbury later in the day.

The largest group, 50 men commanded by Captain Samuel Wadsworth and supported by the experienced and successful Amerindian fighter, Captain Samuel Brocklebank, had a safe journey to within one mile of the town. There they fell prey to the same trick as the one practised on Captain Pierce for, sighting a small band of warriors, they gave chase only to find themselves in an ambuscade:

> The woods seemed alive with the terrible foe. They poured a terrific fire on this devoted band, but the brave Englishmen were undaunted, and at length succeeded in reaching the top of Green Hill, where for hours they held the red fiends at bay.[14]

There now followed a Spion Kop moment,[15] with the English lying on the hilltop, running short of water and ammunition but still keeping up a sufficient and accurate fire to deter the Amerindians from a direct assault. An attempt was made to reach them by Watertown's Captain Mason. With the help of some Sudbury soldiers, he succeeded in driving a few of the town's attackers back across the river but the weight of enemy numbers was eventually telling and he was forced to return to the defended garrisons.

Back on Green Hill, the attackers deployed another of their weapons. Several rain free weeks had left the underbrush tinder dry and with the wind blowing in the right direction, the Amerindians set fire to it and waited. Very soon, overcome with thick smoke and fierce flame, the soldiers scattered like quail, only to be picked off one-by-one as they burst through the smoke. Most did not make it. Some 20 rushed towards the shelter and safety of the abandoned Noye's Mill nearby; 14 scrambled inside, six were captured. They left behind over 50 of their dead comrades who soon to be joined by the six captives. The Amerindians withdrew, celebrating 'the dishonour of a victory'[16] but at a cost.

Mary Rowlandson, witnessing the return to their Wachusett base, felt them to be somewhat subdued. They too were suffering losses but unlike the English, who immediately could and did despatch reinforcements to the contested zone, there was no source of reserve soldiery upon which Philip and his allies could call. Braves could not be bred to replace their fathers or brothers and as their numbers reduced, so did their chance of success. With

---

14   E. W. Mc Glenen, *The Sudbury Fight*, address given at the battle site, 17 June 1897.
15   Spion Kop – in South Africa 1900, 2,000 English soldiers on an isolated hill top, were surrounded and slaughtered by the Boer.
16   D. Gookin, *An Historical Account* 1836.

the advent of spring, the Amerindians needed to sow crops and catch fish – both occupations requiring to be unsafely, sedentary.

To retain the morale of a dispossessed, pursued, hungry and itinerant people trudging through narrow forest tracks whatever the weather, never knowing when they might be surprised by their enemies – required leadership of a high order and a belief both in the rightness and eventual success of the cause espoused. For the Amerindians, this meant trust in their *sachems* who had the treble task of keeping the group united and fed, retaining links with other tribes and if possible, negotiating favourably with their enemies. Without such leadership things would fall apart.

Although the capture of Philip had been an objective from the outbreak of the conflict, the destruction of the tribes through the slaying of the *sachems* was an almost opportune strategy but a very effective one.

Connecticut was foremost in the hunting down of Narragansett foraging parties heading back to their old lands to gather hidden stores of grain. The colony search parties consisted of a potent mix of English militia supported by native guides. At the start of April, one group led by Captain George Denison, were tracking down those responsible for the raids on Rehoboth, and Providence (and probably, the slaughter of Pierce's troops) when they surprised an Amerindian camp and opened fire. As the Amerindians scattered, one caught the eye of the attackers and as he ran, he threw off a smart blanket and coat and then a belt of *wampum* but held on to his musket. Trying to run at speed through across a river, the fugitive slipped, soaked his gun, and lost his advantage. A fleet-footed Pequot tackled him and found that he had captured Canonchet, the great Narragansett warrior.

The *sachem* was led in triumph to Stonington where he scorned the offer of pardon in return for persuading Philip to stop fighting. Under interrogation, the proud warrior told the young interpreter Robert Stanton, 'You much child, no understand matters of war; let your brother or your chief come, him I will answer'. When sentence was passed, he said, 'he liked it well, that he should die before his heart was soft or he had spoken anything unworthy'.[17] To ensure no chance of their Amerindian allies changing allegiance, the English ordered that the Pequot shoot him, the Mohegan cut off his head and the Niantic burn his body. In order for this proud, brave man to retain some of his dignity, his executors were Oneco (son of Uncas, his lifelong enemy) and two *sachems* of the Pequod of equal rank. His head was sent to Hartford to be mounted on a pole. A few days later, a Connecticut force slew 25 of the enemy and captured double that number without suffering a single loss.

By May, the war changed in favour of the English. This did not come about through strategy, tactics, competence or even superior firepower but because the fight was now a numbers game with English addition versus Amerindian subtraction. In the next major engagement, the unequal toll of casualties made the future outcome very apparent.

In mid May, a large group of Amerindians gathered by the Peskcompscut rapids on the Connecticut River in the disputed region above abandoned

---

17   N. Philbrick, *Mayflower, A Voyage to War*, (Harper, 2006).

Deerfield. Here they enjoyed successful fishing as well as planting seeds in Deerfield's fields and rustling cattle from Hatfield. However, their presence was reported by an escaped soldier, to Captain William Turner who was commanding the garrison at Hatfield. Unable to deploy all the men away from their duties, Turner gathered a mixed group of soldiers and local volunteers, many of whom may have offered themselves up having been told that the opposition consisted mainly of the elderly and women and children.

On 18 May, this mishmash of 150 men marched or mostly rode, without reliable and up-to-date intelligence, reconnaissance or scouting. Indeed, the enemy do not appear to have had scouts stationed there either. They travelled past Bloody Brook and the razed ground of Deerfield, apparently not being jolted into tactical thinking by the tales of these sad sites. Undetected, at dawn they dismounted a ten-minute walk away from the falls and moved forward towards the sleeping Amerindians, their stealth aided by the noise of the raging torrent.

Unlike Pequot or the Great Swamp, this was a settlement with no palisades so the attackers were able to creep up to the entrances of the wigwams before Turner gave the order to fire. Shouts of 'Mohawk, Mohawk', indicated that the startled defenders did not know where the assault came from and by the time they realised who their foe was, many were unable to gather weapons or respond by anything other than flight. Some leapt into canoes without paddles, only to be washed over the falls; some capsized; some dived into the stream and were drowned; others hid only to be flushed out. 'Captain Holyoke killing five, young and old, with his own Hands from under a bank'[18], it being no concern of these Christians' conscience to massacre the innocents. Only one Englishman died.

Content with his actions, Turner ordered the wigwams to be set alight. During the search, the English found the remains of two forges, a stockpile of ammunition and sufficient lead to make thousands of bullets; all these were heaved into the river.

Leaving some 100 or more dead, the victorious English turned for home. Now no longer stealthy and probably excited, garrulous and unguarded, they did not consider that other groups of Amerindians may have been hastening to the site bent on revenge. The first band got to the tethered horses first and would have driven them all off had not the leading group of retreating soldiers arrived in time to save most of the mounts. They left a significant number of attackers to return on foot or behind a mounted comrade.

The attacks turned the retreat into a rout until well beyond Deerfield. Turner himself fell early on. His deputy tried to marshal the scared men with some success but by the time the ambushes ended, some 40 members of the assault force had died. It was not a pyrrhic victory.

In a few days, replacements – double the number of English losses – were heading for the troubled towns. No such reinforcements were available to compensate for the Amerindian losses for whom the pain of losing wives and children was an added hurt and disincentive to continue the struggle.

---

18   The Avalon Project, *Charter of Connecticut*, <Avalon.law.yale.edu/17th_century>

At this point, whatever their sex or age, any Amerindian was fair game for the English. Few accounted for more of these non-combatants than the Connecticut forces led by Major John Talcott. He was Connecticut's most prominent, professional and experienced soldier commanding a mixed force of volunteers, militia and friendly Amerindians drawn from the Pequot, Mohegan and Niantic tribes. In June 1676, such was the state of Amerindian resistance, Talcott was able to roam Narragansett Country at will, rounding up and slaughtering sheltering groups with little fear of an armed response. His company's enthusiasm for their mission was reinforced by the hope of booty and profit from the sale into slavery, of captured Amerindians.[19]

Among those hiding away, was a group of about 200 survivors of the Great Swamp massacre who had sheltered with the *squaw sachem* Quiapen in her small stone fort. Perhaps, believing her enemies had moved away, she headed north. Not all joined in this flight. Her chief adviser Potuck, believing a safer policy would be to surrender, led a smaller group of about 80 into Providence to negotiate terms.

Quiapen's movements were reported to Talcott who on 2 July, surrounded the squaw's campsite and launched an attack on the unsuspecting Amerindians. Some fled into a nearby swamp but even these onetime safe havens had lost their potency due to unseasonal drought drying the land. The English plunged in after them and slew at will. In a short time, 171 Amerindians of both sexes and all ages, were either dead or captured. The squaw herself, was amongst those killed.

The triumphant Talcott, his losses limited to one dead allied Amerindian and a few injured volunteers, was now keen to join Bradford for the final hunt for Philip, who was known to be in the vicinity of Swansea or his home territory, Mount Hope. However, his Amerindians weighed down with booty, were not so keen, preferring to head homeward. Without this key element in his arsenal Talcott, reluctantly, did not march towards Bradford.

Any disappointment was soon salved by reports that Potuck's weary refugees were on the coast road at Warwick travelling in the open under the assurance of a promise of safe passage. The niceties of such an arrangement did not concern Talcott who, it must be remembered, was operating within the boundaries of Rhode Island without clearance. At Warwick he descended and killed or captured nearly 70 of the refugees. This time, there was no doubt about the use of torture. Talcott handed over one of the captives to his friendly Amerindians and watched as the victim's body was ripped apart.

With this demonstration of English might and Amerindian frailty, the Connecticut men dispersed homeward feeling their job had been done. Talcott's reward included a grant of 700 acres of good agricultural land. There had been a cunning in his cruelty. Connecticut was very aware of the designs its more powerful colonial neighbours had on the Narragansett lands. By destroying the native population, his colony could pre-empt the opposition by having a legal claim to the territory by right of conquest. Connecticut

---

[19] J. W. Warren, *Connecticut Unscathed* (University of Oklahoma Press, 2014).

could also claim royal approval and legitimacy. Its Charter of 1662 stated that the colony could:

> … from tyme to tyme and att all tymes hereafter, for their speciall defence and safety, to Assemble, Martiall, Array, and putt in Warlike posture the Inhabitants of the said Colony, and to Commiffionate, Impower and authorise such Person or Persons as they shall thinke sitt to lead and Conduct: the said Inhabitants, and to encounter, expulse, repell and resist by force of Armes, as well by Sea as by land, And alsoe to kill, Slay and destroy, by all fitting wayes, enterprizes and meanes whatsoever, all and every such Person or Persons as shall att any tyme here after Attempt or enterprize the destruccon, invasion, det riment or annoyance of the said Inhabitants or Plantacon.

Talcott had killed, slain and destroyed the enemy and the Narraganset ceased to be an armed, potent force. All they could hope for was a negotiated peace. For many, this was too uncertain and more and more Amerindian families trudged into settlements to surrender and crave mercy having heard the lenient terms published by Massachusetts on 19 June.

Whatever the circumstances, it was up to the government or local magistrate to decide who might be a rogue and worthy of execution or being sold into slavery. There was little compassion, the attitude of the colonists having been summed up in the blunt statement that the Amerindians, 'might try the difference between the friendship of their neighbours here and their service with other masters elsewhere'.

Ironically, those so-called 'Praying Amerindians' who had opted for friendship and neighbourliness by espousing the Christian religion and congregating in special villages such as Natick on the Charles River, found themselves treated with suspicion and open hostility. Many were shipped off and interned on the desolate Deer Island in Boston Harbour where they suffered and died due to minimum support provided by their co-religious – some of whom even planned to slaughter them. Over half of the Christian Amerindians starved or froze to death during their winter of internment. The survivors were released in mid May 1676.

The Deer Island internment is just one example of the way Amerindians, whatever their background or behaviour, were treated by the New Englanders into whose control they passed. Captives, either captured or voluntarily surrendered, or refugees of either sex, young and old or the innocent, could expect harsh treatment including enslavement which provided a useful income for those who organised such traffic. The going price was £3 a head. In the period between 25 June and 25 September 1676, Massachusetts raised £397.13s from 188 sales. Many of these were on board the slave ship *Seaflower* which sailed from Boston for Barbados later that year with 180 Amerindians crammed below; 110 were captives from Plymouth with the remainder captured near the Bay.

A contrary, illogical and self-justifying certificate penned by Governors Leverett and Winslow, accompanied Captain Thomas Smith on the voyage. This stated that prisoners had joined in an uprising against the colony and had committed 'many notorious and execrable murders, killings, and outrages'. This was plainly untrue; the English had made sure that any found guilty, or even suspected of carrying out such 'outrages', were hanged – it was the innocent, including women and children, who were shipped southward. Indeed, the court at Boston had stated that those who had 'imbrued their hands in English blood shall suffer death and not be transported to foreign parts'.

Towards the end of July, a foraging party led by the elderly Narragansett *sachem* Pomham, was surrounded by men from Dedham who slew many of them. Pomham himself was shot but tried to crawl away into the woods only to be pounced on by one of the soldiers. A wrestling match ensued as the *sachem* tried to bury his hatchet into his opponent. He might have succeeded had not another soldier come to the rescue, killing the old man whose corpse lay bloody before his captured son.

Not all died as nobly. On 27 July, the Nipmuck Sagamore John, marched almost 200 of his tribe into Boston to surrender. As proof of his penance, he brought with him a bound prisoner, the notorious and detested *sachem* Matoonas whose raid on Mendon a year earlier, had been the first such attack within the boundaries of Massachusetts. Without bothering with a trial, Matoonas was tied to a tree on Boston Common and shot by his fellow Nipmucks.

The Narraganset *sachem* Quinnapin and his wife, the Pocasset *squaw sachem* Weetamoo, provided one of the very few lighter moments in this otherwise dark and savage war. On 1 May, the night before Mary Rowlandson's release, in the presence of herself, her English negotiator John Hoar and Philip, the pair dressed up in their finery and started to dance. She was in a kersey coat, bejewelled with strings of pearl like *wampum*, bangles and bracelets. He was in a shirt with silver buttons, white stockings and garters from which silver shillings jingled as he danced. Unfortunately for the dignity of the couple, Quinnapin had persuaded John Hoar to give him 'one pint of liquor'. Consuming this had made him both amorous and disinhibited – resulting in giving chase to his wife with his intentions pretty clear. She avoided him and darted away to another wigwam. After giving up, he took comfort in the arms of one of his older wives and gave Mary and the others 'no more trouble that night'.

On 6 August, a posse operating out of Taunton, surprised and captured

The death of Philip in August 1676, shot by one of Church's native troops just a few miles from his original home at Mount Hope. (Harper's Magazine, June 1883)

almost 30 Amerindians who had camped nearby. Among those who escaped was Weetamoo, who took to the river on a makeshift raft only for it to capsize and her drowned body to be washed up a day or so later. Instead of treating her unidentified corpse with dignity, she was beheaded and the head stuck on a stake at Taunton where the 'diabolical lamentation' of the captured Pocasset identified it as that of their 'Queen'. Her husband Quinnapin (who had earlier stood against a peace treaty arguing for a fight to the finish), having kept company with Philip on the return to Mount Hope, was captured and taken to Newport where he was executed on 25 August.

As for the less important Amerindians who came seeking clemency, the English had the easy option of executing them, or the profitable opportunity to sell them into slavery or servitude. They could, like the Praying Amerindians, have been resettled in closely controlled villages but where was the profit in that? Servitude was a conscience-saving way of handling the children. Soon, the various governments came up with laws to control such dealings with Connecticut, whose harsh handling of the Narragansett had been a feature of the war. Rules were established directing the length and type of servitude that, for the time and circumstances, were the most lenient. Whatever and wherever the treatment, it paid dividends; King Philip's War was to see the last full-scale attack on the colonists by the greatly reduced and cowed native population.

With Philip a fugitive, only one other notable tribal leader remained at large, the much-respected warrior Annawon who had managed to slip out from Church's trap. He was not free for long.

Philip, far from being 'the greatest man that ever lived upon America's shores'[20] remains a shadowy figure. The war named after him was rather like the Anglo-Spanish war of 1739–1748 which, although named The War of Jenkins' Ear, did not much involve that gentleman. While Philip was at large, the colonies could not consider their work done. However, they slew many other Amerindians, indentured them as servants or sold them into slavery.

The man who was believed most capable of tracking down the Wampanoag *sachem* was Benjamin Church. His plan for doing so depended on enlisting the service of friendly Amerindians and learning from their field craft.

The Amerindians that Church had in mind were the Sakonnet. While in their presence the previous year, he witnessed the war dance of the visiting Wampanoag youths in early June, just days before the attack on Swansea. A year later, Church believed the *squaw sachem* Awashonks (whom he had always considered a friend), might turn to him despite her wandering away with Philip. She was now back in her own territory and Church, without being sure of either her allegiance or the enmity of her warriors, bravely paddled off to arrange to meet her with a proposal (sanctioned by the Plymouth government), to form a joint company to seek out and destroy the enemy on the borders.

Church agreed a site for a rendezvous with Awashonks and returned two days later accompanied by just two Amerindians, a bottle of rum and a wad

---

20   W. Apess, *A eulogy on King Philip*, 1836.

of tobacco. For a heart-stopping moment, he must have feared he had walked into a trap. He sat down alone with Awashonks on a stone only for the tall grass to part and for 'a great body of Amerindians' to emerge menacingly 'armed with Guns, Spears, Hatchets and with their hair trimmed and faces painted, in their warlike appearance'.[21].

Despite their threatening appearance, the sharing of rum and tobacco with Awashonks did the trick. If she could be reassured her people could return unmolested to their own lands, she was happy. With this understanding, she surrendered herself and 90 Sakonnet to the army camped nearby under the command of Major William Bradford. Bradford was not ready to trust turn-coat Amerindians and it was not until Church called on Governor Winslow on 5 July, that the governor's higher authority endorsed Church's proposal.

Following a celebratory dance and dinner with the Amerindians at Buzzards Bay, Church led his new warriors back to Plymouth before they set out together in search of the foe. His independent company also included several volunteers who joined him in the hope of booty and a share of the profit from any subsequent slave market.

At the same time Church's company were notching up the first of their many successes – the killing and capture of a group of Amerindians on 11 July at Marlborough – William Bradford, with no friendly native scouts in his company, was demonstrating in the swamps and woods surrounding Swansea, the advantages of Church's mixed force. On several occasions the major and his men had flushed out groups of Amerindians but mostly had to be content with the capture of the elderly and infirm; the agile, including Philip, eluded them. As for the women and children, many were taken on as servants with both Massachusetts and Plymouth stipulating the youngsters were to be released from such servitude in their mid twenties.

At this stage, Church's company were busy ferrying captives into Plymouth and supplies out to the settlements. On one of these trips, his scouts captured several Amerindians who revealed that Tuspaquin, the Wampanoag *sachem* who had been responsible for a number of raids, was hidden nearby. Church and his trackers set out in pursuit, entering the swampy region of Assawompsett Pond where they were fired on but sustained no casualties. Dividing his forces, Church sent his scouts along one promising track while he took another and captured a different group of foraging Amerindians. They told him that *sachems* Philip and Quinnapin had taken shelter in the Great Cedar Swamp with a strong enough band of warriors to deter Church's own force. Nevertheless, Philip was not safe. With Bradford holding the banks of the Taunton River and Church roaming at will around the woods and swamps, it was only going to be a matter of time before the two groups collided.

The inevitable meeting was made more certain by Philip's movements. Far from seeking safety over the border in New York, even if it meant humbling himself before the Mohawk, the *sachem* was returning to his home territory where he could be easily flushed out. Why? Did he realise that after all these

---

21 T. Church, *Entertaining Passages relating to King Philip's War* (Boston: 1716).

defiant months, a bitter end was inevitable and that he would be more at ease with death were it to occur in the land the loved? It is impossible not to draw parallels with the search and killing of the *Al-Qaeda* leader Osama bin Laden who, with the whole world his hideaway, was tracked down to a compound on the Pakistan/Afghanistan border not far from the country which had been his home for so long. Mount Hope would belie its name for Philip as 'it proved but a prison to keep him fast till the messenger of death came by divine providence'.

With the outcome no longer in doubt, the governments wanted to bring matters to a swift conclusion. On 24 July, Church, the man most likely to succeed, was given virtual *carte blanche* in his pursuit of the remaining enemy. This included pardoning all but the most senior, although this probably meant they would be sold into slavery rather than executed.

So desperate was Governor Winslow for results, that on 30 July he rode over to drag Church from his Sunday service to inform him that the enemy had been sighted near Bridgewater. By late afternoon, Church was on his way and the next day he was welcomed into Bridgewater. The militia there had just completed a successful foray against the prowling foe, killing Philip's uncle Unkompoin. Where the old gentleman was, his nephew was certain to be close.

Indeed it came about, for on the next day, while preparing to cross a stream by log bridge, Church noticed an Amerindian watching him from the opposite bank. He raised his musket only to be shouted at by one of his own that the target was a friendly Amerindian. Church lowered his weapon and in the moment before the other man disappeared, he realised his mistake – Philip had been in his sights. Church and his men slithered over the tree trunk and set off in pursuit but none of the Amerindians they captured was Philip. However, they did catch the next best thing – his son and wife. They were sent to Plymouth under escort and paraded as captives before a serious, biblically based discussion took place on how to treat the son.

Those who wanted to kill the young child claimed authority through *Exodus* 34:7 '… visiting the iniquity of the fathers upon the children, and upon the children's children'. Meanwhile, those more leniently minded, quoted passages like *Ezekiel* 18:20 'The person who sins will die. The son will not bear the punishment for the father's iniquity'. A neat compromise was agreed so that the boy was sold into the living death of slavery. His distraught mother became a servant.

Church called off the chase in the evening, leaving his scouts out to glean information. He returned to the pursuit the next day and by late afternoon, they could hear their quarry preparing to camp out for the night. Giving the recently captured prisoners the option of either sitting quietly and walking meekly into captivity along with the hope of mercy or attempting to escape and being hunted down and shot, Church left them unguarded while he positioned his men around Philip's camp. Unfortunately for his plans, his two reconnaissance scouts were sighted by two of Philip's own. They gave out a monstrous warning holler in sufficient time for the Amerindians to rise, run from their evening meal and take shelter in a swamp.

Church's small band endeavoured to surround them too but were but too thinly spread. The Amerindians burst out only to be bluffed in their own language by a fellow countryman who told them they were surrounded by a large force and would be shot if they did not lay down their arms. Amazingly, the bluff worked and the exiting Amerindians meekly handed over their weapons. However, Philip was not one of them. The frustrated Church headed into the swamp just as the wily Philip leapt out, killing a far from sober soldier and making good his escape.

Church almost did not make it out himself. He confronted 'a great stout surly fellow', the *sachem* Totoson, who did not have surrender on his mind. Instead, following a duel with two damp muskets (neither of which fired), Church gave chase and Totoson turned to attack him only to be dissuaded by the discharge of several muskets by his pursuers which almost succeeded in killing Church.

When the excitement subsided, Church found himself in possession of the field with 173 captives but neither of the two *sachems*. Nevertheless, it had not been a bad day's work for a party of 18 Englishmen and 22 natives. Momentarily disgruntled, Church went home to Aquidneck Island for a bit of tea and sympathy. He had no time for either; his wife fainted at the sight of him. By the time she was revived, two horsemen had galloped up to tell the fighter they had left at the ferry, a disgruntled Amerindian who knew exactly where Philip lay. With a farewell as hasty as his greeting, Church remounted and headed off.

The deserter reported that Philip was camping at the base of Mount Hope within a protective swamp. Church had just 24 men – English, Sakonnet and Pocasset – who were available to finally trap Philip. They paddled over to the Mount Hope shore and were led inland. After an overnight camp on 11 August, Church's plan was to place a group on one side of the swamp; from there, they would launch an early morning attack driving the fleeing Amerindians into an ambush laid by Church and the other group.

When the first gun fired, Philip was first in flight – his rout leading him on to the guns of an Amerindian and an Englishman. The latter fired first but his gun failed to go off. The aim and fire of Alderman, the Amerindian, was surer. The running man dropped dead at their feet. They turned him over– it was Philip.

The body was dragged into the open where all gathered around the famous fugitive. In Church's words he now lay like 'a doleful, great, naked, dirty beast'. He was to have no dignity in death. Church, denying him the comfort of a burial, had him beheaded and his body quartered. One scarred hand was severed and given to Alderman as an exhibit. The head Church bore in triumph to Aquidneck, perhaps causing his wife to faint again. It was eventually displayed skewered onto a palisade of the fort at Plymouth where it remained grisly and staring for another 20 years.

Totoson remained at large with his wife and son but the little lad caught a disease and died followed soon afterwards by his father. His wife scraped out a shallow grave for him and surrendered to the authorities. She offered to take them to her husband's grave only for her to die of the same illness before this could happen.

With Philip dead and dismembered, only two other significant native leaders remained at large. They were Philip's 'general' Annawon and the Black Sachem of Nemasket, Tuspaquin. The former had fled from Church's trap but was believed to be sheltering around Mount Hope while the latter had been sighted near Plymouth. It was the capture of Tuspaquin that Church first directed his attention to in late August. The trawl was only partially successful with the *sachem*'s wife and children being seized. Ever cunning, Church released a few of his Nemasket captives with the message that should Tuspaquin surrender, there would be a place for him in command of Church's Amerindian volunteers. Although the war in Massachusetts was ending, the Abenaki Amerindians in Maine were still fighting with some success. Having left this bait, Church returned to the Mount Hope area where Annawon had again been sighted.

Church set off on 7 September with just five Englishmen and 20 Amerindians to track down Annawon and his still loyal company of about 60 followers. As was now usual, they came across and captured many subdued survivors who offered up no fight and indeed, found comfort in capture.

One of these captives led Church's company into a swamp where his father and a young girl were resting while taking provisions to the chief and his men. They were willing to lead Church to the warrior's camp and it was only a matter of his company deciding whether or not they wished to enter the lion's den with such few men. At first, the Sakonnet troops havered but Church's enthusiasm won them over and they replied, 'We will go'. They pressed on until dusk when the old man called a halt saying that Annawon always posted sentries at sunset to check for intruders, it was best to wait for night.

Under cover of darkness, they crept stealthily forward until they heard the sound of corn being ground with pestle and mortar. They could not launch an attack. The 'subtle savage' had chosen his camp site with care. It lay beneath a steep cliff and was surrounded on all other sides by swamp. Church crawled to the lip of the rock and looked down. What he saw convinced him that a surprise assault would be successful. The Amerindians were spread out around several campfires but just below Church, resting against the branch of a tree, they had placed all their arms.

Cautiously, Church and his men slithered down the rock face until on reaching the ground, Church dashed to commandeer the weapons while at the same time, threatening Annawon's son with his axe. Seeing his son in such peril, the warrior surrendered without a fight as did also his men who had been quickly rounded up by the Sakonnet.

When all were subdued and possibly, seeing the symbolism of the moment, Church turned to Annawon and invited himself to dinner. With great grace the warrior gestured him to be seated and the two great leaders supped on roast beef and corn as did, presumably, the rest of those present. In a little while, all but Church and Annawon had fallen fast asleep.

These two, although not possessing a common tongue (as far as Church knew), managed a sort of conversation as they lay either side of the fire. With the rising of the moon, Annawon got up and moved into the shadows. Suspecting treachery, Church moved to a position where he could threaten the chief's son but the latter returned carrying a large woven basket. Having put this down, he spoke in English what must be taken as the formal surrender of his people.

'Great captain', he said, 'you have killed Philip and conquered his country, for I believe that I and my company are the last that war against the English, so I suppose the war is ended by your means and therefore these things' he said, gesturing towards the basket, 'belong unto you'.

With that, he proceeded to hang around Church's shoulders, several long and neatly decorated belts of *wampum*, the personal regalia of Philip which were worth a fortune. He also handed over a deep red blanket and some powder horns. Such noble gestures much affected Church and he and Annawon talked until dawn. By this time, the Englishman was convinced he had made a new, and probably very loyal friend.

With the camp broken up, Church marched his prisoners off to Taunton where they were handed over to the army for conveying to Plymouth. All apart from Annawon who Church took with him to Newport to be introduced to his Rhode Island friends. They would probably have remained together had not Massachusetts Governor Leverett, summoned Church to discuss ongoing action against the Abenaki in Maine.

Church departed, having thought he had persuaded Plymouth's Governor Winslow, to grant both Annawon and Tuspaquin clemency should they hand themselves in. He returned to find the heads of the two warriors alongside Philip's on the posts of Plymouth's palisade, dumbly demonstrating the war was over. In October, Massachusetts felt confident enough to officially declare this so – however, this was not true in Maine.

9

Maine

The First Abenaki War: 1675–1678

> No attempt to relate in daylight all the incidents of the war along the Maine coast has here been made; some known to the writer have been omitted and undoubtedly many occurrences of these times are now absolutely unknown to any person.[1] – Ellis & Morris, 1906.

The war in Maine lasted longer than it did in southern New England. It continued not only after Massachusetts claimed it ended in October 1676, but also after the formal Treaty of Casco was signed with the Abenaki in September 1678. One reason for this being that after Philip's death, neither Connecticut nor Plymouth had any interest in supporting Massachusetts' continuing campaign in the north. The conflict also enabled tribal groups who had been defeated further south, to take refuge with the still warring Abenaki and their allies in Maine. Yet many accounts, both contemporary and later, ignore this theatre of war completely. Perhaps the disregard was due to this being the conflict the Amerindians won.

Jennings mentions Maine just once [2] while Douglas Leach in *Flintlock and Tomahawk* (probably the best and most thorough book about King Philip's War), apart from acknowledging that 'In Maine the Indian menace persisted longer', spares the conflict just one paragraph. This lack of information was eventually rectified by John Noble in his doctoral thesis *King Philip's War in Maine*.[3] It involved incidents that illustrate the problems of the whole campaign as well as having its own unique aspects. In the space available,

---

1   G. Ellis & J. Morris, *King Philip's War*.
2   F. Jennings, *The Invasion of America*.
3   <digitalcomms@UMaine>

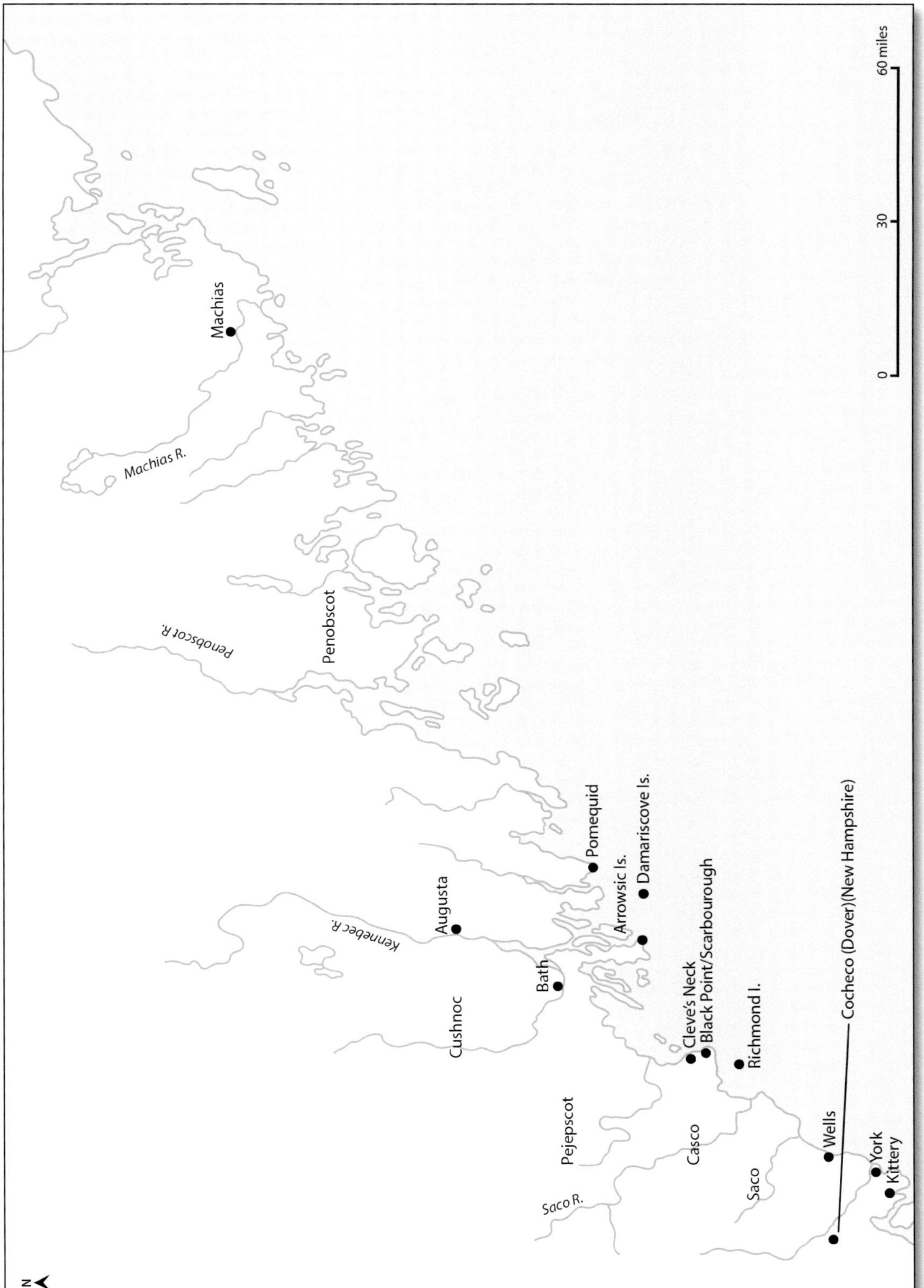

MAINE

Maine in King Philip's War

bearing in mind the charming words of Ellis and Morris quoted above, these will be considered by examining selected incidents and the individuals involved.

If New England bore a resemblance to Old England, then Maine was its West Country. This affinity was recognised in the creation of Cornwall County in 1665. This encompassed a vast domain stretching from St. Lawrence to the Atlantic, between the Kennebec and St. Croix Rivers. From this area, Devonshire County was carved in 1674, only for both counties to be assimilated by the Abenaki in 1675.

Although the area was vast, for the time being, the incomers clung to the fractured Atlantic coast. There was a broken necklace of 13 small settlements which were dotted along the coves and inlets from the Piscataqua River in the South to Acadia in the North. According to Hubbard, inland was 'a barren and rocky country' such that, regarding its protection, 'the whole being worth scarce those means that have been lost these past two years in trying to save it'. Ellis and Morris summarised the situation succinctly:

> There were in this region but few of the conditions existing in the United Colonies. No well-fortified and defended towns to be set upon in warlike fashion by a furious enemy. No well-equipped force to surprise the Indian fastness in a moment of unwatchfulness. Here was border warfare only. The sharp and unexpected attack upon the undefended cabin of the settler; the still more unexpected surprise upon the little garrison, and always, common to all sections in which the English fought, the deadly ambush, offering a lesson which was apparently never learnt.[4]

The very nature of this thinly populated and isolated colony meant there was little reason to encourage an assault on the settlers by the 'barbarous and perfidious' Amerindians. Before 1675, Maine provided an example of how the incomer and the indigenous might become friendly trading partners. No great numbers of land-hungry immigrants were forcing the natives from their traditional grounds. Instead, most of the incomers wished to fish, an occupation which they could carry out side-by-side with the Amerindians – not without the occasional dispute over catches of cod but these were localised and short-lived.

Inland, the settlers were establishing saw-mills to take advantage of the country's magnificent forests. These were dominated by the tall, straight white pine, *Pinus strobus* which was ideal for ship's masts and which gave Maine its sobriquet of the 'Pine Tree State'. Mary Beth Norton observed: 'In 1675, about 440 fishing boats operated off the coast between Boston and the Kennebec … and at least fifty saw-mills each produced up to a thousand feet a day of white pine boards'.

Within the forest, with its many rivers and lakes, the Amerindians were left undisturbed to hunt and trap beaver and other skins which they could trade with the English. They in turn, were content to provide the (mainly)

---

4   G. Ellis & J. Morris, *King Philip's War*.

Abenaki Amerindians with firearms, powder and shot to increase the size of their catch.

However, by 1660 the fur trade had considerably declined and by 1670 wampum had ceased to be the dominant currency. Now, the very geography of the colony impacted on the relationship between the two communities. Maine covered the area where the horticulture of the warmer south gave way to the hunting region that stretched northward. By the late seventeenth-century, with the loss of the fur trade, the native population became more reliant on firearms to survive. This was a fact which the agricultural colony of Massachusetts neither wished to be acquainted with – nor to accept. Before their tragic interference, Maine had managed.

There were some who were quite prepared to take advantage of the trust that had been established. At the top end of such malpractice came those who seized Amerindians from the shoreline and sold them into slavery. Only slightly less pernicious were the rogue traders who used rot-gut whisky as a route to gain advantage in their dealings. The Abenaki, typical of societies that keep no written record, had long memories and many innocent settlers would suffer from the mistrust engendered by these practices.

Colonial Maine also suffered from a flawed hierarchy, its settlements being 'places of unhonourable exile … where many were sent to shift for themselves, without being of further trouble to those nearer home'. This inadequacy was present from the first attempt to settle along this coast in 1607 when the ships *Gifte of God* and *Mary and John*, sailed from Plymouth to the mouth of the Kennebec River. Here, on 18 August, 100 passengers disembarked to establish the Popham Colony under the leadership of George Popham and Ralegh Gilbert. Neither man had the required attributes; their sponsor Sir Ferdinando Gorges, wrote of them:

> The President himself [George Popham] is an honest man, but old, and of an unwieldy body and timorously fearful to offend or contest with others that will or do oppose him, but otherwise a discreet careful man. Captain Gilbert is described to me from thence to be desirous of supremacy, and rule, a loose life, prompted to sensuality, little zeal in religion, humorous, head-strong, and of small judgement and experience.[5]

These traits would seem ideal ingredients for a similar personality clash to the one undergone at Jamestown. The fierce winter reduced the colonists (who were now settled within their palisade at Fort St. George) down to 45 only. In February, George Popham also died. In early September, Ralegh Gilbert learnt that he had inherited the family estate at Compton Castle in Devon and promptly took passage home. The surviving colonists, unwilling to be abandoned, decided to return with him.

Further settlement in Maine was at best desultory and the occasional European visitors left a virulent virus behind them. Between 1616 and 1619, the tribes of the north-eastern coastal region lost almost 90 percent of their

---

[5] D. B. Quinn, and A. M. Quinn, (ed.), *The English New England Voyages*.

numbers in the 'Great Pandemic' through diseases, principally hepatitis, for which they had no natural immunity.

Slowly and disjointedly, the English established settlements along the coast establishing the towns of Pemaquid, York, Cape Porpoise, Saco, Kittery, Scarborough, Falmouth, North Yarmouth and Wells; these lacked the cohesion of the townships being created in Plymouth and Massachusetts. The Maine folk were fishermen with axes and ploughs who wished to have the freedom to bring up families unfettered by ancient land laws or rigid religious rules. From the South, as the rule of the saints became less tolerant, they were joined by dissenters, mainly Anglican by inclination, who drifted into the colony to escape persecution. Thus, a community was created which valued its independence. Further north in Acadia, the French were settling with a desire to push south into the Sagadahoc region.

Concerned as to French intentions and the seemingly relaxed attitude of the Anglican settlers, Massachusetts in 1652, decided to incorporate the territory under its own administration using the borrowed authority of the Puritan victory in the English Civil War. One-by-one, the settlements yielded to the Bay's militia-backed persuasive suggestions. There was no organised resistance; the settlers were too dispersed and besides which, they had to spend most of their time struggling as subsistence farmers in this bleak northern land. Neither did they have any wish to take up arms against their Abenaki neighbours; Maine would have to be pressured into taking part in King Philip's War.

During this time, the Abenaki were suffering from the 'Beaver Wars', an inter-tribal war over control of the fur trade. Although peripheral to the main action which was fought along the St. Lawrence and the Lakes, the Abenaki became increasingly involved. Their access to the dwindling beaver population became critical. The English were less sympathetic to their plight than the opportunist French, whose Jesuit priests saw that conversion opportunities could be created along with the provision of guns and ammunition, which were essential to the tribe if they were to keep from starving. Equally important, however, was an agreement between the Amerindians and the English:

> If any mischief should happen to be done by the English or Indians one against another, though it were to the killing any person, neither side should right themselves, but complaint should be made to the *sagamores* if the Indians did the wrong and to the court if it was done by the English.

In the autumn of 1674, Massachusetts banned the sale of shot and powder to the 'subtle brood and generation of vipers', who at the time, had not bitten any settler. In July 1675, news of Philip's insurrection arrived at Kennebec along with an instruction to disarm the Amerindians. A few days later, this demand was conveyed to the Amerindians upstream. In response, a few weapons were handed over but insufficient to satisfy the most hostile of the English. The journey and the demand was repeated leading to the sachem Madockawando, saying 'That if the English were their friends as they pretended to be they would not suffer them to die for want of powder'.

The local incomers realised the gravity of what was being initiated. The trader Thomas Gardner, wrote to the Massachusetts Governor Leverett in September 1675, drawing his attention to the fact they were in danger of bringing about a war through their own actions:

> Sir, I Conceive the Reason of our Troubles hear may be occationed not only by som southern Indianes which may Com this way But by our owne Acctings … Sir, upon the first Newes of the warres with the Indianes at Plimouth divers persone[s] from Kenibek & Shepscott got togeather makeing themselves officers & went up Kenibeke River & demanded the Indianes Armes. And seeing these Indianes in these parts did never Apeare dissatisfied until their Armes wear Taken Away I doubt if such Acctions may force them to go the French for Releife or fight Against us having nothing for their support Almost in these parts but their guns.[6]

He also reinforced Madockawando's words by stating: 'these Indians Amongst us live most by Hunting as your Honnor well Knoweth how we can't take away their armes whose livelihood dependeth of it'.[7]

Along with arms, the English also required the provision of hostages to ensure compliance. However, the hostages had no wish to assume that role and 'trusting more to the celerity of their own feet, than to the civility of their English friends', they swiftly fled. Skirmishes soon followed and before long, open hostilities broke out in Maine. There was an outbreak of killing and captive taking, beginning with the killing of the Nichols (husband and wife) at Blue Point in September 1675.

The combination of killing and capture at the start of the war with the Abenaki, is illustrated by the incidents at the onset of hostilities. The Indian assaults were similar to those taking place further west. Isolated homes had their barns and crops set alight and any settler outside a defended house was slain. Although aware of this danger, the elderly Weakley was too slow in removing himself, his wife, son, pregnant daughter-in-law and three grandchildren to a place of safety. A patrol, investigating a plume of smoke, came across the burnt building where they found 'the body of the old man half consumed with fire, the young woman killed and three of the grand-children having had their brains beat'. One eleven-year-old girl was taken into captivity and 'having been carried up and down the country some hundreds of miles' was returned by the *sagamore* Squando, unharmed.

Squando also led an attack on the Soco River settlements, burning many houses and stores. On 1 October, the fight moved inland when a Sokiki and Canibas force attacked a garrison house on the Salmon Falls River in which 15 women and children had taken shelter. Leaving a young girl to bravely bar the door, they all escaped. The girl was tomahawked and left for dead but, miraculously survived.

---

6 L. Brooks, *Our Beloved Kin*.
7 J. P. Baxter, (ed.), *Documentary History of the State of Maine* (*Baxter Manuscripts*) (Portland, ME: Maine Historical Society, 1900).

The Waldrons and Captive Taking

Captive taking was a feature of the war in Maine with the Amerindians aiming to use their hostages as bargaining chips. Most of those held appear to have been treated firmly but without any lasting harm or violation. At least they were kept within the territory. Those who the English took prisoner were often sold out of the country into Barbadian slavery with its harsh treatment and no hope of return. When the Reverend John Easton objected to the 'selling away … as a usage worse than death', he was threatened with a lynching.

A typical example of the methods pursued is shown when William Waldron, cousin to the soon to be notorious Richard Waldron, received the following authorisation in November 1675:

To William Waldron

The Insolency of ye Indian enemy being such as that in ye Eastern parts they have Made sundry Assaults upon us to ye great prejudice of ye people there both in ye loss of ye lives and Estates of many of them & as yet no considerable damage done them by ye soldiers or Inhabitants[.] that yourself being bound into those parts these are to Im[power] and commission you with what company shall [g]o along with you as opportunity presents to pursue kill & destroy & by all ways & means to Annoy ye said Indian Enemy[.]

> Attending such further order as you shall receive from myself or other superior authority

Richard Waldron

Ignoring another letter that advised him 'not to take any Indians east side of Kenibek River because we had made peace with them', the slaver did precisely that by capturing several dozen Amerindians. Among these were 17 Mi'kmaq, including a chief and his wife who were seized from Cape Sable Island off the southernmost point of Nova Scotia, although the tribe was not even at war with the English. He took them to the Azores to be sold as slaves. Unusually, the Massachusetts Court viewed William's action dimly and charged him as he 'did unlawfully surprise & steale away seventeen Indians men weomen & children & in your vessel called the endeavor of Boston Carrjed & sent them to ffyall & there made sale of them'. The case was dismissed. Nevertheless, for many, it was William Waldron's actions that led to the 'first Indian Warr in those parts'. It certainly caused the Mi'kmaq, well north of the struggle's epicentre, to seek their revenge.

Richard Waldron was a man whom a reader instinctively dislikes and for good reason. In 1662, while serving as the crown magistrate in Dover, he sentenced three Quaker women missionaries to be bound behind a cart and to walk 80 wintry miles through 10 townships. On arrival at each place, they were to be stripped to the waist and flogged. Luckily, at the third town of Salisbury, the local magistrate freed them and gave them medical attention.

The incident inspired John Greenleaf Whittier to write a poem which included the verse – accurate through hindsight:

> And thou, O Richard Waldron, for whom
> We hear the feet of a coming doom,
> On thy cruel heart and thy hand of wrong
> Vengeance is sure, though it tarry long.[8]

Powerful in his own territory of Dover, New Hampshire, and its environs (Waldron also served as a Deputy to the Massachusetts General Court for 25 years from 1654), he ended his career, ironically, as Chief Justice of New Hampshire in 1683. Before then, as a leading citizen and Amerindian trader, he was appointed as the senior officer to prosecute the Amerindian war.

In mid October, a large body of Amerindians resumed attacks on the home of Richard Tozier at Salmon Falls a short distance from the garrison defended by Lieutenant Roger Playstead. Hearing the sound of fighting, Playstead despatched seven men to go to Tozier's assistance as well as writing the following letter to the garrison at Dover:

> Salmon Falls
>
> Oct. 16, 1675
>
> Mr. Richard Waldern and Lieut. Coffin:
>
> These are to inform you that just now the Indians are engaging us with at least one hundred men, and have slain four of our men already – Richard Tozier, James Barron, Isaac Botts, and Tozier's son – and have burnt Benony Hodsdon's house. Sir, if you have any love of us, and the Country, now show yourself with men to help us, or else we are all in great danger to be slain, unless our God wonderfully appears for our deliverance.
> They that cannot fight, let them pray, nought else, but I rest
>
> Yours to serve you
>
> Roger Playstead
>
> George Broughton.[9]

In the meantime, the seven men had been ambushed and severally mauled. On the following day, Playstead along with 20 men and an ox-cart, sallied forth to recover the dead but they too were ambushed. Playstead, his two sons and a number of his men were killed. The hoped-for support from Waldron at Dover, arrived too late.

In the spring of 1676, the Amerindians attempted to negotiate a peace treaty but made their feelings very clear when they stated:

---

8   *How the Women went from Dover.*
9   W. Hubbard, *The Present State of New England*

> We were driven from our corn last year and many of us died. We had no powder and shot to kill venison and fowl. If you English were our friends, as you pretend to be, you would not suffer us to starve as we did.

Instead of recognising this as a supplication, even a surrender, the English felt their best response would be to tighten the screws, or even use trickery to gain an advantage. A peace treaty was agreed at Cocheco (Dover) in July 1676 but was not enacted.

At the start of September, Richard Waldron reported to Governor Leverett that the Nashaway leader Shoshanim (also known as Sagamore Sam), had arrived in Cocheco to renew his calls for peace. Instead of warmly welcoming him, Waldron told him that he was 'too late' and had him seized and sent to Boston where, without the niceties of a trial, he was hanged along with three of his countrymen on 26 September.

Back in Cocheco, Waldron found himself 'hosting' 400 Amerindians who had arrived in anticipation of the July peace being ratified. By coincidence, a large number of colonial troops were also in the vicinity having arrived with orders to 'seize all Indians, who had been concerned in the war'. Rather than initiating a bloody fight, Waldron, all smiles, suggested the two sides engage in a 'sham' friendly fight, like a game of rugby with guns, the English being led by Captain Frost from Kittery. Once he was satisfied with the positions taken on the field, Waldron 'caused the Indians to fire the first volley', after which they were surrounded and disarmed without either side suffering casualties. One source even suggest that Waldron first plied the Amerindians with drink to stupefy them before they were imprisoned.

English accounts state the Amerindians were then divided into two groups with those who had not been involved in the conflict sent on their way. Meanwhile the warriors, some 200 of them, were despatched to Boston under guard where 'Seven or eight of them, who were known to have killed Englishmen' were hanged, while 'the rest were sold into slavery in foreign parts'. Later research implies that there was no such separation of the sheep from the goats; rather they were '*all* sent down to determine their case at Boston' apart from '10 young men to Serve in ye Army with their families'. As Waldron wrote in a letter that accompanied the prisoners:

> This Day I drew up ye Indians at Cocheco upon ye open Ground before my house under ye Notion of takeing them out into ye Seruice, such of y[m] as I saw meet, upon assembled I made them eate & Drink, & then surrounded y[m] with ye Army & calling ye chiefe Sagamores into ye Center I told y[m] what must bee don, only yt ye Innocent should not be damnified, they surrendered their Armes 20 in Numbr. We have taken 80 fighting Men & 20 old men, & 250. Women & children 350 in all.

It is significant that only 20 weapons were seized, a clear indication that this large group did not intend to pose a threat. Waldron, along with the army commanders at Cocheco, were also very aware that the consequences of their actions would lead not to peace but to further war. He went on to say that:

> We find among y[m] (as I [have?] Information) Narraganset Indians, Groton & Nashaway Indians & c I shall [torn] it very necessary & judge it safe to use severell of ours in ye Warre. I humbly request Advice to ye Army to stay a while to search ye Woods, at least an Expresse Order of yt Captn Hunting may stay with his Indians & 40. of the English, such as he shall chuse which may be suitable number to doe service among us. Wee expect eury houre to [several words torn] upon us but hope yt by yt meanes we now) bee capeable of I [several words torn] war.[10]

Even the 10 scouts were not free from indignity. In a notorious case, Mary Namesit, the wife of the newly recruited scout John along with her suckling child, were not only flung into prison in Boston but sold by Waldron, into slavery. When the issue was raised with the Boston magistrates, instead of admitting fault, Waldron argued his case, even blaming Mary for her plight, writing to her advocate, Major Gookin:

> … as to ye Squaw you mention belonging to one of Capt. Hunting's Souldiers, there was such a one left of ye first Great Company of Indians 1st [sent] down which Capt. Hunting desired might Stay here til himselfe & her husband Came back from Eastward which I consented to & how she came among ye company I know not I requiring none to go down to Boston but those that came in after ye Armies departure neither knew I a word of it at Boston when I disposed of them so twas her own fault in not acquainting me with it.

The incident did little to darken Waldron's reputation among his compatriots. In February 1677, he was appointed by the council at Boston to lead a party of 200 men on a raid into enemy territory inland from Arrowsic Island. Captain Frost accompanied him as his second in command. As the council was also hoping for some negotiated settlement, their choice of these two men who had done so much to destroy the native trust in an Englishman's word, was ill-founded. Indeed, the Amerindians had stated: 'Major Waldron do lie. We were minded to kill no man but Major Waldron did no wrong to give cloth and powder but he gave us drink and when we were drunk killed us'.

As the English were disembarking their troops, a delegation of Amerindians paddled up, proposing peace talks. To this suggestion Waldron replied: 'We came to fetch off the captives and make war as we see good'. Nevertheless, during a face-to-face meeting with the senior *sachem* Squando, a captive exchange was negotiated and arranged – only for the *sachem* to fail to show. Several days of skirmishing followed before another meeting was arranged. Waldron schemed to 'fight them or surprise them' yet again. For their part, the elderly *sagamores* stated: 'only a few of our young men, whom we cannot restrain, wish to enter upon the warpath'. They however, wanted peace and would release each captive for 'twelve bearskins and some good liquor'.

In the early afternoon, Waldron, convinced that drink and sweet talk had relaxed the Amerindians, pulled out a lance hidden in a pile of goods

---

10 L. Brooks, *Our Beloved Kin*.

and waving it over his head, summoned his troops ashore. They arrived and unleashed a swathe of fire. In the panic, an escaping canoe overturned drowning five of the Amerindians while others struggled ashore and surrendered. Two chiefs and five other Amerindians were shot, as was the old *sachem* Megunnaway. The triumphant English, their mission a mess, sailed back to Arrowsic laden with plunder, where they continued to shoot unfortunate Amerindians. They returned – self-pleased – to Boston having ensured that hostilities would continue. This happened with the Arrowsic garrison having to be abandoned after a series of ferocious attacks.

The Amerindians did not forget what happened at Cocheco in September 1676. During King William's War which was fought between 1688 and 1697, they got their revenge. On 27 June 1689, a native woman, having been invited to spend the night within the garrison of Cocheco, opened the doors to let the warriors in. In the massacre that followed, 23 residents were killed and a further 29 taken into captivity. Richard Waldron was tortured and mutilated before he died. In 1697, Major Charles Frost, Waldron's accomplice at Cocheco, was ambushed and slain near Kittery.

Joshua Scottow

The man in whom most believed could bring a successful conclusion to the war, was Benjamin Church. Indeed, over the next decades he would make five sorties into the north-eastern province, arriving portlier and less mobile on each occasion. However, having snared Philip in 1676, he wanted to spend more time with his family so he declined the invitation. Instead, Maine was presented with gentlemen who lacked Church's charisma and so were unable to offset their worst failing – as far as the inhabitants of Maine were concerned – being that they were from Massachusetts.

The first incomer appointed to command the dispirited Maine folk was the Boston merchant, Joshua Scottow. In 1671, he had moved to Black Point, Scarborough, having bought up much of the land in the area. Here he built a fine house and a stockade to protect both it and the small adjacent town. However, his behaviour towards his neighbours earned much resentment, including an accusation of murder of a rival merchant. As a result, when he assumed the role of the captain of the garrison at Black Point, he lacked local support and had difficulty keeping the fort manned at a level sufficient to meet the threat. Reinforcements sent from Massachusetts resented their deployment so much that of the 50 soldiers despatched, 22 failed to arrive and many of those who did, were 'insufficient for service'. Others were so mutinous that Scottow could not award the punishment their behaviour warranted. Elsewhere, soldiers abandoned their posts and made it very clear that they had no intention of risking their lives in defence of the people of Maine. At the same time, the locally enlisted found themselves tasked with jobs such as paving Scottow's yard which had nothing to do with defence and more to do with the captain's self-aggrandisement. They complained, raising a petition that stated:

Wee whose names we have underwritten, doe declare that we were never in ye least privie to ye sending for ye souldiers which came from Boston to Blackpoint, neither during ye time of their stay did we in any sort receive advantage by them; but yt they were maintained upon ye acct. of Mr. Scottow: for all the while his fishermen were thereby capacitated to keep at sea for the whole season; and much worke was done by them which was greatlie turned to his profit; as removing of a great barn, paving before his house and cutting of Palisado stuff for a pretended fortification where there is no occasion nor need. And many more such courtesies Mr. Scottow (got) by the soldiers. And that other men should pay for his work, done under pretence of defending ye country, wee hope in behalf of the rest of ye sufferers in these sad times, you will please to take it into your serious consideration, and heape no more upon us than wee are able to beare, but where the benefit has been received, there order ye charge to be levied.

Richard Foxwell, Giles Barge, Rol Allanson, Joseph Oliver, William Sheldon, John Cocke, John Tinney.

Scottow seemed reluctant to despatch soldiers on recce and interception missions. On one occasion, when the neighbouring garrison of Blue Point requested the release of some gunpowder that Scottow was holding for them, he declared, 'if Boston Soldiers wanted powder, they could have it, but if the inhabitants wanted it, they must buy it'.[11]

In the autumn of 1675, Scottow's behaviour sorely angered the people of Maine. In response to a fatal Amerindian attack on nearby Dunstan, Scottow was asked to send soldiers to protect the survivors. This he refused to do, stating bluntly that as they refused to come to Black Point 'they must take what follows'. Shortly afterwards, the unprotected Alger brothers were killed.

In October, a company of a sixteen-man patrol led by Lieutenant John Winckoll, disembarked at the abandoned but burnt settlement of Winter Harbour. They had arrived to provide support for those settlers still isolated and defenceless in the Saco area. Immediately they came under attack from a large force of Abenaki and were forced to take shelter behind some timber near the shore – but within sight of the Black Point garrison to which Winckoll sent requests for help. Scottow refused to supply support although his 40 strong garrison could easily have despatched relief. Instead, it was the other local garrison, Blue Point, that rushed five of its seven-man force to Winckoll's aid. They were too late to prevent the death of nine of Winckoll's patrol.

Such incidents further sullied Scottow's reputation and authority and it was not long before he was recalled to Boston to answer charges of 'falsifying his trust', leaving his deputy Henry Jocelyn, to try and impose military authority upon the reluctant garrison and local inhabitants – both of whom felt a desire to 'desert their country'.

However, Scottow was tardy in taking up the order to return to Boston, apologising for his failure to appear at the end of a letter written in mid September to Governor Leverett. This vividly describes the unchecked

---

11   J. H. Pulsipher, *Subjects unto the Same King*.

rampaging of the enemy in the vicinity of the fort, as well as indicating that the French were providing the Abenaki with military advisers (Appendix III).

Scottow was to return and in August 1677, as the war was drawing to a close, he sailed from Black Point with a cargo of Abenaki captives to be sent home in exchange for concessions.

Mogg Heigon, Henry Jocelyn and Black Point (Scarborough)

Black Point was the epicentre of the war in Maine and the site of one of the few farcical incidents of the whole campaign, at the time when the hapless Jocelyn was in charge of its reluctant defenders. That he had no liking for the task is made clear in a letter he wrote to the absent Scottow, signed by both him and the third-in-command, Walter Gendall:

> Capt. Joshua Scottow
>
> We underwritten being of ye committee with serjeant Tippen, and both of you now being absent, shall desire you to acquaint ye Governor & Councill of ye averseness of the generality of ye Inhabitants to obey Military orders; yet they would be pleased to direct some especial order to such in this town as may bring ye Inhabitants to ye obedience of ye Military Laws of the Government yet we may be in some capacity to defend ourselves against ye common enemy; and we shall remain,
>
> Yr friends to serve you
>
> Black Point, Aug. 9, 1676. Henry Jocelyn, Walter Gendall.[12]

Following a scouting voyage between Black Point and Casco in September 1676 (where evidence of Amerindian activity was apparent but none of the enemy sighted), the garrison relaxed – only to be startled into activity on 12 October when 100 Amerindians under the able command of Mogg Heigon arrived outside the fort. A parley was organised and Henry Jocelyn, who knew the Amerindian leader, went forth and was persuaded to negotiate terms of surrender. These included the peaceful departure of the inhabitants complete with their possessions. When he returned to the garrison to report this arrangement, he found that apart from his family, everyone, including his troops, had fled, creeping out of the back and into boats. Left behind were the absent Scottow's possessions and for which (for many years), he pursued a claim for the massive sum of 250 pounds.

Jocelyn's decision to flee rather than fight, was roundly criticised but there was a twist to his decision. A few days earlier, Mogg's men had attacked a group of soldiers who had sailed to Richmond Island to collect stores. Greatly

---

12   G. M. Bodge, *Soldiers in King Philip's War*.

outnumbered, the soldiers were forced to surrender to the Amerindians. Among them was Walter Gendall who, overhearing the Amerindians' plan for attacking Black Point, volunteered his own, obviously well informed, idea as to how the garrison could be taken without bloodshed. For this scheme, he was later to be put on trial for treason and sentenced to run the gauntlet, followed by banishment from the colony with all his property forfeit.

The fall of Black Point panicked the neighbourhood, among whom, talks of an attacking force of 500 Amerindians assisted by 300 Frenchmen, gained credence. Families fled, mostly by boat, taking few possessions with them. In their absence, Massachusetts militia men went on looting patrols. They were even recruited by Sergeant Bartholomew Tipping precisely for this task so that when the inhabitants returned, they found all their tools taken, and the hinges ripped off their doors.

The capture of Black Point gave Mogg a bargaining chip and he used it to sue for peace. This involved him bravely travelling down to Boston for discussions with Governor Leverett. Although the terms with which he was presented, including the return of all English hostages and goods, were not ones that he felt authorised to agree without the approval of his *sachem*, Madockawando, Mogg consented. He then returned to his tribe to issue a threat to burn Boston and destroy the Maine fishing fleet.

Black Point, having been abandoned by the Abenaki, was re-occupied by the English in early 1677; an initiative from Scottow who was much concerned with the recovery of his property. Among those returning was Sergeant Tipping who was considered to be:

> … a fitt person to take the charge of such as are to land, in case he shall judge the place tenable, he shall be & hereby is impowered to impresse the company now sent, and any other of the inhabitants, or any other persons which maybe there found, to looke after plunder or their owne estates, and to defend & keepe the place from the enemy untill further order.

He did indeed prove to be fit, for when Mogg returned in May to lay siege to the fort, Tippen and his men held firm and 'conducted a gallant defence'. This culminated on day three when the sergeant himself shot and killed Mogg. The dispirited Amerindians withdrew but held firm to their leader's idea of attacking the fishing fleet – wreaking havoc along the coast. A few months later they would seek their revenge.

Squando and Moore's Brook

One of the most implacable enemies of the English in Maine was the Saco *sagamore* Squando, who had converted to Christianity and might thus have been considered a conduit for peaceful negotiations. Such hopes were dashed when, in the summer of 1675, three English fishermen, having noticed Squando's wife crossing the Saco River in a canoe with her baby, took it upon themselves to test the theory that native children were able to swim from birth. Paddling over, they upset the canoe throwing mother and child into the water. The frantic mother managed to recover the infant but the child died shortly afterwards. Squando never forgave the English for this act. As leader of the Sokosis and Ammoscoggins, he gained a reputation for fierceness and brutality, tampered by his willingness – it seemed – to treat captives with courtesy.

In August 1676, following another failed peace conference, Squando launched an attack on Cleve's Neck, near modern Portland. A two-day fight centred on the house of Anthony Bracket who, along with his wife and five children, were taken captive while his brother-in-law and several other settlers, were slain. By contrast, with the English way of dealing with captives, the whole family was 'redeemed' and returned to their homes where sadly, some of them were to be slaughtered in the Amerindian wars in 1691.

On 28 June 1677, three ships anchored off Black Point ready to disembark a mishmash of soldiers at the fort. Here, they would link up with another group of English and Amerindians who had marched up from Massachusetts. Many of the men were impressed while a number were out of work refugees from Maine being 'encouraged' to march home. They were stiffened by several veterans such as Captain Benjamin Swett, who had earned a field promotion from ensign, at the Great Swamp Fight when his commander, Captain Gardiner, had been killed.

Lieutenant James Richardson was a rare example of a military officer who had fought with distinction at the siege of Brookfield and had also won over the trust of the Amerindians – in this case, the Christian Wamesit, many of whom were marching willingly behind. Along with them were bounty hunters who had been promised 20 shillings bounty for each enemy scalp and twice that for any enemy they could make their prisoner and sell on into slavery. The senior officer was the newly commissioned but elderly, Major Clarke who was appointed both as an adviser to Swett and as the government's representative. He had the authority to act as circumstances dictated. His knowledge of the Amerindians had come from his trading days which had ended when his posts were destroyed in the fighting.

Never a good plan, the expedition had two objectives; the first was to march inland and destroy the mighty Amerindian fortress of Ossipee; the second was to re-establish a presence at the frontier village of Pemaquid (Bristol) on the Sagadahoc River. Massachusetts had abandoned this place in April, its soldiers ill-equipped to maintain it against any Amerindian or French enemy. There was an urgency in this aim for the place was coveted by Governor Andros of New York whose own fleet of ships was sailing to claim possession.

The Amerindians imposed which plan to pursue when a small group of them appeared around half a mile away near the ferry for Blue Point. Being religious men from Massachusetts, the English first mustered for prayers before 100 of them set out to meet the foe, who slowly withdrew as the soldiers approached – marching through blackened pastureland that sloped down to abandoned fishing jetties, evidencing the domination of the Abenaki in the region.

Given the fact that some months earlier, a platoon under Swett's command had experienced an ambush at Wells, what happened next might seem surprising. It seems that the English, marching in files, did not send out scouts or outriders. When they arrived at Moore's Brook on the edge of the marshes, they were unprepared for the sudden up-springing of Amerindians from behind every bush and out of the marsh – every one of them a marksman. The inexperienced, youthful company did not stand a chance.

The first volley swathed the clustered force. Richardson fell immediately along with many of his troop. Some sought shelter in the shrubs. Although a few fled, there was no possibility of an ordered retreat. Swett tried to rally the rout but the slaughter continued all the way back to the garrison. Just six soldiers returned through the gates uninjured. Swett was not one of them; surrounded, he was hacked to death. Of Major Clarke's contingent of 20, just one man returned. Maybe as many of 60 of the New England men died. None who were taken captive lived. Their work done, Squando and his men left the field, their leader heading to the sanctuary of Canada. The English were left in peace to bury their dead, probably in a mass grave. The wounded were carried off for treatment at Salem or Boston.

In October, one of the soldiers Thomas Dutton, wrote a vivid description of the fight in a petition to the government in which he asked for the support that a wounded veteran might have expected (Appendix IV).

Excellent research has identified most of the English dead, wounded and many of those who participated in the action.[13] Among those were the men of Essex County who had contributed many and lost many in the war and featured noticeably on the casualty list.[14] Of the names of their native allies, none of the Wamesit are known, while from the village of Natick, only three are recorded. These included Abraham Speen, whose faithful but persecuted family had served the English well. He himself had been arrested for a murder he did not commit in Lancaster and was only released when no evidence was forthcoming. The English got the Amerindian servants they did not deserve.

As for the enemy, Squando's name must serve for them all. It seems, after he had agreed a peace at Casco in 1678, he travelled north to Canada where he appears to have committed a religiously inspired suicide. It is recorded by Scottow in a letter to Increase Mather, that the *sagamore* had a vision of a Christian Minister who told him that if he hanged himself, he would find himself in paradise. Brushing aside the tearful restraints of his family, this is, apparently how he met his end.

The Island Wars

Arrowsic Island is a seven-mile-long, narrow island near the mouth of the Kennebec River. It was purchased from the Amerindians in 1661 by two trading military men from Boston, Major Clarke and Captain Lake. They built a fortified trading house with outhouses some two miles from a smaller

---

13   S. Hunnewell, *The Maine Genealogist*, May 2003, August 2003.
14   K. F. Zelner, *A Rabble in Arms*.

post owned by William Hammond. Neither establishment appears to have earned a reputation for fair dealing.

On 13 August, an Amerindian force launched a savage attack on Hammond's home, killing some 15 people. From there they crept forward to hide close by the gates of the larger fort. When they were in place, two women walked up to the gate and asked to be let in to purchase some goods. As soon as the gates were open, the Amerindians rushed in and attacked the occupants. Lake and three companions jumped into a canoe and paddled away to neighbouring Mill Island with the Amerindians in close pursuit. As they disembarked, Lake was shot dead but the other three (although Davis was badly wounded), managed to hide. Back at the fort, the raiders took away all they could carry and set everything else ablaze before canoeing over to small Jewell Island to attack several refugees that had fled there. They were repulsed and returned to the mainland.

Many of the isolated settlements on the mainland, realising that they were under immediate threat, headed in the other direction by paddling out to the nearby islands. From these temporary refuges, they could see a semi-circle of smoke indicating just how far along the shoreline the destruction was being wrought. Over the following days and nights, they carefully contacted other families and gathered together in a few fortified homes. In their haste, they had left food, provisions and gunpowder and had to send out foraging parties at night in their small sailboats.

On 20 September, a glimmer of hope arrived in the form of Captain William Hathorne (an ancestor of Nathaniel Hawthorne [15]) who being a Massachusetts man, commandeered the survivors' boats and pressed their men into service. He was, however, very short of supplies himself, due to contrary winds delaying the arrival of his victuals. Hathorne therefore authorised seven men to make a journey to Munjoy Island where it was known a flock of sheep were grazing. Either they were spotted or the native Amerindians had also coveted the sheep for when the foragers arrived, they were immediately attacked. They fled up the slope to take refuge in a ruined stone house but this provided only a temporary shelter. None survived. The whole incident was witnessed by Hathorne and his men who, having no boats themselves were unable to row to the rescue.

Captain Hathorne

Hathorne was an experience soldier. He had been present at the Great Swamp Fight and had taken charge of his company when Captain Joseph Gardiner had been killed inside the fort. Following the 'surrender' of the Amerindians at Cocheco, Hathorne had been ordered to march with a force of 400 men, including volunteers both English and native, with the intention of attacking

---

15 Hathorne was a notorious flogger of Quakers. His son was the even more notorious judge at the Salem Witch Trials, thus providing much grist to their descendant's writing mill.

the Abenaki stronghold at Ossipee. The aim was to do unto them what had been done to the Pequot and the Narragansett.

Hathorne did not enjoy his expedition into Maine, finding the terrain too broken for ease of movement and the natives too ready to set ambushes and then flee in canoes. He, like so many from the Bay, did not take to the Maine English. He felt they were a people not worth sacrificing the lives of his soldiers to protect. This he made clear in a letter which stated:

> … att blackpoint, the people there are in great distraction and disorder; I know not of former Neglects but now they are a people ungoverned, & Attend little to ye Government there established soe that ye most of ye towne desert ye place, though we told them of a law they were Ignorant of wch we think we doe perfectly remember of 20lb penalty for any that desert ye frontiers, wch we thinke is most Rationall, ye Inhabittants there having little to doe; we are ready to thinke they might better be Imployed there than many of ours, who have famillys att home.[16]

Unlike Church, Hathorne suffered from the less-than-useful bias of a commander of a joint force; he did not trust his native troops but realised he could not campaign without them especially if he was to complete a successful attack on Ossipee. As it was, after a hard four-day march inland, he found the fort abandoned and had to be content with burning it without roasting anyone trapped inside. The fort was to be rebuilt and burnt down again in the war of 1725 which was focused in the same area.

The War at Sea

The Maine campaign was unique among all the Amerindian wars in that it had a maritime element. Given the naval supremacy of England, it was surprisingly dominated by the Abenaki who concentrated on destroying livelihoods rather than lives by capturing or sinking the settlers' fishing boats. The role of Admiral of the Abenaki was undertaken by Mogg Heigon who built up a small flotilla of 40 sloops and 12 larger vessels that raided small coastal towns. In one attack on Salem, it was reported that over 20 ketches were captured or destroyed. Before Scarborough in May 1677, the sea war continued.

A memorable instant in the maritime war began off Port La Tour, Nova Scotia, close to Cape Sable Island where William Waldron had seized and enslaved 17 Mi'kmaq. In July 1677, the Mi'kmaq sighted six New England fishing boats operating from Port La Tour. Paddling out, they boarded the boats and took the crews prisoner before ordering them to sail to Maine. During the passage, the skipper of one of the boats fooled his captors and was able to take back command imprisoning some while others leapt overboard. He then sailed back to his base at Marblehead where the tightly secured Amerindians were surrounded by the fisherwomen, many who had been

---

16   G. M. Bodge, *Soldiers in King Philip's War*.

widowed in the war. The women showed no mercy and beat and stoned the captives to death. This gruesome episode is best related in a deposition by the ship's mate, Robert Roules (Appendix V).

Roules's words certainly serve to contradict the opinion of William Hubbard that the fishermen were not known for their fighting ability 'being a dull and heavy-moulded sort of People, that had not either Skill or Courage to kill anything but Fish'. The deposition also illustrates the difference in character between the settlers of Massachusetts and Maine. All the former, including Hubbard, recount the story of the war with frequent biblical references and justifications as well as using vitriolic language concerning their enemy. By contrast, Roules reports factually what he witnessed with no disparagement of the Amerindians who captured him; nor does he feel the need to quote biblical chapter and verse. In fact, the nearest he comes to offering a criticism, is on the behaviour of the women of Marblehead.

The fight off Port La Tour led to the authorities despatching an armed ketch from Salem to administer punishment but it had to return having not encountered a single enemy vessel. The tide turned with the death of Mogg before the gates of Scarborough. After this, ships despatched by Governor Andros of New York, aided by Royal Naval vessels, took command and control of the inshore waterways.

Treaties

There can be few conflicts where overtures for peace were made so frequently and so often either disregarded or spoilt by distrust or betrayal. Unusual also is that it was the winning side, the Abenaki, who were most fervent in their pleas for peace. Yet, time after time they found themselves having to deal with people, such as Waldron, who they knew to be untrustworthy but whom the English still considered a suitable negotiator.

This mismatch was most apparent in the message carried to the English by the captive Elizabeth Hammond who, ironically, had her estate, mills and ironworks utterly destroyed by the rapacious Waldron. The report she made records the Amerindians' justified disappointment. In it, the visionary Madosquarbet states: 'You all ways break the peace' yet the Amerindians were willing to live peaceably and that 'we will not fight without they fight with us first'.[17]

The Amerindians also pointed out the unfair way in which the English dealt with their neighbours: 'We must pay 100 skins if we break a tobacco pipe'. Yet they were very aware as to which side had the advantage: 'We are owners of the country and it is wide and full of Indians and we can drive you out'. This was a defiant statement set against what he saw, as the English desire they would 'not leave war as long as an Indian is in the country' and their 'fashion to come and make peace and then kill us'.

---

17   L. Brooks, *Our Beloved Kin*.

MAINE

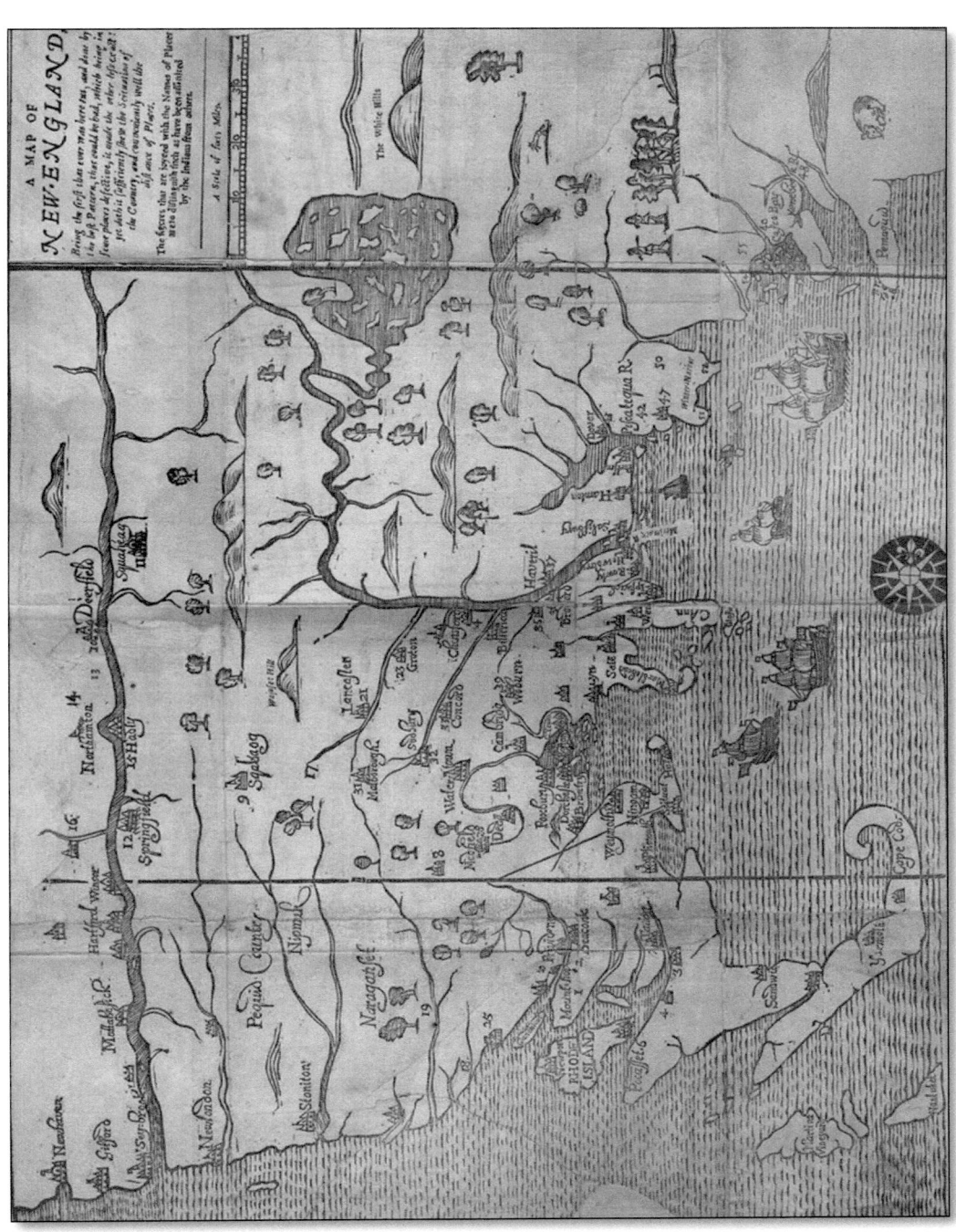

This was the fist map to be cut and printed in New England. it was propably designed by William Hubbard to illustrate his account of King Phillip's War (1675-76) in "The Present State of New England: Being a narrative of the troubles with the Indians, 1677." The map was printed from a 1677 woodcut by John Foster, who is considered to be North America's first printmaker. (Public Domain)

What the Abenaki did not appreciate was the role of Major Waldron who, as Madosquarbet stated 'did lie' and although they 'were not minded to kill nobody, Major Waldron did wrong … he gave us drink and when we were drunk killed us' and 'Major Waldron has been the cause of killing all that have been killed this summer … We have killed none of your English prisoners. If you had any of our prisoners you would have knocked them on the head'.

This last point, if one included selling into servitude, slavery and summary executions, provides a stark contrast between the cruelty of the civilised Christians and the attested, good treatment of prisoners by the so-called, savages. Even those people who came into Boston or elsewhere, voluntarily as part of a process of peace and reconciliation, could find themselves bundled into boats and despatched to Barbados.

Now, the Amerindians wanted to find 'all ways for peace' offering to resume trade and return the captives that they held. To this end, during July and August, the two sides met at Pemaquid, near the mouth of the Sagadahoc River. But there was one major change; the English negotiations were headed by men from Governor Andros's state of New York whose authority and direct link with the King of England, the Abenaki freely acknowledged. Massachusetts had little option but to grudgingly acknowledge this undesired leadership, if only because of the rights that New York had achieved by rebuilding a fort at Pemaquid.

The death of Waldron, killed in 1697, in revenge for his treatment of the Abenaki in 1676. (Author's collection)

Early on, Madosquarbet and the Kennebec *sachem* Moxon, agreed to a cessation of hostilities and to summon their allies to surrender the captives they held, inviting the English to do likewise. This agreement was sent post-haste to Massachusetts with a firm statement that expected acquiescence. The Bay acted honourably, even despatching a ship to the Azores to bring back those Amerindians who had been taken their as slaves. They then shipped the notorious Joshua Scottow off to Pemaquid with a hold full of captives. He arrived on 5 August, one week before canoes carrying the Abenaki *sachems* paddled to the place for 10 days of talks. Their number included the previously intransigent and adamantine Squando who had reluctantly agreed to return to the peace talks under the acknowledged authority of Moxon.

Both sides agreed they were 'subjects to the same king' and that future disputes should be forwarded either to the *sagamores*, the New York commissioners at Fort Pemaquid or to Henry Jocelyn who had returned to Black Point. Without discussion, they insisted that despite the release of English prisoners, their captives could not be released until the Abenaki returned the fishing boats they had seized. This demand 'threatened to spoil all'. The Abenaki could see and hear their captives crowded below decks on Scottow's ship – he refused to release them. The situation looked likely to come to blows as the Amerindians mustered to 'rescue the captives by force'. An attempt to seize one of the youngsters failed when force was threatened. Scottow then allowed the prisoners to come on deck but not to go ashore. On 18 August, the Amerindians agreed to the return of the boats and the frail prisoners were carried ashore (Appendix VII).

The negotiations continued the following spring when Squando led a delegation to secure the Pemaquid agreement. This time, the two sides met at Casoak to put in place arrangements for the return of the beaten English to Maine. Unlike elsewhere, it was the English who had to agree to pay tribute to the Amerindians; each family to surrender a 'peck of corn' annually except for the larger landowner, Major Philips of Saco from whom a bushel was required.

Casoak itself took on a significance rather like that held by Runnymede in England where Magna Carta was signed. In 1701, following further fighting, the treaty was renewed and two cairns were raised side-by-side to signify the brotherhood between the two groups. Future agreements were also marked by additional stones being placed here at Two Brothers Point.

For the English and Abenaki, this 'brotherhood' was more akin to that of Cain and Abel rather than David and Jonathan. The peace was not permanent. The war just ended was the first of seven fought by the Abenaki to defend their territory.[18] When they took up arms again in 1688, they gave their reasons as being:

> Because the English refused to pay the yearly tribute of corn.
>
> Because they were invaded in their fishery co, by certain gentlemen, who stopped the fish from coming up the river with their nets and seines.
>
> Because the English cattle were destroying their corn.
>
> The granting or patenting of their lands to some English.
>
> Common abuses in trading such as drunkenness, cheating of which traders were 'seldom innocent'.

In other words, precisely the wrongs that had so upset them at the start of King Philip's War.

---

18 King William's War, Queen Anne's War, Father Rale's War, King George's War, Father La Loutre's War, the French & Indian War.

NEW WORLDS, OLD WARS

The disputes and attacks continued. For example, in July 1694 during King William's War, 250 Abenaki, led by the Frenchman, Claude de Villieu, attacked the English settlements on the Oyster River killing some 104 settlers and taking a further 27 into captivity. The Europeans were thus recruiting the tribes for the colonial wars that would soon break out culminating in the Seven Years War of 1756 to 1763. These years would decide the future rulers of Canada and the continuing demise of the native population.

The little change in the mutual hostility between incomers and indigenes might be best summarised by a proclamation read to the House of Representatives in Boston in 1755; it offered the following inducements to hunters of humans:

> For every Male Penobscot Indian above the Age of Twelve Years, that shall be taken within the Time aforesaid and brought to Boston, Fifty Pounds.
>
> For every Scalp of a Male Penobscot Indian above the Age aforesaid, brought in as Evidence of their being killed as aforesaid, Forty Pounds.
>
> For every Female Penobscot Indian taken and brought in as aforesaid, and for every Male Indian Prisoner under the Age of Twelve Years, taken and brought in as aforesaid, Twenty-five Pounds.
>
> For every Scalp of such Female Indian or Male Indian under the Age of Twelve Years, that shall be killed and brought in as Evidence of their being killed as aforesaid, Twenty Pounds.
>
> Given at the Council-Chamber in Boston, this Third Day of November 1675, and in the Twenty-ninth Year of the Reign of our Sovereign Lord GEORGE the Second, by the Grace of GOD of Great-Britain, France and Ireland, KING, Defender of the Faith, God Save the King.

They certainly did not expect Him to save the natives.

A Penobscot chief greets a fellow chief at a modern ceremony in Maine in 1951. (Author's collection)

10

Conclusion and Consequences – How the East was Won

'We are owners of this country and it is wide and full of Indians and we can drive you out'. – Madosquarbet, 1667.

This land is your land, and this land is my land

From California to the New York Island,

From the Redwood Forest, to the Gulf stream waters,

This land was made for you and me. – Woody Guthrie, 1940.

Every native population in the world resists colonist if it has the slightest hope of being able to rid itself of the dangers of being colonised – that is what the Amerindians in America did. They persisted in this as long as there remained a solitary spark of hope they would be able to prevent the transformation of the native lands known as Tsenacomoco and Norumbega into New England and Virginia.

Leach considered that 'the two races had fought a war of extermination' but this was not so as the Amerindians were not ruthless, united or organised enough to achieve this aim. Tactically brilliant, unsurpassed in fieldcraft and ambush, the tribes never had a unifying strategy nor a general who could lead an army towards the cities on the shore. Jamestown, Boston and Plymouth remained inviolate and if that continued, the English were bound to win. Regrettably, they would then continue their assault on the indigenes until they had long ceased to pose a physical threat. Even now, the small communities descended from those enemies still exist; the Wampanoag, the Pocasset, the Narragansett and others still have to struggle for recognition of their treaty rights and federal statutes to apply to their legal claim for land rights.

At the start of the century, English settlers were precariously placed in a few settlements that clung like loose limpets to the coast of North America where their success was far from guaranteed. By the start of the next century, they dominated a wide and lengthy tract of land having virtually irradicated the threat from the Amerindians who had contributed so much to their earlier survival.

Future conflicts in this region would be fought mainly between the two competing colonial powers of France and Britain; both of whom would recruit native allies, followed by an internecine strife over governance. These were wars of the immigrant whites – for the red man had ceased to exist as an independent combative presence east of the Appalachians. He had even, in many cases, ceased to exist as a cohesive tribe or a recognisable society.

To begin with, the opposing sides were reasonably evenly matched. There was little difference between the settlers and the settled in their requirements for surviving in the often-hostile environment – this being food, shelter, fire and water. In addition, the English had metallurgy, liturgy, the law and livestock; they weaponised all four. They also had numbers and these embodied in the replacements, the reserves and the breeding potential would be their most significant and unmatchable advantage. Whatever setbacks they suffered, however precarious the hold on the shore, a settler could be sustained by the inventions and industrial production of English manufacturers and the continual immigration of his countrymen. The Amerindian might out-master him in weapon skills and fieldcraft but he was never able to produce his own guns or ammunition nor repair the ones he had. For him, as the fighting continued the number of firearms and braves he could muster, decreased significantly. The English could lose 1,000 men and still gather the same number a month later – no papoose could mature as quickly to take the place of his dead father.

Tobacco and livestock cultivation also contributed to the destruction of the native way of life, by clearing and grazing in green pastures that had once been pristine and essential hunting grounds. If tribes objected to this insertion of alien animals, the settlers produced laws that allowed them to do what they liked. It became worse as the natives became the pursued. They had no secure storehouses to replenish their supplies, no strongholds inside which food could be sown, harvested or stored, few rivers which could be fished in safety. Hunger stalked them, weakened them, starved them, broke up the cohesion of the groups including women and children who had been forced to travel with their braves. This was in stark contrast to the colonists whose families, away from the front-line, were fed, watered and secure.

The tribes also contributed to their downfall by being disunited and even hostile – one against the other. Thus, the English could utilise the Mohegan and Narragansett against the Pequot; the Niantic and Mohegan against the Narragansett; and the Mohawk, Praying Indians and Sakonnet against the Wampanoag. Only the Powhatan stood united but they lacked the strategy and ruthless leadership to press home their advantage. They all lacked the numbers – the numbers necessary to fall upon Jamestown, to assault Boston, to besiege Plymouth – all of which could in any case, be reinforced by sea.

The English also had time to learn from their mismanagement and mistakes. Principal amongst these was how best for an isolated community to hold out until help arrived. Fortified buildings and palisades obviously helped but most important of all was that every man had to be able to defend his own house through possession of his own arms and ammunition. From this arose the belief in an independent militia to which every man, by virtue of his living in the land, belonged, both by duty and right, including his private ownership of arms. This meant that in minutes of an alarm being raised, a village could become a platoon; a township into a company and a city – an army.

By 1645, Massachusetts was designating part of its militia as 'minutemen companies', which comprised fit young men able to deploy almost immediately. The system, supported by a system of riders and alarms, was further reinforced in 1653 when Massachusetts declared that one eight of its militia must be available to deploy within one day. Obviously, such a rapid response would fail if those available for summons did not have their arms to hand and were not at home. The Revolutionary War made an icon of the 'minutemen' but their foundation was created in the early Amerindian wars.

A study of the 1625 audit of land holdings in Virginia shows how widespread was this individual ownership of arms. For example, Captain William Eppes, the commander of the settlements on the eastern shore of the Chesapeake, was recorded as possessing, inter alia, five guns, 120 pounds of powder and 200 pounds of lead, six suits of armour and four coats of steel mail. These last three items indicate how backward some of the fighting equipment was in the colony.[1]

The need for immediate access to arms is no better illustrated than in the words of the Reverend William Hubbard who wrote: 'Like Nehemiah's builders, each one toiled with his weapon of war in one hand, and his instruments of labour in the other; exposed every moment, from a watchful, unseen foe'.[2]

This need lasted a long time and became a tradition. It changed into an irrefutable belief held by a majority of Americans, that they have a fundamental right to possess private weapons, even their own arsenals. The Second Amendment to the Constitution merely acknowledges this right in law.

On offensive operations, the English also adopted and adapted the local fieldcraft which they for a long time had sneered at being mere 'skulking', scorning such skills as the ambuscade, tracking and living off the land. John Smith showed the way claiming that with 10 men, he could successfully range the land. However, the first true exponent, the man credited with being the father of 'The Rangers', was Benjamin Church who learnt from the warriors.

Church wrote down no fighting instructions but from his writings and recorded statements, a number of tactics can be deduced. These include:

Planning each operation in advance, not leaving anything to chance.

Ensuring that soldiers under his command were properly trained, fed, and equipped.

---

1 <www.virtualjamestown.org/Muster/muster 24> quoted in J. Potter, *The Jamestown Brides* (Atlantic Books, 2018).
2 *The Present State of New England*, 1677.

Building alliances with potential allies (i.e. Native Americans), who may have been overlooked or mistrusted by other commanders.

Not inflicting unnecessary damage or harm.

Using stealth and surprise to tactical advantage.

Understanding how a tactical operation fits in with strategic objectives.

Leading by example and from the front.

Maintaining communications with higher and lower echelons.[3]

Important as these military developments were, the major impact of the Amerindian wars and the way they were conducted was the development of the relationship between the white and red tribes.

The new Israelites had conquered the promised land and made, in a reference with which most of the settlers would have been familiar, Moab their washpot. There would be no serious attempt either to assimilate the defeated or to recognise their situation; they would become sojourners and outcasts in the land in which they had lived symbiotically for centuries. This land, which had endured for millennia with its unchanging landscape of forest, lakes, rivers and wildlife, through which man had moved and left scarcely an imprint, would now be ripped apart by plough, saw, mill, road and town in a major ecological destruction. This would only be halted (and to an extent, reversed) once the bare mountains had slid mud onto the stump-pocked valleys and villages beneath.

Unlike European conflicts, these wars depended on the supremacy of two superimposed, contradictory populations confined to a small country with conflicting aspirations and no common concepts. Neither side could envisage blending their cultures to form a new, united, unique and flourishing society. It was easier to behave with anger, antagonism and animosity than to attempt harmony through understanding, appreciation and admiration. The most obvious analogy for this oil-and-water incompatibility is Palestine, post the Balfour declaration, where Jewish immigrants flooded in to claim rights to a land already occupied by another race with an alien culture and creed. Ironically, the Holy Land of Israel was also exactly how the seventeenth-century immigrants viewed America.[4]

Could it have been different? The result suggests otherwise. What could have been different was the future relationship between the two sides. Yet the English preferred hegemony to harmony. Once the natives had been beaten in war, they were not going to be allowed to resume their way of life; they were not even allowed to assimilate. Those who converted to Christianity were kept apart as second-class citizens. The verse of the Bible that stated that peoples from both east and west shall share the kingdom of God, was

---

3   B. Church, *Diary of King Philip's War*, (ed.), Simpson A. & M. (Pequot Press, 1975)
4   I. Black, *Enemies and Neighbours, Enemies and Neighbours, Arabs and Jews in Palestine and Israel, 1917–2017* (Allen Lane, 2017).

CONCLUSION AND CONSEQUENCES – HOW THE EAST WAS WON

not one frequently quoted.[5] Neither was there the promise of having no bond or being free.[6]

The English converted people with the *New Testament* but occupied, opposed, and slaughtered them with books from the *Old Testament* – especially *Deuteronomy* and *Joshua*. This was their promised land and they insisted on sole occupancy by using the methods advocated by the God of the *Old Testament*. Once in control, it was their laws, their land management, their settlements, their livestock and their needs that would dominate. Having beaten the opposition, there was no way that anything like the status quo ante was going to be tolerated. The natives could wander in bedraggled bands, no longer have a place to call home, starve, even beg, but they would not be allowed to coalesce once more into proud communities. They found themselves dumped in green ghettos or gulags, concentration camps which were called reservations, where even their rights to these limited acres are still frequently challenged.

The callous treatment of the tribes established a pattern that would travel with the settlers. They continued to cross this vast continent from sea to shining sea, claiming this land as their land, gaining control by treaties which would be broken once control had been taken. All this time, biblical or theological justification would be used to justify this treatment of lesser breeds without the law. The good book even inspired the puritanical attitude towards the native women whose role, position and emancipation was very different from the domesticated women of England. Many, to the consternation of the newcomers, had considerable sexual freedom and formed part of the hospitality dispensed to important visitors to Amerindian towns.[7]

John Smith was certainly one such important visitor. In 1607, a very sensuous dance was organised by the Powhatan ladies who displayed much of their lithesome beauty. Smith was even taken away to their 'changing room' where he would have been most dense not to recognise what was on offer – he rejected any advances.

Unlike the French and Dutch, who found comfort and contentment with local liaisons, for the English, such relationships could be almost sinful. One only has to read the grovelling letter from John Rolfe to Governor Dare, requesting permission to wed Pocahontas, to realise how controversial his act of miscegenation would be viewed. This was in the more relaxed colony of Virginia which, unlike New England, was not ruled by 'saints' who, in taking a literal interpretation of the Old Testament would have been very familiar with the order laid down in *Deuteronomy*, chapter 7, 'Neither shalt thou make marriages with them; thy daughter shalt not give unto his son, nor his daughter shalt thou take unto thy son'.

This ban on social mixing, settlement integration and intermarriage, either by custom or law, became observed wherever the British established

---

5   *Luke* 13:29.
6   *Galatians* 3:28.
7   H. C. Rountree, *The Powhatan Indians of Virginia* (University of Oklahoma Press, 1989).

their colonies: 'A deep instinct kept them perpetually apart from their subjects of other races'.[8] They both lived and loved apart.

If one was looking for a basic review of the settlers attitude towards the 'savages', it could be found in a paragraph by Bradford. He describes the apprehension of his company onboard *Mayflower* as they approached New England in 1620. He used words such as: 'savage', 'sharp', 'severe', 'fierce', 'desolate', 'wild', and stated that the 'savage barbarians when they met with them were readier to fill their sides full of arrows'. He also likened the Separatists' arrival to the children of Israel on the borders of the promised land, bemoaning the fact that he was unable, unlike Moses, to 'go up to the top of Pisgah' to view Canaan.[9] This biblical reference was taken from the final chapter of *Deuteronomy*; it is followed immediately by the devastating *Book of Joshua*, a record of genocide inspired by God.

If proof was needed to indicate the English used this scripture as precedent, it can be shown by the simple expedient of changing a few biblical names – Hittite, Amorite, Perizzite, Canaanite with the names Powhatan, Pequot, Wampanoag, Pamunkey, Narragansett – and one has the parallel story and identical circumstances of two sets of slaughtered peoples.

> And they utterly destroyed all … both man, and woman, young and old … *Joshua* 6:21.
>
> And it shall be, when you have taken the city, that ye shall set the city on fire: according to the commandment of the Lord shall ye do it. *Joshua* 8:8.
>
> And the king of Ai he hanged on a tree. *Joshua* 8:29.

Those left alive were made to be 'hewers of wood and drawers of water', or in the context of New England and Virginia, sold into slavery. All with the blessing of the Lord, for were these settlers not also a chosen people? This an aim of the English is confirmed by Philip Vincent who wrote of the Pequot War:

> For having once terrified them, by severe execution of just revenge, they shall never hear of more harm from them, except (perhaps) the killing of a man or two at his work, upon advantage, which their sentinels and corps du guards may easily prevent. Nay, they shall have these brutes their servants, their slaves, either willingly or of necessity, and docile, if not obsequious.[10]

If this seems harsh, it is worth considering that on 27 October 1659, Marmaduke Stephenson and William Robinson, both Quakers, were executed on Boston Common, for holding to their beliefs. If that is not sufficient evidence of the barbarity and savagery that had been unleashed upon New England, consider that between February 1692 and March 1693, there were 200 persons accused of witchcraft in Salem and adjacent towns

---

8   J. Morris, *Pax Britannica* (Faber & Faber, 1968).
9   W. Bradford, *Of Plymouth Plantation* (Boston: The Massachusetts Historical Society, 1912).
10 *A True Relation of the Late Battell fought in New England* (London: 1637).

CONCLUSION AND CONSEQUENCES – HOW THE EAST WAS WON

– of which 14 women and five men were hanged and one man crushed to death. These were not 'savages', these were, with one exception, the kith and kin of the settlers. If such gross action could be taken against their own folk, what chance did the native population have? Even a light-hearted example highlights the intransigence of the 'saintly' supervisors. In New Haven on Christmas Day 1639, a celebratory cricket match drew to a rapid close when the church elders confiscated the bats.[11]

One of those persecuted for providing succour to Quakers was Thomas Macy, a well-regarded citizen of Amesbury, Massachusetts, who was fined 30 shillings for sheltering the above-named Quakers during a rainstorm in 1657. Discontented by such treatment, he headed for the coast and bought some land on Nantucket Island from his cousin Thomas Mayhew, who was establishing himself on neighbouring Martha's Vineyard. Both men managed to live in harmony and friendship with the islands' native population. So much so, that when King Philip's War broke out, the islanders remained neutral. They practised a different faith to that of the clergy on the mainland of whom Easton wrote:

> I am so persuaded of New England priests that they are so blinded by the spirit of persecution … that they have been the case that the law of nations and the law of arms have been violated in this war.[12]

The treatment of the native populations of the eastern seaboard set a sad precedent that was to reach its climax on the Great Plains. It was here that much more famous forts, battles and Amerindian Chiefs would become the subject of popular films and at last, sad reflections.[13] Of this lengthy campaign, Nye and Morpurgo wrote a clear summary:

> For close on four hundred years the white man had to fight for the control of the American continent against those who had owned it before he came. Often, he suffered disaster at their hands, sometimes, particularly in the early days of settlements, his hold on the newly won lands seemed about to be broken, but always he had behind him the inventive and industrial genius of Europe and which provided him with weapons of destruction which the Indian could not equal. At least his peer in the skills of pitched battle, and, to the very end, his master in fieldcraft, the Amerindian soon learnt to use the white man's weapons – and soon learnt to steal them – but the manufacture of firearms, their invention, and their improvement, he never learnt. By the time the Indian had the muzzle-loader, the white man was already at work on a breech-loader, by the time the Indian had the breech-loader, the white man was rifling his weapon, when the Indian had caught up with this development, his enemies were preparing repeaters and machine-guns. The organization, both industrial and military, which is necessary for the use of artillery, the Indians never mastered.[14]

---

11   T. Holland, *Dominion, The Making of the Western Mind* (Little Brown, 2019).
12   J. A. Easton, *A Relation of the Indian War*.
13   P. Cozzens, *The Earth is Weeping* (Atlantic, 2017) and *Bury my Heart at Wounded Knee*.
14   R. Nye & J. Morpurgo, *A History of the United States*, Vol. 1, Penguin, 1955

NEW WORLDS, OLD WARS

James Axtell wrote:

> In every 'Indian' war in colonial America, the warring Indians invariably *reacted* to European provocations, usurpations, or desecrations, arrogations much more specific and serious than mere trespassing on Indian soil. Because quickly outnumbered by the prolific and technologically superior newcomers, the warring tribes or confederacy had to have their collective back to the wall or their stoical patience exhausted before they would risk armed conflict.
>
> Their caution and forbearance were well placed, for once the aggressing colonists felt the sting of attack, they became in their own minds, aggrieved victims, with holy vengeance for their cause. Their retaliations were usually savage, if not particularly swift; their lack of defensive preparations was predicated on their disbelief that anyone could doubt their innocence.[15]
>
> For the Indian's record is the background and not seldom the foreground of American history in which his endless contest with the invader were but a counterpart of the unwritten, or recorded, struggles … In that long strife the bitterest charges against him is his barbarity, which constitutes in the annals of pioneer settlement and aggression a chapter of horrors.[16]

But the barbarity and horrors were extended by the white settlers to all those whose colour was not white. Their treatment of the native Indians taught them how they could manage the slaves that would soon flood into their lands. They were to take a pride in their prejudice so much so they saw no anomaly in the fact that a wedding, similar to the much-celebrated marriage of John Rolfe and Pocahontas, would become, for centuries afterwards, an illegal act of miscegenation.

One of the major significances of the long, seventeenth-century wars in the New World, was it set a precedent for how the British would fight their non-European foreign foes and how they would treat those they defeated. From the hot-headed Richard Grenville's firing of a village at Roanoke, to similar incinerations by Argall and Percy; from Cape Cod to California, the Anglo-Americans would leave an indelible, sooty smudge in the written record of their behaviour towards the Amerindians. This ugly weapon would then be wielded wherever and whenever imperial forces clashed with native populations, whether it was in the Ashanti Wars, the Indian Mutiny or the Zulu and the

Boston today – the City on a Hill – less than 0.3 percent of the population of Massachusetts are Native American. (Author's collection)

---

15   *Beyond 1492, Encounters in Colonial America* (Open University Press, 1992).
16   C. Mair, Introduction to E. Pauline Johnson, *The Moccasin Maker*.

CONCLUSION AND CONSEQUENCES – HOW THE EAST WAS WON

Opium wars, to name just a few. So significant is this feature of excessive violence heaped upon whole communities, that Lord Blachford, a long time serving Permanent Under-Secretary-of-State at the Colonial office, wrote the British were: 'the great exterminators of aborigines in the temperate zones'.[17]

This disregard of normative Christian values when in contact with other races, lingered on. Winston Churchill, the veteran of several colonial wars, pronounced he could not …

> … admit, for instance, that a great wrong has been done to the Red Indians of America, or the black people of Australia. I do not admit that a wrong has been done to these people by the fact that a stronger race, a higher-grade race, or, at any rate, a more worldly-wise race, to put it that way, has come in and taken their place … I do not think the Red Indian had any right to say, 'The American Continent belongs to us and we are not going to have any of these European settlers coming in here'. They had not the right, nor had they the power.[18]

Those views are not dissimilar to those held today by both Christian fundamentalists and White Supremacists. It is a long shadow, an indelible blot, first cast by the behaviour of the early American colonists.

The Amerindian wrote none of the chapters of their history, nor were they lorded for their natural desire; a wish to rid the invaders from their land; to object to its seizure; to protect their way of life. Abraham Lincoln once said, 'I don't like that man. I must get to know him better'. The tragedy for the Amerindians was that among the immigrants, there was no Lincoln; no one wanted to get to know the natives better; no one desired to make them their friends or equals; no one was prepared to share the land on which they both wished to live.

Yet whatever one's views on the way these seventeenth-century wars were conducted, they were the wars that paved the way for the creation of the United States of America. This fact alone confirms their supreme importance.

---

17 Records of the Colonial Office, 1811–1889, National Archives, Kew.
18 Evidence to the Peel Commission, 1937. *Palestine Royal Commission Report Presented by the Secretary of State for the Colonies to Parliament by Command of His Majesty, July 1937*. His Majesty's Stationery Office, London, 1937.

Appendix I

The Virginia Charter of 1606 (extracts)[1]

JAMES, by the Grace of God, King of England, Scotland, France and Ireland, Defender of the Faith, &c. WHEREAS our loving and well-disposed Subjects, Sir Thorn as Gales, and Sir George Somers, Knights, Richard Hackluit, Clerk, Prebendary of Westminster, and Edward-Maria Wingfield, Thomas Hanharm and Ralegh Gilbert, Esqrs. William Parker, and George Popham, Gentlemen, and divers others of our loving Subjects, have been humble Suitors unto us, that We would vouchsafe unto them our Licence, to make Habitation, Plantation, and to deduce a colony of sundry of our People into that part of America commonly called VIRGINIA, and other parts and Territories in America, either appertaining unto us, or which are not now actually possessed by any Christian Prince or People, situate, lying, and being all along the Sea Coasts, between four and thirty Degrees of Northerly Latitude from the Equinoctial Line, and five and forty Degrees of the same Latitude, and in the main Land between the same four and thirty and five and forty Degrees, and the Islands hereunto adjacent, or within one hundred Miles of the Coast thereof;

And to that End, and for the more speedy Accomplishment of their said intended Plantation and Habitation there, are desirous to divide themselves into two several Colonies and Companies; the one consisting of certain Knights, Gentlemen, Merchants, and other Adventurers, of our City of London and elsewhere, which are, and from time to time shall be, joined unto them, which do desire to begin their Plantation and Habitation in some fit and convenient Place, between four and thirty and one and forty Degrees of the said Latitude, alongst the Coasts of Virginia, and the Coasts of America aforesaid: And the other consisting of sundry Knights, Gentlemen, Merchants, and other Adventurers, of our Cities of Bristol and Exeter, and of our Town of Plimouth, and of other Places, which do join themselves unto that Colony, which do desire to begin their Plantation and Habitation in

---

[1] New Plymouth was never in receipt of a Charter, making its incorporation into Massachusetts, an easy acquisition.

THE VIRGINIA CHARTER OF 1606 (EXTRACTS)

some fit and convenient Place, between eight and thirty Degrees and five and forty Degrees of the said Latitude, all alongst the said Coasts of Virginia and America, as that Coast lyeth:

We, greatly commending, and graciously accepting of, their Desires for the Furtherance of so noble a Work, which may, by the Providence of Almighty God, hereafter tend to the Glory of his Divine Majesty, in propagating of Christian Religion to such People, as yet live in Darkness and miserable Ignorance of the true Knowledge and Worship of God, and may in time bring the Infidels and Savages, living in those parts, to human Civility, and to a settled and quiet Government: DO, by these our Letters Patents, graciously accept of, and agree to, their humble and well-intended Desires;

And they shall and may begin their said first Plantation and Habitation, at any Place upon the said-Coast of Virginia or America, where they shall think fit and convenient, between the said four and thirty and one and forty Degrees of the said Latitude; And that they shall have all the Lands, Woods, Soil, Grounds, Havens, Ports, Rivers, Mines, Minerals, Marshes, Waters, Fishings, Commodities, and Hereditaments, whatsoever, from the said first Seat of their Plantation and Habitation by the Space of fifty Miles of English Statute Measure, all along the said Coast of Virginia and America, towards the West and Southwest, as the Coast lyeth, with all the Islands within one hundred Miles directly over against the same Sea Coast; And also all the Lands, Soil, Grounds, Havens, Ports, Rivers, Mines, Minerals, Woods, Waters, Marshes, Fishings, Commoditites, and Hereditaments, whatsoever, from the said Place of their first Plantation and Habitation for the space of fifty like English Miles, all alongst the said Coasts of Virginia and America, towards the East and Northeast, or towards the North, as the Coast lyeth, together with all the Islands within one hundred Miles, directly over against the said Sea Coast, And also all the Lands [etc.], ... from the same fifty Miles every way on the Sea Coast, directly into the main Land by the Space of one hundred like English Miles; And shall and may inhabit and remain there; and shall and may also build and fortify within any the same, for their better Safeguard and Defense ... Moreover ... they, and every of them, shall and may, from time to time, and at all times forever hereafter, for their several Defences, encounter, expulse, repel, and resist, as well by Sea as by Land, by all Ways and Means whatsoever, all and every such Person or Persons, as without the especial Licence of the said several Colonies and Plantations, shall attempt to inhabit within the said several Precincts and Limits of the said several Colonies and Plantations, or any of them, or that shall enterprise or attempt, at any time hereafter, the Hurt, Detriment, or Annoyance, of the said several Colonies or Plantations:

Appendix II

Extracts from letter of John Rolfe to Sir Thomas Dale (extract) 1613, published in Hamor's *True Discourse*[1]

The coppie of the Gentle-mans letters to Sir Thomas Dale, that after married Powhatans daughter, containing the reasons moving him thereunto.

Honourable Sir, and most worthy Governor:

When your leasure shall best serve you to peruse these lines, I trust in God, the beginning will not strike you into a greater admiration,1 then the end will give you good content. It is a matter of no small moment, concerning my own particular, which here I impart unto you, and which toucheth mee so neerely, as the tendernesse of my salvation. Howbeit I freely subject my selfe to your grave and mature judgement, deliberation, approbation, and determination; assuring my selfe of your zealous admonitions, and godly comforts, either perswading me to desist, or incouraging me to persist therin, with a religious feare and godly care, for which (from the very instant, that this began to roote it selfe within the secret bosome of my brest) my daily and earnest praiers have bin, still are, and ever shall be produced forth with as sincere a godly zeale as I possibly may to be directed, aided and governed in all my thoughts, words, and deedes, to the glory of God, and for my eternal consolation. To persevere wherein I never had more neede, nor (till now) could ever imagine to have bin moved with the like occasion …

But to avoid tedious preambles, and to come neerer the matter: first suffer me with your patence, to sweepe and make cleane the way wherein I walke, from all suspicions and doubts, which may be covered therein, and faithfully to reveale unto you, what should move me hereunto.

---

[1] <virtualjamestown.org>

EXTRACTS FROM LETTER OF JOHN ROLFE TO SIR THOMAS DALE

Let therefore this my well advised protestation, which here I make betweene God and my own conscience, be a sufficient witnesse, at the dreadfull day of judgement (when the secret of all mens harts shall be opened) to condemne me herein, if my chiefest intent and purpose be not, to strive with all my power of body and minde, in the undertaking of so mightie a matter, no way led (so farre forth as mans weakenesse may permit) with the unbridled desire of carnall affection: but for the good of this plantation, for the honour of our countrie, for the glory of God, for my owne salvation, and for the converting to the true knowledge of God and Jesus Christ, an unbeleeving creature, namely Pokahuntas. To whom my hartie and best thoughts are, and have a long time bin so intagled, and inthralled in so intricate a laborinth, that I was even awearied to unwinde my selfe thereout. But almighty God, who never faileth his, that truly invocate his holy name hath opened the gate, and led me by the hand that I might plainely see and discerne the safe paths wherein to treade …

Nor was I ignorant of the heavie displeasure which almightie God conceived against the sonnes of Levie and Israel for marrying strange wives, nor of the inconveniences which may thereby arise, with other the like good motions which made me looke about warily and with good circumspection, into the grounds and principall agitations, which thus should provoke me to be in love with one whose education hath bin rude, her manners barbarous, her generation accursed, and so discrepant in all nurtriture frome my selfe, that oftentimes with feare and trembling, I have ended my private controversie with this: surely these are wicked instigations, hatched by him who seeketh and delighteth in mans destruction; and so with fervent praiers to be ever preserved from such diabolical assaults (as I tooke those to be) I have taken some rest.

Likewise, adding hereunto her great apparance of love to me, her desire to be taught and instructed in the knowledge of God, her capablenesse of understanding, her aptnesse and willingnesse to receive anie good impression, and also the spirituall, besides her owne incitements stirring me up hereunto.

What should I doe? …

At your command most willing to be disposed off

John Rolfe

Appendix III

Letter to Massachusetts Governor John Leverett

Blackpoint 15 September1676 Honoured Sir After all humble submission, these are to acquaint the present posture of affairs with us, upon the 12th current the enemy after they had fired all the houses on this side of Casco Bay, moved towards us within a mile of our garrison & broke up a house in the night & within two miles fired two houses, slew one man, took another prisoner, & wounded a third who escaped, with another who hid himself in the bushes & lay within two or three rods of them, heard all their discourse, who the other side of the river where he lay, & also that there are two or three Frenchmen with them, one who leads being brave with blue, black & yellow ribbons on his knees, a hat buckled with a silver buckle, brown[?] belt & C[?] & heard him inquire in French by an Indian Interpreter who spoke very good English of the Captives, whether it were difficult to take Richmond Island & Blackpoint of the number of our men, & that their design is to carry all before as they have done along the Eastern a fright (that those who have stood by it all this war) being in expectation of relief from our army & none appearing, the body of them removing, though we hope so many will abide, as with the assistance of the 12 county soldiers will leave us in a capacity to defend ourselves until help come in, which we daily look for having dispatched a post to our Maj. the same day this accident befell. We feare the Army unless they bring bread with them or soon to be sent them, will not be in a capacity to manage a pursuit of them, though the enemy, if they keep their station being for nigh[?] the seah[?] & capeland, giveth opportunity of a defeat[?]. Sir we are at the present the frontier garrison, which if not maintained fear little security this side Piscataquay river knowing the travaile[?] of the spirit for the safety of the whole, beg that the little remnant may be preserved, our poor people having lost 2 crops sink under discouragement, & the rather because Mr. Richworthe[?] & complices designe being effected, as they are informed, of making this County a peculiarity, thereby have excluded them the association of the united Colonies, whereby we shall without your Christian compassion be inevitably exposed to the ruins &rage of the heathen, for want of ability to beare our own charges, but we hope to find favor from those who have taken us under protection as well as government, thus humbly craving pardon for our boldness, we rest.

Yours Honours and humble servants

One of us humbly craveth that if by reason he should misse personall appearance at the General Court it may not be esteemed as a failure but admitted to answer by Attorney or his case be returned, Scottow and Jocelyn

Henry Jocelyn
Josh Scottow

Appendix IV

Petition of Thomas Dutton to the General court in Boston, 1678

Bilerikye this 1st of 8th [October]: (1678)
To the honered govener & the Rest of the honered members of the Generall Court now sitting in boston : this 2:8:1678
The petetion of Thos Dutten Junr: most humbley sheweth: thatt som time in June :: I was imprest into the contrey serves from Billeriky : & was sent with sum others to the estward : under the Command of the honered major clarke esq^r & the wise providence of the allwise god : so ordered if I was in th^t fattall scirmish : In which cap^t swett : th^t worthey comander : was slaine : and allmost all his officers : with about 50 men besids & : 21 more that were wounded [to my best Rememberance] of which my self was one : I was shott therow the side of my belle : and thorow my left knee & so fell doun wounded amongst the rest not able to help my self : I being of a child lame one my right thigh my hipp bone was putt out of Joynt and never sett againe so if I was now lame one both sides : beside the shott which went thorow my side : as afores^d : I therefor hid my self amongst amongst [sic] the bushes: not being able to stand nor goe : the battell being over : the indians came forth out of the swamp and one of them espied me in a bush : and seing my gonne in my hand : aprehended more danger th^n there was : and spake to the rest and they all ran away the which I perceiveing : with much deficoltie : crept into the swamp and Covered my self with mudd & dirt : the Indians qicklie returned to the place to look for me : & fiered into the bush where the indian did se me : & they sought diligentlye for me : but It pleased the lord : they coold nott find me : then in the night after all was still : I crept out of the swamp towards the gareson about a mile & a halfe and whatt with my bleeding and great paine : I was not able to goe one rodd farther : it was the more deficolt for me to creep becase I was shott thorow one of my knees: but there I laye doune & thought I must dye before mornig but the lord who ordereth all things acording to the counsill of his own will : so ordered th^t an other wounded soldier came bye me : in the night a letle before daye : and so took my condetion to the Capt of the gareson : who sent forth men imediatelye : and found me and brought me into the gareson who had much adoo to keep life in me : & I was sent by the first opertunitye to salem : where I came upon the 2nd of July : from th^t time till the : 28th : of Janeuary I Remained under the hands of docter welds : as will appeare by his certeficate which I gave it to to [sic] the honured counsell

Appendix V

Statement by Robert Roules concerning the slaying of captives at Marblehead by the Fisherwomen

I Robert Roules of Marblehead, mariner, aged thirty years or thereabouts, belonging to the catch William and Sarah of Salem, do upon oath say, that Joseph Bovey went out master of the said ketch upon a fishing voyage to the eastern coast. After we had caught, and being about half laden with fish, and riding at an anchor at port La Tour, near cape Sable, and on the easterly side thereof, on the 7th of this instant, July, it being saturday, purposing here to take in wood and water, and in two days to be again upon our fishing design, but on the Lords day) being the 8th instant, in line dawaning of the day, there came suddenly on board of us a canoe of Indians, in number nine or ten, as near as could judge, with their arms ready fixed, loaded and cocked. I first discovered them, and dropped down upon deck to save myself from their shot. They immediately fired upon us, and their shot chiefly struck against the windlass, and so did not hurt us. I then called to them, and said What for you kill Englishmen? They answered me, If Englishmen shoot we kill—if not shoot, we no kill. They then ordered us to come up. By this time they had boarded us, and we were obliged to surrender without conditions. The[y] then proceeded to bind me, and the other four men with me, the master, Capt. Bovey being one. They stripped us, one after the other of all our clothes, only leaving tie a greasy shirt and waistcoat, and drawers we used to fish in, our shoes and stockings being in the cabin. They then gave us liberty to sit upon deck, bound as we were all, till about two of the clock in the afternoon. After this they unbound us, and commanded us to sail our vessel towards Penobscot, which we endeavored to do; but the wind shortening we were forced to come to an anchor again, and lay there till the second day of our capture. In the meantime, they told us they intended to kill all of us, and all the Englishmen, being in number twenty-six, including boys, except three. They had taken four other vessels besides ours. On the second day they commanded us and the other ketches to sail together for Penobscot. The

Indians had dispersed themselves into all the ketches; there being seventy or eighty of them. As we sailed onward we espied a bark and gave her chase and soon took her, and found it Mr. Watts vessel. The Indians compelled us to haile him, and he answered us he was from Boston, bound on a fishing voyage. To prevent the murder of him and his men, as soon as we came up with him we told him he was taken, but he thinking it only a joke, laughed at us. The Indians now rose-up and told Capt Watts if he did not strike they were all dead men. All but four of the Indians then went on board him, divided and mixed the Englishmen in the different vessels with themselves; sending master Bovey with one man more of our company, onboard another ketch, and left me as master of the ketch (they wholly disliking the said Bovey) with an old man, whom I desired. And now being on board with Capt. Watts, the Indians having sent two of their number away, took two of Capt. Watts' men in their place, whereof one was William Buswell.

We had not been thus situated but a short time, when another sail was discovered, and we were commanded to give chase. We did so till it began to grow disky [dusky], and then the Indian Sagamore of our vessel ordered me, who being at the helm, to bear up; but I refused. Thereupon the Sagamore grew angry, and was about to fall upon me, which William Buswell observing, seized him by the throat, and a close scuffle ensued. Buswell however soon tripped up his heels, fell upon him, and kept him down with his knee upon his breast. Meantime, another of my companions in captivity, named Richard Dowries, closing with a second Indian, succeeded in getting him down also; and in attempting to throw him overboard, his legs became entangled, which Buswell perceiving, left his man, and seizing upon him too, they quickly threw him into the sea.

While this was going on the other Englishmen were enabled to confine the other Sagamore in the cook room, by shutting down the scuttle upon him. All hands then grasped another Indian and threw him overboard. It was a desperate attempt, but the victory was now certain. The two remaining Indians were Sagamores, one was an old man the other was a young man. One was fast in the cook room, and the other was glad to surrender to save his life.

We next proceeded to bind the two Indians, and then made all the sail we could to the southward, and on the fifteenth day [Sunday], a little before sundown, we came to an anchor in the harbor of Marblehead.

News had reached this place that we were all killed and many people flocked to the water side to learn who we were and what other news they could, concerning the many vessels that had been taken by the Indians. They hailed us, and then some came on board; and when they saw the Indians, they demanded why we kept them alive and why we had not killed them. We answered them, that we had lost everything, even to our clothes, and we thought if we brought them in alive, we might get somewhat by them towards our losses, But this did not satisfy the people, who were angry at the sight of the Indians, and now began to grow clamorous. We told them we should take them on shore and deliver them into the hands of the constable of the town, that they might be answerable to the court at Boston; and so we carried them on shore with their hands bound behind them,

STATEMENT BY ROBERT ROULES

Being on shore, the whole town flocked about them, beginning at first to insult them, and soon after, the women surrounded them, drove us by force from them (we escaping at no little peril,) and laid violent hands upon the captives, some stoning us in the meantime, because we would protect them, others seizing them by the hair, got full possession of them, nor was there any way left by which we could rescue them. Then with stones, billets of wood, and what else they might, they made an end of these Indians. We were kept at such distance that we could not see them till they were dead, and then we found them with their heads off and gone, and their flesh in a manner pulled from their bones. And such was the tumultation these women made, that for my life I could not tell who these women were, or the names of any of them. They cried out and said, if the Indians had been carried to Boston, that would have been the end of it, and they would have been set at liberty; but said they, if there had been forty of the best Indians in the country here, they would have killed them all, though they should be hanged for ii. They suffered neither constable nor mandrake, nor any other person to come near them, until they had finished their broody purpose.

Taken upon oath this Robert Roules.[1]

---

1   Deposition, MS 252, E. Edward, Ayer Collection, The Newberry Library, Chicago, IL., reprinted in James Axtell, '*The Vengeful Women of Marblehead: Robert Roule's Deposition of 1677,*' *William and Mary Quarterly* 3rd. Ser., 31 (Oct. 1974), 650–52.

Appendix VI

Thadeus Clark to His Mother, 14 June 1676

Honoured Mother After my duty & my wifes presented to your Selfe these may inform you [page torn] present health of our present being when other of our friends are by the [page torn] barous heathen cut off from having a being in this World The Lord [page torn] late hath renewed his witnesses against us & hath dealt very bitterly with us in that we are deprived of the Societie of our nearest friends by the break in in the morning ing of the advesarie against us. On Friday last your own Son with your two Sons in Law Anthony & Thomas Bracket & their whole families were killed & taken by the Indians, we know not how, tis certainly known by us that Thomas is slain & his wife & children carried away captive, of and ^ Anthony & his familie we have no tidings & therfore think that they might be captivated the night before because of the remoteness of their ha bitation from neighbourhood, Gm Corban & all his family Gm Lewis & his wife, James Ross & all his family, Gm Durham, John Munjoy & Dan Hadwell iel Wakely Bejamin ^ Martin & all his family are lost, all slain by Sun an hour high in the Morning & after, Gm Wallis his dwelling are house & none besides his is burnt. we there ^ of men slain 11, of women & children 23 killed & taken, we that are alive are forced upon Mr Andrew's his Island to secure our own & the lives of our families we have but little provision & are so few in number that we are not able to bury the dead till more strength come to us, the desire of the people to your Self is that you would be pleased to speak to Mr Munjoy & Deacon Philips that they would entreat the Governour that forthwith aid might be sent to us either to fight the enemie out of our borders that our english corn may be inned in wherby we may comfortably live or remove us out of danger that we may provide for our Selves elsewhere having no more at present but desiring your prayer to God for his preservation of us in these times of danger, I rest. Your dutifull Son Thaddeus Clark. from Casco Bay 14.6.76. [written vertically on left edge] remember my love to my Sister

Appendix VII

Joshua Scottow's relation to the Massachusetts Council, August 1677

1677 28 August. Narrative of ye Voyage to Pemmaquid,

We sailed from Boston, In ye afternoon. 4 h We came up with Blackpoint In ye morning early, Saw 3 Shallops who ran from us. about 4 o Clock In ye afternoon came up with Sagwin, Saw a Catch, took her for an Enimy, & provided accordingly, came In to Pemmaquid about 9 o Clock that night. I Landed at Fort Charles presented your Honours Respects, & Delivered your Letter from to Captain Brockers. & was civilly Intertained, who hearing ofMcPerson of Boston who had arrived there 3 or 4 hours afore me. That I was in yr sloope who cam came In so late that night, before he told me Captain Brockers told me that he had dispatcht away an Indian that morning very early to Penobscut, so desire Medockawando to come to him, to know his mind as to Salem Catches and their Company, & to a peace. Captain Brockers Capt Nicols & McPerson, went up Damariscotty River In this Linnaer, & came down that night.13 Cannoes came down Corbinsound to Pemaquid about an hour afore sunset, Capn to Capt.n Brockers Commanding all ye Soldiers in his fort. I went aboard ye Sloope. after 8. Capt.n Brockers sent for me ashore, when soon came Squando Sagamore of Said & Tererumkin & another Sagamore of Amoscoggin, with ye Sagamore of Pegwackett, who had Come down ye Day before with their Retinnue, Simon & 2 more Indians came down that morning In a Cannoe, who after a debate Confirmd & signd ye Articles formerly agreed to by Mosey &c, & promised to deliver up 9 Captives with all speed, 8 of them being Pegwakitt; The Same day Returned ye Indian who had been sent to find Medockawando, Saying that he could not find him, & that Casteen & the french had left theire house with ye doores open, & 4 barrels of Flower in it, Simon and Diogenes that day by order from Captn Brockers came aboard to see ye Captives that we had In Hold, Simon Toke ye Lattle boy out of ye Hold & would have carried him away, but being Hindered put him down again. Gooddy Mills & Mrs Hammons Son Came in with another Sagamore of Amascoggin, who made his peace allso & delivered them up. Disturbance by ye Indians arose because we would not deliver up or Prisners. they saying they had delivered up a great many to ye English, & why should we keep. Insomuch as I was or advised by Captn Brockers to go to Munhiggin or Damariscove with my Sloope. I told him I would not for there we were under ye security of his Fort d. & ye other vessels which Rode by us. Diogenes Sent aboard with our Indian man & a squaw to see ye Prisners, about noon Captn Brockers sent for me ashoare & desired me upon ye Complaint of ye Indians to him, to let ye prisners aboard have ye Priveledge of ye Decke, which was very acceptable to us, having Cleansed ye Hold that Day. Medockawando arrived at Fort Charles with his Retinnue, 3 indians sent aboard to see or Prisners. Captn Brockers. Sent a guard early for to have or Prisners carried ashoare, which was performed accordingly. I went spedily ashore, when after some Little Space Madockawando Came again in ye Fort, when after Reading Hearing of ye Articles were which was signed by Moxy, & and all ye other Sagamores, he Consented unto them, & sig ned them allso. ye substance whereof followeth. That them should be a peace with between him & all ye English, they being Subjects to ye same King. of hostility &2. That there should be an Oblivion of all acts, of all former Injuryes 3 – That there should be a delivering up of all Prisners on both sides, & they to deliver -er up all vessels or catches that they had in their Possesion. 4 – That upon any Injury done by them to ye English Complaints should be made to their Sagamores, for their Reparation. 1677 If any Injury were done by ye English to them, they were to Complaine to those Gentlemens, which said Articles were Signed by Captn Brockers Capt Knapton Capt Nicols Commisoners & by Mr Jocelin Justice Medockaw and a said that Major Clarkes Sloop was Lost, Stavd upon ye Rocks, that he had brought 4 Catches to Penobscot, one of which he came In, and Left at Miscontus, 2 at Penobscot one Falls, and ^ he had delivered to Casteen, for which ye English Prisners (who were Interchanged upon ye signing of ye Articles above), told me that the French on Casteen did deliver, on Casteen to Medockawando 2 barrels of flower, one barrell of wine, one barrell of Tobacco, & about 12 yards of Trucking Cloth & that Casteen was gone last for him, & that there was one or two more left of ye Catches Left at Mount Desarts. The Captives then Delivered up by Medokawando were 5 men belonging to ye Catches of Salem and Marblehead th which we Received aboard. Medockawando further said that he wanted that Catch that he brought to Miscontus to Returne home with & that all ye other Catches with him should be brought In to Pemaquid as soon as his men which were abroad at Hunting should Returne, which would be about a month hence ye Captives In his Hands were said to be one at Penobscott, and 5 at [crossed out] Mount Desarts 20, -- We saild from Pemaquid, arrivd that night at Black point Corperall 21 -- Being a Very Rainy Day we Landed, Sergaint Johnson & ^ Honnywell ye day before were sent with 13 Indians to Wells 23 -- Sergant Johnson arrived. being 12 24 -- The Soildiers that were apointed to stay, 8 of them drew up a Protest, against my acting, both in Regard of ye Insufficiency of ye number left and of their Commander &c, one of them being laid neck and Heels d & threatned to be sent bound to Boston, they all Submitted, & Continued who there, except one to Refused to Tarry upon an oath that he made against it as he pretended, who is at your Honoures dispose, we all got aboard 25 –– About midnight we intended to Saile, having a fair wind all and to put for at York to attend your Honours orders, but ye wind failing I arose at midnight to dispatch away a soildier with expresses to york & Wells by Land, according to my Instructions. 26 –– We set sail In ye Evening with a fair wind 28 –– We arrived at Boston. Josh Scotto.

Bibliography

(*Contemporary accounts of the seventeenth-century wars in North America were only produced by the English and were written to justify their actions. Only recently have historians attempted to consider the events from the standpoint of the native Americans.*)

Abbott, J. S. C. *The History of King Philip's War*. (Harper & Brothers, 1901)
Adams, L. C. and Rountree H. *Breaking the House of Pamunkey* (Crofton, 2017)
Adler, W. A. *A Savage Embrace: The Pequot War, 1636–1637* (Biblioscholar, 2012)
Altham, E. Pory, J., De Rasieres I. *Three Visitors to Early Plymouth* (Applewood Books, 1997)
Apess, W. *A Eulogy on King Philip*, 1836
Andrews, C. M. *Narratives of the* Insurrection, 1675–1690 (New York: 1915)
Ashler, G. M. Henry Hudson the Navigator: the Original Documents in which his Career is recorded. 1860
Axtell, J. *The Rise and Fall of the Powhatan Empire* (Williamsburg Foundation, 1995)
Bacon, N. *Declaration of the People of Virginia, 1676*. (Wikisource, 2020)
Baxter, J. P. (ed.), Documentary History of the State of Maine (Baxter Manuscripts) (Portland, ME: Maine Historical Society, 1900)
Bilodeau C.J., *Creating an Indian Enemy in the Borderlands: King Philip's War in Maine 1675 -1678*, Maine History, Vol. 47, No. 1
Black, I. *Enemies and Neighbours, Arabs and Jews in Palestine and Israel, 1917–2017* (Allen Lane, 2017)
Bodge, G. M. *Soldiers in King Philip's War* (Boston:1906, Clearfield: 2009)
Bradford, W. *Of Plymouth Plantation* (Boston: The Massachusetts Historical Society, 1912)
Brogan, H. *The Penguin History of the United States of America* (Penguin Books, 1986)
Brooks, L. *Our Beloved Kin* (Yale University Press, 2019)
Cave, A. A. *The Pequot War* (University of Massachusetts, 1996)
Childs, D. J. *Invading America* (Seaforth, 2012)
Church, B. *Diary of King Philip's War*, (ed.) Simpson A. & M. (Pequot Press, 1975)
Church, T. *Entertaining Passages relating to King Philip's War* (Boston: 1716)
Clap, R. *Memoirs*, in Young A. (ed.) *Chronicles of the First Planters of the Colony of Massachusetts Bay* (Baltimore, 1845)
Coleman, V. *Rogue Nation* (Blue Books, 2002)
Cooper, J. F. *The Last of the Mohicans*, (H.C. Carey & I. Lea, 1826).
Cowper, W. *The diverting history of John Gilpin* (Boston: Frederick Warne and Co 1796)
Cozzens, P. *The Earth is Weeping* (Atlantic: 2017) and *Bury my Heart at Wounded Knee*
CSP Colonial, Vol. I, 1574–1660, May 1607.
CSP Colonial America, Vol. 9, 1021, 12 August 1676
CSP Colonial, America & West Indies, 1675–1676, Vol. 9, 876, April 1676
Cunningham, J. (ed.), Jute's *Journal* (New Jersey Historical Society, 1959)

BIBLIOGRAPHY

Drake, J. D. *King Philip's War; Civil War in New England, 1675–1676* (University of Massachusetts, 1999)
Drake, S. H. G. (ed.), *Early History of New England* (Boston; 1864)
Easton, J. A. *A Relation of the Indian War*, 1675, in Lincoln C. *Narratives of the Indian War 1675 –1699*, C.H. Lincoln. (ed.) (New York: 1913)
Ellis, G. & Morris, J. *King Philip's War* (Grafton Press, 1906)
Evans, J. *Emigrants: Why the English Sailed to the New World* (Weidenfeld & Nicolson, 2018)
Fausz, J. F. *The Barbarous Massacre Reconsidered* (Maryland Historical Society, 1978)
Fiske, J. *The Beginnings of New England* (Boston: 1892)
Foster, J. *Chronology of some memorable Occurrences happening in New England*, 1676
Fraser, R. *The Mayflower Generation: The Winslow family and the Fight for the New World* (Chatto & Windus, 2018)
Grenville, K. *The Secret River* (Canongate Books, 2006)
Gookin, D. *An Historical Account* 1836
Haile, E. W. *Jamestown Narratives: Eyewitness Accounts of the Virginia Colony, 1607–1617* (Round House, 1998)
Hamor, R. *A True Discourse of the Present Estate of Virginia*, 1614, virtualjamestown.org
Hakluyt, R. *The first voyage made to the coast of America*, in: *The Principal Navigations, Voyages, Trafficks and Discoveries of the English Nation*,1598
Harriot, H. *A Brief and True Report of the New-found Land of Virginia 1588.*
Harris, W. 1902, Harris Papers, Clarence S. Brigman, (ed). Collections of the Rhode Island Historical Society, Vol. 10. Standard Printing Co. Providence: RI.
Hatch, C. E. *The First Seventeen Years; Virginia, 1607–1624* (University of Virginia, 1957)
Hardman, S. H. *Pilgrims, New World Settlers & the Call of Home* (Yale U.P., 2007)
Hersh, S. M. *Eyewitness accounts of the My Lai massacre* (The Plain Dealer, 20 November 1969)
Hibbert, C. *Cavaliers and Roundheads* (London: Harper Collins, 1993)
Holland, T. *Dominion, The Making of the Western Mind* (Little Brown, 2019).
Hubbard, W. *The Present State of New England* (Worcester, Mass. 1801)
Hubbard, W. *A Narrative of the Troubles with the Indians in New England*, Boston, 1677
Hunnewell, S. *The Maine Genealogist*, May 2003, August 2003
Hutchinson, T. *Hutchinson Papers*, Harvard University Press:1936
James, S. V. *Three Visitors to Early Plymouth* (Applewood Books, 1997)
Jennings, F. *The Invasion of America*, Institute of Early American history (University of North Carolina 1975)
Kingsbury, S. M. *The Records of the Virginia Company of London* (Washington: 1906)
King, S. *Subjects under the Same King*, University of Pennsylvania Press: 2005
Konig, D. T. *Dale's Laws and the Non-Common-Law Origins of Criminal Justice in Virginia.* (American Journal of legal History, 1982)
La Croix, L. K, *Captain Pierce's Fight* (Masters Dissertation, University of Boston, 2011)
Leach, D. *Flintlock and Tomahawk* (Parnassus, 1992)
Lepore, J. *The Name of War* (Knoft, 1998)
Lincoln, (ed.), *Narratives of The Amerindian Wars* (New York: 1913)
Mair, C. Introduction to E. Pauline Johnson, *The Moccasin Maker*
Mather, C. *An History of Remarkable Occurrences in the Long War, which New England hath had with the Indian salvages, from the year 1688, to the year 1698*, in C. Lincoln (ed.) *Narratives … Thus*
Malone, P. M. *The Skulking Way of War* (John Hopkins U.P., 1993)
Mc Glenen, E. W. *The Sudbury Fight*, address given at the battle site, 17 June 1897
Morris, J. *Pax Britannica* (Faber & Faber, 1968)
Moore, Susan Hardman, *Pilgrims, New World Settlers & the Call of Home* (Yale University Press, 2007)
Morton, T. *Manners and Customs of the Indians of New England* (Boston, 1637)
Noble, John O. Jr. *King Philip's War in Maine* (digitalcommons@UMaine, 1970)
Norwood, H. *A Voyage to Virginia.* (Gale, Sabin America, 2012)

Nye, R. B. & Morpurgo, J.E. *A History of the U.S.A. Vol. 1* (Penguin Books, 1955)
Orr, C. (ed.), *History of Pequot War, The Contemporary accounts of Mason, Underhill, Vincent and Gardiner* (Cleveland: 1897)
Percy, G *Trewe Relacyon*, reprinted in *Tyler's Quarterly, Historical and Genealogical Magazine III*, (1922)
Philbrick, N. *Mayflower, A Voyage to War* (Harper, 2006)
Potter, J. *The Jamestown Brides* (Atlantic Books, 2018)
Powell, A. P. *Grenville & The Lost Colony of Roanoke* (Matador, 2011)
Price, D. A. *Love & Hate in Jamestown* (Vintage, 2005)
Pring, M. *A voyage … for the discovery of the North part of Virginia*, in Purchas, *Pilgrimes*, iv, 1654
Pulsipher, J. H. *Subjects unto the Same King: Indians, English, and the Contest for Authority in Colonial New England*, (University of Pennsylvania Press: 2005)
Purchas, S. and Hakluyt, R. *Hakluytus posthumus, or Purchas his pilgrimes: contayning a history of the world in sea voyages and lande travells by Englishmen and others.* Volume 4 (Cambridge University Press: Cambridge, 2014)
Quinn, D. B. *The Roanoke Voyages, 1584–1590* (Hakluyt Society, 1955)
Quinn, D. B. *The Discovery of North America* (Heritage, 1971)
Quinn, D. B. and Quinn, A. M. (ed.), *The English New England Voyages, 1602–1608* (Hakluyt Society, 1983)
Rountree, H. C. *The Powhatan Amerindians of Virginia.* (University of Oklahoma Press, 1989)
Rowlandson M. *A Narrative of the Captivity and Restoration of Mary Rowlandson* (Boston: 1682)
Saltonstall, N. *The Present State of New England with respect to the Amerindian War*, 1675
Sheehan, B. *Savagism and Civility: Indians and Englishmen in Colonial Virginia* (Cambridge University Press, 1980)
Schultz, E. and Tougias, M. *King Philip's War* (Countryman, 1999)
Smith, J. Barbour, P. (ed.), *The Complete Works of Captain John Smith (1580–1631)*, University of North Carolina: 1986
Snader, J. *Caught Between Two Worlds: British captivity Narratives in Fact and Fiction* (Kentucky University Press, 2000)
Spelman, H. *Relation of Virginia*, 1613
Strachey, W. *A True Report of the wreck … in the Bermudas*, in *Purchas his pilgrimage*, 1617
Symonds, W. (ed.) *The Proceedings of the English Colonie in Virginia since their first beginnings from England in the year of our Lord 1606, till this present 1612, with all their accidents that befell them in their Journeys and Discoveries* (London: 1624)
The Virginia Company of America, *Instructions Given by the way of Advice*, 1607
Thorpe, G. *Virginia Colonial Records* (Richmond: 1874)
Tougias, M. *King Philip's War: The History and Legacy of America's Forgotten Conflict* (Countryman Press, 2017)
Underhill, W. *Newes from America* (London: 1638) <http://digitalcomms>
Virginia Colonial Records, vol. 4.
Vincent, P. *A True Relation of the Late Battle Fought in New England, between the English and the Pequot Salvages*, in Orr, *History of the Pequot War*, 1897
Warren, J. W. *Connecticut Unscathed* (University of Oklahoma Press, 2014)
Waterhouse, E. *Declaration of the State of the Colonyn and Affaires in Virginia; With a Relation of the Barbarous Massacre in the time of peace and League, treacherously executed by Native Infidels upon the English, the 22 March last.* (London:1622)
Wilson, D. *The World Encompassed* (Hamish Hamilton, 1977)
Winslow, E. *Good Newes from New England, 1624* (Applewood Books, 1996)
Winthrop, J. *Journal, 1630–1649* Dunn R.S. Savage, J. and Yeandle, L.(ed.) (Harvard University Press, 1996)

Woolley, B. *Savage Kingdom, The True Story of Jamestown* (London: Harper Collins, 2007)
Wright, R. K. *Massachusetts Militia Roots*, 1986, Army Historical Services, <https://history.aemy.mil>
Zelner, K. F. *A Rabble in Arms: Massachusetts Towns and Militiamen during King Philip's War* (New York University Press, 2009)

Web Sites:

<www.avalon.law.yale.edu> – contains all the Charters issued to the Colonies
<Gerald-tondu.blogspot.com> – the most thorough timeline for seventeenth-century colonial history
<www.virtualjamestown> – contains most of the contemporary accounts of early Jamestown
<www.historicjamestowne.org>
<www.encyclopediavirginia.org> – *Preservation of Racial Integrity*, 1924
<www.fairfieldhistory.org>
<www.warpaths2peacepipes.com>
<digitalcomms@UMaine>